a
Secret
star

a
Secret
star

....

KRYSTYNE F. ALEKSANDR

TAG Publishing, LLC
2030 S. Milam
Amarillo, TX 79109
www.TAGPublishers.com
Office (806) 373-0114
Fax (806) 373-4004
info@TAGPublishers.com

ISBN: 978-934606-52-0

First Edition

Quantity discounts are available on bulk orders.
Contact info@TAGPublishers.com for more information.

Author photo by Mason Gray, Gray's Studio, Amarillo, TX
Make-up by Chelsea Cheshire, First Impression, Amarillo, TX

Published in the United States of America

~ *Dedication* ~

To the people who were ever without a home,
For the individuals who have ever felt alone, To the
one who has fallen into despair,

For the souls who have no one to care, To
persons who have only sorrow,

For the heart that has known many a great
woe, To the parents who now protect from above,
For the children who were ever without love.

~ Contents ~

~ *Wish Upon a Star* ~

. . . .

*There was my name up in lights. I said, "God,
somebody's made a mistake." But there it was, in
lights. And I sat there and said, "Remember, you're not
a star." Yet there it was up in lights.*

—Marilyn Monroe

. . . .

I t was late summer, about mid-July. I never was a big fan of the
summer. I hated the feeling of being hot, especially while riding
in the van. The thing was like a sauna on wheels—extremely
stuffy with a stark odor of sweat. Our van was air conditioned,
but Faye, my foster mom, never turned it on. She said it burned
up the gas, which we didn't have the money to replace. We rarely
went anywhere, but Faye had to leave town, so she was taking me to
another foster family's home to stay with them until she returned.
They lived way out in the country. Despite the drive, I was excited.
I thought of the next few days as an adventure. A new place. But
better yet, a place without my foster parents, Faye and Jack.

We arrived after what seemed like a really long drive. Looking
out the windows, there was nothing. Just wide-open space, with a
cow or horse spotted here and there. There is something to be said,

though, about Texas landscape; you see nothing but so much all at the same time. In the distance I could see a group of trees and what looked like a chimney protruding through the tops of them. I assumed that's where they lived, the Thomas'. I met them before at the monthly foster parent meetings. They seemed nice enough, but I never did trust a first impression.

When we pulled up in the drive, the house became more apparent. It was very large and very pretty. I placed it as the type of house one imagines when thinking of a family. The sight, for me anyway, was breathtaking. As I stepped out of the van, I wandered up the gravel path. Their house was beautiful, like a mansion or something. It was so big and inviting. The stairway led to the front door, where the other kids sprung from behind to greet me. They were very friendly and liked to give hugs. That made me a little uncomfortable at first. I wasn't really used to people touching me in an affectionate way.

Faye dropped off my bags and said she would be back for me in a few days. "You better behave yourself," she warned. "Or you'll be in big trouble."

"Yes, ma'am," I said promptly while thinking, *Take your time in coming back.* I was glad to be away from her and Jack for a while. I had a week to imagine that they weren't in my life, and I also had some time to wish for my dad to come rescue me.

"Bye!" I waved. *Good freaking bye,* I thought as she drove away. Yes, I'd do a lot of wishing and pretending that week while they were away. I knew the danger, though, of dreaming. I had to make sure to have a grasp on reality. If not, the truth of my life would slam down too hard on my six-year-old heart, crushing me in a way that was hard to recover from. It was easy to get caught up in thoughts of having another life, but too soon Jack or Faye would wake me into the reality of what my life actually was.

Around five o'clock in the evening, the family was preparing dinner. They had so much food. It was like a feast. I asked one of the girls sitting next to me if they always had dinner like this. She said yes. That surprised me. There was a lot to eat. Honestly, I don't think I'd ever seen that much food in one setting. We didn't have food at our house most of the time. I was really happy to be spending the next few days here, and I was really excited about getting three meals a day. It had been a long while since that was the case, if it was ever was. I just knew that I had to be good. I didn't know how they disciplined here. With my other foster parents, if you were bad, you didn't get food, and I certainly didn't want to miss one of these meals.

We ate together, and everyone was laughing. They were very… happy. That was nice to see. I didn't say much; I just observed. That's my normal way of dealing with most situations: just sitting back and watching people. You can learn so much by observation. I watched the kids giggling while Mr. Thomas told silly jokes. I watched him stroke Mrs. Thomas hand sweetly. They loved each other. I'd never seen that in real life.

Honestly, the whole thing kind of seemed surreal. I didn't know that people actually lived like this. They were like…a family, even though all of the children were foster kids. Plates were passed, and Mrs. Thomas gave generous helpings. I think I probably ate three plates. I was always hungry, and anytime I was presented with food, I was sure to eat as much as I could. Most of the time, I didn't know when the next meal would come. After the third plate though, I started to feel a little sick but comforted still that tonight I wouldn't go to bed hungry for the first time in a long while. She never told me no either, Mrs. Thomas. She never said there wasn't enough food or that I was eating too much. She just filled my plate with a smile. She was very kind and pretty. And she was a mom. You could just tell. She loved taking care of kids. I became a little jealous of the others. I wondered if one day I would have a mom like this. Their dad, Mr. Thomas, was really funny, too. He always joked and teased. In between spoonfuls of food, I was laughing. Definitely a new experience, to say the least. My giggle wasn't a regular occurrence.

They were all wonderful people. And I couldn't help but notice that they talked about God and spoke of His blessings. I knew of God. And I don't know how, but I felt I always knew Him. I knew that He was big on the whole right-and-wrong thing and that I should always try to do what was right, even if it was hard. I knew that He loved us and would always protect us. But there were also many things I didn't understand. *Why would God let so many bad things happen? Why did he let the babies in our house die? Why wouldn't he bring my daddy back?* But I knew I was supposed to try to be good. And I wanted to please Him. I knew He was the keeper of heaven, and one thing for sure was that I wanted to go to heaven. My life was hard and unfair, and if hell was worse than this, I sure didn't want to go there.

Later on that evening, after cleaning up the table, we all stepped outside. It was dark, but there was light by the full moon; it was a very strange experience and not something I'd ever seen in the city. Wondering down the pathway, as I stepped past the trees, I looked up. Then I saw the most miraculous thing that I had ever seen in all my life. Stars. Millions and billions of stars. They were infinite. And beautiful. I couldn't turn away from the sky. It was so amazing. I wandered out farther into the field, far past the house to get a better look. The Texas sky was as clear as a crystal glass. I stood there and gazed endlessly, trying to take it all in. I couldn't wrap my head around the vastness of them. There were so many.

"You are going to break your neck if you stretch it any farther up," Mr. Thomas said.

Startled, I replied, "Oh, haha. Hi. I was just looking at all of these stars. I've never seen so many!"

"Yes, ma'am. The countryside has its perks. The sky is one of them," he said.

We stood there for a moment, just looking up. I wondered about those stars. What were they made of? How were there so many? Mr. Thomas was a smart man, I knew, so I decided to ask.

"Mr. Thomas?"

"Yes?"

"What do you think those stars are made of? How are there so many of them? How does God make them?" I questioned.

He answered, "Well, I think he made them like he made us."

"Oh." I thought about his answer.

"Don't you know the story about stars?" he asked me.

"No. What story?" I wondered aloud.

"Well, when people die, God represents them as stars to remind those of us that are still here about all the others that came before us. Each star represents someone's life. And the more you work for God and please him, the bigger and brighter you'll be."

This mesmerized me. Stars were once people? And now they became bright stars?

"Like the *Lion King*?" I asked.

His laugh bellowed. "Yeah, something like that," he said.

"Wow, so all of those stars are people who have done good things?"

"Yep." He chuckled at my sudden excitement. "I believe so."

"Well, I believe, too," I stated. "Hey, do you think the North Star is George Washington? But, oh, the sun! Who could be the sun? Perhaps Jesus. He did pretty good things. Did you know that the sun is actually a star? Most people don't."

"Haha, I didn't know that. But yeah, I suppose that perhaps Mr. Washington is the North Star!" He entertained my ideas. I appreciated that.

"I wonder if we could figure out who was who…" I pondered aloud.

"Haha, well, I'm afraid we won't tonight, sweetheart. We better get inside. It's getting late, and the coyotes come to eat little girls when it gets late," he warned teasingly.

"Really?" I questioned with a hint of fear. This was the country after all.

Chuckling, he said, "Yep, so you better get inside."

"Yes, sir," I agreed as I gazed up to take one last look before heading in.

We all got ready for bed, but I knew I wouldn't be sleeping. That night, I thought a lot about what Mr. Thomas had said. I wondered about all of the people who I had learned about in school who were probably now stars. I remember thinking that I should really try to figure out who was who. I needed to find them so I would know what was expected to be bright.

Excellence has always been one of my priorities. I knew it would be hard. Certainly, I would have to work for it. I mean, George Washington was the first president of the greatest nation! That's a lot to compete with for a young girl. I would have to do something miraculous. I was going to have to make a change in the world or something incredibly wonderful to impress the Lord.

As I lay there, I began to think of things I could do to please God. Things that could ensure that I would, one day, illuminate the sky. I set my mind to it. I wasn't quite sure what I was going to do, but one day, I was going to be a star. A bright, shining star.

~ *Born into Burdens* ~

· ·

For you formed my inward parts; you knitted me
together in my mother's womb.

—Psalm 139:13, nkj

· ·

May 27, 1991, was a day that didn't go as planned. I had been in my mother's womb for six months and was still developing, but the pregnancy had lasted as long as it could under the conditions. My mother had not received proper prenatal care and was not a healthy person in general. When I was born, I weighed merely 1.3 pounds. I was barely viable. But, truth be told, the world was a much better place for me. My mom, Charlotte, was addicted to drugs. Anything and everything that could get her high, she would ingest, although cocaine and alcohol were probably her favorite combination, as it is for many addicts. When those two substances are mixed, cocaethylene is produced in the body, maximizing the feeling and duration of the high. However, the complications of this combination forced her into labor, and I was born.

After months of ingesting the toxins my mother was taking, I had begun the processes of withdrawal. I tested positive for cocaine and alcohol. Alcohol is the worst of the two, because it is the single most dangerous drug to quit abruptly. The fight for life had begun.

I stayed in the hospital for the first three months of my life. During that time, my mother's rights were being questioned by Child Protective Services. However, she started to clean herself up. She wanted to be a part of my life. My father, John Welch, was still in the picture, too. He was also a drug addict, and the man loved his whiskey, but he loved me and came to the hospital every day. Child Protective Services said that if he and Charlotte   promised to clean up, they wouldn't take me away. They both worked very hard, and after I was discharged from the hospital, I went home with my mommy and daddy.

I was still a very sick child when I left the hospital. I had been receiving drugs, most likely, from the moment of conception. They had altered my body chemistry and severely affected my development. These complications, the doctors were sure, would follow me for the rest of my life, which was most likely to be short lived. My diagnoses were a long list of fetal alcohol syndrome, cerebral palsy, failure to thrive, and mental retardation. As I began to grow, severe developmental delays became readily apparent. At six months old I was still unable to bend my legs. I was not easily soothed; my body was stiff. A touch of any sort, calming or not, alarmed me. I screamed constantly, which only created more problems. Because of my lack of tolerance to physical contact, this affected my eating and normal bonding mechanisms. In addition, I had a very hard time sucking a bottle and swallowing. It was a battle for me to eat, and weight gain was a huge obstacle, which added to the problems of normal development. I had many doctor and physical therapy appointments weekly. I had lists of medications and procedures that had to be done. But my physical problems were just the beginning of the issues.

Somewhere along the way, my mother gave up. Change is hard, I suppose. My father worked hard, but he was a heroin addict. And though he was my dad, he was a heroin addict first. I can't imagine how hard it was for my parents during that time. Fortunately, my daddy was a little more persistent than my mother. He was trying to clean himself up so that he could take care of his little girl. Neither of us was in great physical condition and, oddly enough, because of the same thing. But I was difficult, and there is only so much one person can take on. My daddy was trying to become an adult and parent all at the same time. My mother was in and out of the picture. She wanted me one week, rejected me the next. The situation was counteractive to any sort of progress.

We were in poverty; neither of my parents held jobs. We were living in a dangerous neighborhood, and when one problem arose, many others followed.

My parents didn't get along. Several times the two of them were in domestic violence disputes. They weren't able to take care of themselves, much less a sick little girl. It just became too much for either of them to handle. My father had grown tired and was no longer willing to try. He called Charlotte to come and get me. Before long, the two were fighting over who would take me. The two started arguing, which soon broke out into fist fighting. The cops were called. Both my mother and father agreed that they could not handle parenthood at this time, and Child Protective Services took me into custody. So that was my next stage: foster care. Because I was a sick child, I was going to be placed in a "special needs" home to ensure I would receive proper care. A home that ensured I would be safe; one to ensure that I would not be in any danger. At least, that was the idea. That was what was supposed to happen.

Cold Winter Frost

. . . .

Fate is not an eagle, it creeps like a rat.

—Elizabeth Bowen, *The House in Paris*

. . . .

I was placed in the home of Faye and Jack Winters. They had been fostering for about two years and just began to take in medically sick children. I cannot remember our first meeting, but their impressions will forever be burned into my brain.

Faye and Jack had been married for fifteen years. Faye was forty-seven, and Jack was fifty years old. They rented a small house in a lower middle-class side of town. Jack worked as a truck driver and was previously in the United States Navy. Faye had always been a stay-at-home mom during the marriage but was a hairdresser before that. She had two biological daughters, Adrianna and Molly. Both, at that time, were still living at home. Adrianna was a senior in high school, and Molly was considered a junior; however, she was in specialty classes because of mental disability. Unfortunately, Molly was considered to be on the borderline of mental retardation. She was barely functional on her own. On their application, Faye and Jack emphasized this and stated that was why they were interested in helping children with disabilities. They looked good on paper.

Neither had criminal backgrounds. They went through fostering classes, had taken the tests, and were certified to care for children in the State of Texas. So it was there that I was placed.

Faye was a large woman, and she did not care much about appearance. She was about 5'4" give or take, but weighed about 250 pounds. She had short spiky hair that was bleached blonde. When she did style it, it would stick out crazily all over her head, as if lightning or something had struck her. Her attire consisted of a T-shirt and sweatpants most days. But when good impressions were necessary, she followed through with a blouse and a skirt.

The features on her face were disproportionate. Her eyes were green. They appeared to be nice, but if you looked closely, you could see that was just a glaze that hid her true intention. However, most never looked that deeply, because she made sure no one got that close. Her nose was large and appeared to have been broken a few times. Her mouth was set in a constant frown, like she had been unhappy since the beginning of her days.

Jack was the complete opposite in terms of size and proportion. He was about 5'8" and had a very lanky figure. In all reality, the man looked malnourished. He wore dark-shaded glasses that constantly slid off his sunken in face. He had facial hair, a mustache and somewhat of a beard. His hairline had receded over the years, but what remained was mostly gray. He always wore button-down, checkered, flannel shirts with jeans that were usually too big. Jack looked, as most would describe him, as creepy. He was a very awkward individual. From the time I was a little girl, I noticed he never really knew what to say or how to respond in conversation. He was very off in social situations. Perhaps psychology would say he was introverted, but Jack was just an odd individual. He had discomfited body movements, and it was like he never knew what to do with his hands.

Independent in their physiques, they were my temporary parents. At this point, I was a little over one year old and still had many complications. My development was still very delayed. I was irritable. I cried constantly and still did not take any comfort in being touched or held. The doctors' diagnosis held true. I was not normal, and I would still need significant therapy and treatment. But more than anything, I needed love. I needed someone to not give up on me, and the Winters family was given that role.

Jack was gone most of the week, only home during the weekends. Faye was my primary caregiver. I will admit that I was a difficult child to take care of, but Faye was certainly not Mother of the Year. As I got older, I remember feeling she didn't like me; any child can pick up on that, no matter the age. But those feelings were mutual. Faye was harsh in nature. As I grew, the feelings did as well. She was not a nice person. She was an angry individual, but I was never really sure why or with what she was so angry. And Jack was just awkward and in no way demonstrated characteristics of a father.

Though I cannot recall my exact thought processes as a young toddler, I can say that I didn't like Jack or Faye very much. Ever since my memory serves me, I felt uncomfortable around them. They were confusing people, saying one thing but doing another.

But good news held, as my dad started a rehabilitation program. He was fighting for himself and for me. John Welch had an addiction problem, but he wanted to be my daddy, and I longed to be with him again. It is a long process to rid oneself of an addiction, but my father was trying. He had to do monthly drug testing and maintain a stable job and living conditions. When I was almost two, he met with a judge and was granted visitation. Over the next few months, I was to be eased back into his care. I had three four-hour supervised visits a week with him. If my case manager reported that they had gone well, I would begin spending weekends with him, and soon, I would live with him. We would be together. We were going to be a family.

I was so excited to see my daddy. I loved our visits. My speech still wasn't very good, but I kept asking Faye, "Daddy comes?"

"Yes," she would answer. She seemed to be as excited as I was when visitation time came.

My daddy always came to pick me up in his old red truck. Every time I saw it, excitement overtook me. The old rusted truck was my cue that daddy was here, taking me with him. My daddy, John, was a tall man, almost six feet and two inches. He had blonde hair. It was long and kind of shaggy, hanging in his face. He always wore jeans, a button-down shirt, and cowboy boots. He was a Texas man. An Alan Jackson character, no doubt. As soon as I saw him, I would do my best to bolt out the door. I could stand at this point, but my leg movement restricted my walking. Most of the time I would just fall over. The excitement of trying to move so quickly didn't help and turned me into a spastic mess. But even though my body restricted me, my mind and heart jumped straight into his arms.

He would come straight to me, pick me up, and throw me into the air. My laugh echoed through the room.

"Hi, Missy Natalie! How's my little girl?" his deep voice would boom.

"H-H-hi, Daddy! Hi! H-h-how's mine daddy?" I shrieked. Between my speech problems and enthusiasm, my language was skewed. But I didn't care. I loved my daddy, and when he came for visits, I was just thrilled!

He would take me to his truck and strap me into my car

seat. I would beg for him not to, because I wanted him to hold me. Sometimes he would. When we were together, we were just that—inseparable. I wouldn't let go of him. He was my daddy, and he spoiled me rotten. He would take me to the corner store and buy me Sugar Daddys, a toffee sucker that is an absolute mess. He said they were made just for me because I was Daddy's sugar. I had a constant smile in his presence.

One time on our visits, he surprised me. When we got home, he took me into the backyard, and there was a swing set with a swing that was an airplane! I squealed with excitement! For hours at a time, he would push me in that swing. And when I say hours, I mean three to four hours constant. I loved it. It was soothing for me. In that swing, I had not a care in the world. I didn't have to worry about walking, because my legs just dangled freely. I didn't have to worry about talking, because there was nothing to be said. During those times, nothing really mattered. I had my daddy, and even if I didn't see him, I knew by the momentum of the swing that he was there. And honestly, that's all I needed to know… that he was there, just for me.

However, those weekends would end, and I would have to go back to the Winters' home. I would scream, shout, and throw a darn good tantrum about it. I didn't like those people, the Winters, and my dad knew it. I know he also questioned it. Was it because I loved him so much, or was it because there were true reasons as to why I didn't want to go back there? He couldn't do much about it at that time, though. His behavior and actions were under a magnifying glass. It was best not to question and just do everything he could to get me back.

"It's okay, little Natalie. I will see you again soon. This Friday! Don't cry," he soothed.

"No. No leave. P-p-please. Do no go." I sobbed.

"My Natalie, don't cry. We'll be together soon. Just you, Grandma, and me. Not to worry. We'll be together soon," he promised.

Homecoming

On January 28, 1994, I was released officially into my father's custody. I remember that day at the courthouse. Looking around, everyone was so well dressed. But the most memorable was the smell. I remember it vaguely as leather and paper, but mostly of importance. The room was dark, and you had to be *so* quiet. I saw my daddy up at the front. The large man in a robe was talking to him. How weird was he dressed? But I knew he was very special. The caseworker was sitting right next to me.

"Natalie, be very quiet and sit still. Okay?" she requested.

"Yes, ma'am," I agreed. Yes, the smell; the place reeked of significance and justice.

"See your daddy? You're going home with him today," she said with a smile.

Happiness was my response. For news like that, there was no need for words. I was a little over three years old, and developmentally,

I had made outstanding improvements. My walking was not always stable, but I was consistent in my attempts. My development was almost at a normal level, which shocked physicians. I still had trouble with weight gain and a few speech problems, but I had made considerable progress. I was going to start preschool in August, which was something I wasn't too thrilled about. I went to daycare twice a week, and I didn't really get along with the others. But the doctors eventually refuted the diagnosis of mental retardation, as my IQ testing was slightly higher than the norm. This was remarkable considering my gestational drug use; however, that somewhat explained my physical development, too. I understood, and therapy became not only about training my muscles but also training my brain.

"Court adjourned," the man in the robe said loudly, hitting the hammer.

That's weird, I thought. But I was interrupted when my daddy came up and grabbed me.

"You're coming home, my Natalie! You are coming home with me!" he bellowed.

"*Yay!*" I screamed. Oh, finally, I was going home!

We left the courthouse in my daddy's truck. We were moving in with my grandma. I was so excited. I loved my grandma. She was so sweet. And that's where my airplane swing was! I would get to swing every day with my daddy. I was the happiest little girl in the world. One thing for certain was that I loved my daddy, and I refused to leave him. I was always scared that I would lose him. Everywhere he went, it was a sure thing that I was tagging along. Sometimes, unfortunately, that wasn't always the best choice.

Though my father gave up drugs, he still had a craving for alcohol. It was more controlled now, but was still a problem. But as a little girl, I didn't mind. I loved going to the bar. When my dad said he was going, I would beg to go with him! It was so much fun!

He'd say, "We're going to see Joe to get Jack!" My grandmother would advise against it, saying it wasn't the place for little girls, but I usually got my way and went with my daddy. He didn't like to disappoint me.

Vividly, I remember those times. We would walk into this smoky place. I thought the lights were really neat. They were so bright, and some of them were flashing on and off. There was a really long table with chairs only on one side. On the other side, there was a man. He was really nice.

"Hey, there's Missy Natalie! How are ya, kitten?"

"I'm good, Mr. Joe!" I would say, holding on to my daddy's belt loop. Daddy would pick me up and set me onto one of the tall stools and sit down next to me.

"Beer for starters," my dad would say.

"What about the little lady?" Joe would ask.

"I want a beer like my daddy." And that's what I would get. A root beer, of course, but I didn't know the difference. And we would drink. Daddy could drink his much faster than I could mine, but he said it was 'cause I was just a little gal.

There were other guys there, and they were nice, too. They were my daddy's friends. We played games. There was this really cool one named darts. My daddy would put me on his shoulders and let me throw these little pegs at a board of circles. There was also a table with a lot of little balls that you hit with sticks. I didn't like that one as much. I couldn't see, and the stick was just too hard to handle. My coordination just wasn't up to that scale yet.

We would stay there for hours, way past bedtime. Sometimes Daddy would start acting really silly. I thought it was funny. He would take me to the open part, and we'd dance. Our favorite song was "I Like It, I Love It" by Tim McGraw. Daddy would go and put quarters into the huge stereo, and it would play instantly. We had so much fun at the bar. I loved it, and I loved my daddy. I never really remember leaving, though. I suppose I fell asleep before we left. But I always remember when we got home. Grandma would be so mad at Daddy. She would yell at him.

"John, you cannot take a little girl to the bar and get drunk. CPS is going to take Natalie again," she warned him.

"Oh, they're not going to take my little girl. And there ain't nothing wrong with having a few drinks," he slurred.

"John! You can't! What if Faye finds out? She'll report you. She's been calling a lot, asking where you were and what you were doing. About Natalie," she explained.

"Well, doesn't matter. I'm not giving her my kid. Natalie is mine, and that old hag just needs to deal with it and leave me the hell alone!" he yelled. "Why does she keep calling? Isn't it against the rules or something?"

"I don't know, John. But she doesn't stop. Just be careful. I don't want Natalie going back there. Those people… I just—I don't know about them."

"Yeah, I know, Mom. I know. I'll stop taking her."

"Okay, Johnny. Okay," she agreed.

I loved my grandma, too. She was very sweet and always liked to hold me. She was sixty-four years old, but she was so pretty. She had long hair, which was white as snow. I loved to play with it. She always smelled of flowers and wore a beautiful smile. Her skin was soft. There were lines on her face that told a story, hard years now that I think about it. But my dad, grandma, and me, we were happy when we were together. We were our own little family.

And even though Grandma got mad sometimes, we were still so happy. I had no worries, no troubles. I was taken care of and loved. And no matter what, everything was okay, or so it seemed. But Daddy did start going to the bar a lot more, and he didn't take me with him as much. I stayed at home with Grandma, and she would sing me to sleep. I would miss my daddy, but he came back in the morning, and would play with me in the afternoon after he woke up. It was great! Everything was fine…or so it seemed.

Road Trip

. . . .

A journey is a person in itself; no two are alike. And all plans, safeguards, policing, and coercion are fruitless. We find that after years of struggle that we do not take a trip; a trip takes us.

—John Steinbeck

. . . .

It was a cold, fall morning. There was a thick fog in the air, but I insisted on playing outside. Of course, my daddy had to come with me. I was playing with chalk on the sidewalk, but my daddy wasn't helping very much. He was being weird, withdrawn, and seemed a little sad.

"What's wrong, Daddy?" I asked.

"Daddy is just sad," he said.

"But why, Daddy? Why are you sad?" But he didn't answer. As I stared at him, his eyes looked different. They had lost their twinkle. My dad's usual smirk was gone. His mouth was in a solid straight line. His face was almost emotionless. I was confused, but I figured he was just having a bad day. A hug would help. They always helped me when I was upset. So that's what I did. I gave my daddy a big bear hug, like he gave me. I squeezed him so tight, but he almost pushed me away.

As he pulled me back, he said, "Natalie, we have to go on a trip."

"Where to?" I asked excitedly. I loved trips!

"Go get your coat," he stated.

But like a normal four-and-a-half-year-old, I argued. "But where are we going? Why do I have to get my coat? I have this one."

"You need to get your big coat. Do what I say," he said firmly.

"But, Daddy, why? I hate that coat. I can't move in it," I whined.

"Natalie! Do what I say now!" he yelled.

His voice scared me. Daddy never yelled like that. I decided I should probably do what he said. I walked into the house while my eyes filled with tears. Why was Daddy so upset?

My grandma asked, "What's wrong, Little Natalie?"

"Daddy is being mean. I have to get my big coat so we can go on a trip," I said. As I spoke those words, my grandmother's face turned harsh. Immediately, she went outside and started yelling. Both my grandma and daddy started screaming at each other. I couldn't make out what they were saying because their voices scared me. I ran to the back room and hid under my daddy's bed. I stayed there for a while until my daddy found me.

"Come on, Missy Natalie. It's time to go on our trip."

He seemed happier or a little more relieved, but I still saw conflict in his face. Whatever was bothering him, I wasn't sure. But I didn't want to make him mad again. I slipped out from under the bed, and he helped me put my big coat on. My grandmother told me bye, but it was kind of strange. She had tears in her eyes, and she was holding me so tight in her hug. Why was she upset? Nothing was really making any sense.

"I love you, Natalie. Know that I love you so much," she said in a shaky voice.

"I love you, too, Grandma. What's wrong? I'm sorry I threw a fit," I apologized. Maybe they were upset because I didn't mind.

"No, darling. You are perfect. Now go with Daddy," she said.

"Yes, ma'am." As I turned, not as worried, I grabbed my dad's hand. "Let's go, Daddy!" As I held his hand, I played with his big turquoise rings. I thought they were so pretty. "Can I wear one of your rings, Dad? Please?"

"Not today, Natalie. Let's go," he stated softly.

We got into the truck. My daddy didn't say one word. I kept asking where we were going, but there wasn't an answer. I suppose I got tired of not getting a reply, so I just stopped asking. Whatever it was, he was being pouty about it.

I watched out the window. We drove for a while until we pulled up into this parking lot. There was a bunch of old buildings around. It looked a little scary. My dad got out of his truck and came to my side. He unbuckled me from my car seat and set me on his hip. We started walked toward this building. It looked very old and rustic. I didn't recognize anything around us. I started to become very nervous. What was going on?

"Daddy, what is this place? Where are we?" I questioned, but there was no answer.

We opened this door, and the thing I remember the most was the smell. It smelled terrible. A strange odor that I can't recall ever smelling before. The air was thick, like the fog from outside had managed to creep in. There weren't any lights. We turned toward this rickety stairway. It didn't look safe. You could barely see anything at all.

"Daddy, I'm scared. I don't like this place." And it was true, I didn't like it. But as we climbed the stairs, parts of me remembered it. Something about the surroundings spurred my memory and heightened my fears. I didn't like this place. I knew that much.

"Daddy, where are we going?" He continued not to answer. We just continued up the stairs until we reached this door. He stopped in front of it and set me down. When he looked at me, there were tears streaming down his face.

"Daddy! What's wrong, Daddy?" I begged of him. "Daddy?"

He looked at me with his blue eyes and said, "My little Natalie, I love you, but I can't be your daddy anymore."

My little four-year-old mind couldn't comprehend what he meant. What was he talking about? I configured the statement and came up with nothing. But he was my daddy. He was *my* daddy. He always was. But when I looked up to tell him that, he was gone. I started crying and screaming.

"Daddy! *Daddy!* You're my daddy! Daddy! *Where's my daddy?*" I screamed as loud as I could. "Please, Daddy! Come back!" I was sobbing now. "*Where's my daddy?*"

Abandonment is horrifying. As I recall that memory, it brings me chills. Honestly, to this day, I cannot remember where we went. Or what happened after that. Perhaps it's a lapse in memory or motivated forgetting because of the trauma and emotional pain. I just know that if I had to name the worst day of my life, that one would be it.

The next thing I recall was being back at the Winters' home. I have no idea how I got there. I had no idea why I was there, but that's where I was. And unfortunately, I didn't have any visits from my dad this go-around. There were no phone calls, no getaway weekends. I always hoped that he would come. I prayed that he would come back for me someday. And after a while, when his absence continued, I started to lie to myself.

"He had to go on a trip. He'll be back," I told myself. "Don't worry. He had something to take care of. Daddy will come back because I'm his little girl. His Natalie. I'm his daddy's sugar."

And so I waited. I waited for him. He was going to come one day. But the hardest thing to overcome was my last memory of him. It was a cold day, and I was being a little brat. He had been upset, and I argued. If I had done what he said, maybe he wouldn't have gotten so angry. Perhaps I shouldn't have hid under the bed. What if he was agitated at the fact that I hid from him? The questions haunted me. What did I do?

At four years old, my daddy's words made no sense to me. *Natalie, I can't be your daddy anymore.* And even as I grew older, time never cured their foreign sound. But I hoped. I had to hope. He would come back for me. He just had too. I just had to wait a little while. I needed to wait and, perhaps, wish.

A Day in the Life

....

*Allison: is a female given name. It was originally
a medieval Norman nickname for Alice, meaning
"truth" or "noble."*[1]

....

I've always found it interesting how we all have subjective definitions and ideas of normalcy. As young children, one begins to devise the schemas of life, from family rituals, religious ideas, and functional relationships to everything else in between. However, as children, we also assume that what we experience and live daily is normal. And why wouldn't it be? For me, I suppose that's what I also construed. At least it was that way until I started school. It was then that I realized that the normal I was living was completely and utterly abnormal.

I was in the third grade, eight years old. The four years that had gone by since I saw my dad were blurry. I don't remember what all happened. I just know that my dad dropped me off at that horrible-smelling place. And for some reason, I ended up back at the Winters' home. But regardless, I was waiting. My dad was going to come back for me when he could.

So I lived, I suppose. I thought. I functioned on the scale of normalcy that the Winters family provided. But that's just the thing, their scale's measurements were off. Way off. I remember when I started noticing things and began to question. It was a subtle finding, but no less dramatic.

But school was always a safe haven for me. I loved school. It was the best place ever in my little world. You got to learn, read, and do math. And if you did all of your work correctly, you would get rewards. I liked that, and I always tried to do my best. Interestingly though, a lot of my classmates hated school. I couldn't understand why. I loved being away from home and being in the classroom. In fact, I was heartbroken when we had holidays off. But the other kids would be so excited, thrilled that we didn't have to come. It never really made sense to me.

I didn't really have friends. I was what's called "a nerd." I was about three times smaller than the other children. I was extremely skinny; grossly skinny would probably be more accurate. In third grade, I appeared approximately the size of a five-year-old. I had very fair skin. In the summer, I gained a little bit of color, but by the time winter came around, I was back to my ghostly, lucid sheer. I usually had bumps and bruises underneath my old oversized clothes. I had long stringy auburn hair that I tried to style different ways. I thought that if my hair was pretty, people wouldn't pay much attention to my face. I wasn't what was considered nice-looking. At least, Faye always told me I looked like my mother, who was ugly, fat, and crazy. I didn't believe the fat part, but I considered myself to be ugly for sure. I always tried to fit in with others, but it didn't really ever pan out. The only way I could get the other children to play with me was if I agreed to do their homework, which was fine with me. It wasn't hard, and I got extra practice. And if I did all of their math papers, I could play tag with them two days out of the week. I figured it was a pretty good deal, and if the others would talk to me, it was just fine.

One Tuesday afternoon, after I had labored the evening before doing about fifteen different sets of worksheets in order to play a round of tag at recess, the other kids decided that they just wanted to relax. They just wanted to sit by the monkey bars and "hang out." I would have rather been running around, but I didn't share my opinion. I knew that they could revoke my ability to participate at any time. So we sat and talked. I mostly just listened and observed, my normal social game plan. Everyone was talking about games they liked to play, things they wanted to do. Just mindless chatter, I suppose. But then one of the girls explained that she was grounded. That was a foreign term to me.

What is grounded? I thought. Unfortunately, the thought was actually spoken aloud. They all turned to me and looked at me like I was a freak.

"You don't know what *grounded* is?" one of the other kids asked.

"No. What is it?" I questioned.

"When you get in trouble, your parents ground you. Like, they take something away, like your favorite toy or the TV. It's punishment," a kid answered.

"Oh," was all I could murmur. *Grounded? Really?* I thought. *That's not punishment.*

"Do you not get grounded?" the girl sitting next to me asked. She was nice. I thought she was also very pretty. She had long blonde hair and a pretty smile. She was always nice to me even when others weren't. I liked her.

"Umm, no, I don't get grounded," I said to her.

"So you don't get into trouble?" a boy shouted. "You don't get punished?"

Quickly, I felt uncomfortable. Yes, I got in trouble. I got in trouble every single day. I was constantly in trouble. But my punishment was much different than any of theirs.

"Do you?" the boy insisted again to me.

"Yes, I get punished. But I...I...I've never been grounded," I stammered.

"Well, what do your parents do then?" a girl sitting across from me asked. It was all very strange to me. None of them were ever interested in me or how my life played out. Now they were all inquisitive, asking me all of these questions. I was unsure as to how to answer. What would they think? Was I weird because I didn't get grounded?

"I get whippings," I replied grimly. Now they were the ones confused, just as I had been when they said they got grounded.

"What do you mean *whippings*?" the blonde girl sitting next to me asked.

"Like, um, I don't know. Just like when your parents hit you 'cause you've been bad. Like when I don't do something right," I tried to explain. They still looked confused. "Like if I don't say 'Yes, ma'am or if I talk too much to the nurses that come to our house."

"Do you always get whippings?" the blonde girl asked. As I turned to answer, I noticed the look of concern in her eyes. It was strange to me. Foreign.

"Well, I get in trouble a lot. I don't do things right," I said. Suddenly, she was looking at me, studying me.

"Is that why you always have bruises?" she asked. I didn't really know what to say. I just know that I felt that I shouldn't be saying anything. Faye always said that what happened in our house was our business, and no one needed to know about it. I wasn't supposed to talk about this, I knew. I was going to get in trouble if she found out. Immediately, my body tensed. I needed to stop. I had to leave. I had to get out of here.

"I...I don't know. I...I-I-I...I have to go." I got up and ran away. My mind was racing as my body was shrieking with panic. I shouldn't have said anything. All of them were looking at me so strangely. I was a freak. I knew I was. And now, I would never get to play tag. I was a nerd. A freak and a nerd, and if Faye found out, I was going to be in trouble for sure.

The next day, no one asked me to do his or her work. Just as I figured. I was weird, and now they really didn't want to play with me. So I just finished up my work. I told myself that it didn't matter. I could play on my own. I'd just go to the library after school and check out some books.

When recess rolled around, I wondered out to the swings. I loved the swings because it reminded me of a happy time. A time when my daddy was there. So when I felt I needed him or if I really missed him, the swings brought me a certain level of comfort. As I got there, I sat down and started rocking back and forth, trying to gain my momentum.

"Can I sit by you?" The question startled me. I didn't expect anyone to come over by me. When I turned, it was the little girl that sat next to me in the circle yesterday.

"Umm, sure you can. I'm just swinging," I said with a slight smile.

"I like to swing, too. Thank you," she said. She was so nice, I thought. But why?

"You don't have to sit by me. The other kids might make fun of you," I warned.

"I want to sit by you, and I don't care what they think," she stated. I was taken aback by her answer. She was going to hang out with the freak? She was the prettiest girl in our class and probably the nicest. And she wanted to swing with me? That was very kind. Yes, I liked Allison. She was always very nice to everyone.

"Thank you, Allison," I said. She just smiled. We didn't speak for a few moments. It was a nice day, and it was nice not to feel obligated to talk. The breeze in the air helped our momentum. Neither of us was going all out in terms of height. We were just slightly moving back and forth. An effortless motion, I guess.

"So did you get a whipping last night?" she asked.

Her voice startled me, but her words frightened me. *How did she know?* I thought. *How did she know I was in trouble?* I just turned to her, panic on my face.

"It's okay. I won't tell anyone," she promised. I didn't really know what to do.

"How do you know?" I questioned.

"This hand mark." She pointed it out. "You didn't have that yesterday."

"Oh," was all I could say. I was always having marks and bruises on me. Faye told me that if anyone asked, I was supposed to say I fell. I was little and frail, so for the most part, it was believable. No one questioned. But I felt bad for lying. I didn't want to lie to Allison. She was kind to me, and it was wrong to lie.

"What happened?" She maneuvered until she was looking me straight in the face.

"I, well, I was being bad," I stammered. I didn't want to lie. She said she wouldn't tell anyone.

"How? What did you do?" she questioned me.

"I… Well, yesterday morning, when I left clothes sticking out of my drawer. My foster mom, Faye, hates that, so I got in trouble." It was weird to be talking about this. No one ever asked, no one ever cared, but it seemed she did.

"How did you get in trouble?" The question made me tense as I replayed the night before. Again, she noticed my body language.

"It's okay," she said. "Natalie, you can tell me. It's okay."

"It was my fault. You're always supposed to fold your shirts, and make sure they are all the way in the drawer before you close it. I didn't do it right. I left the sleeve out, and it got caught. My mom was really mad when I got home."

"What happened?" Allison inquired.

"Well, when I get home, we have nurses there 'cause of the sick babies. They have to have extra care. So I don't get in trouble at first. But I usually know when I will, because Faye has this look in her eyes. It's like a warning. Yesterday, she had the look. So I went to my room and tried to finish all my homework. When I get in trouble, I usually have to go to bed right after, so I try to finish everything before."

"Oh," she said. Her hand was on my shoulder, comforting me. It was very, well, strange. No one had ever taken interest before, so I continued.

"So after the nurses left, she slammed my door open and started screaming, 'How many times have I told you to make sure your shirts are in the g-dd—n drawer before you close it?' She cusses a lot when she is mad. She says really mean things that hurt your heart."

"It's okay. What happened after that?" Allison asked.

"Well, she continued to scream and yell. I don't mind because if she gets her anger out through the yelling, she doesn't hit as much. But yesterday, she was really mad. I was sitting at my desk in my room. And she came over and yanked me off my stool. That's where this one came from." I reached to my arm and outlined the hand imprint on my left arm. "Then she just...hits me. Over and over again. I tried to shield, but that only makes her angrier. Sometimes she uses a belt, but yesterday it was just her hands, but it still hurts. It hurts."

I didn't realize that I started crying while talking to Allison. When I escaped from my memory of the evening before, I realized her arms were around me. She was giving me a hug. She cared. I hugged her back. I cared for Allison.

The bell rang; it was time to get back to class. Recess was over.

Over the next few weeks, Allison and I spent recess together on the swings. She asked me questions about what happened at home, and for the first time, I told the truth. I told her about the beatings, about going to bed without food. Really, about never having food in general. I recalled the stories that had happened the night before. It helped me somehow. Just to talk about it. To tell her. But, Allison, she was very sensitive. Sometimes the things I would tell her upset her a lot. One day, she started to cry. So I decided I would not tell her everything anymore. She was so nice; she was my friend. I didn't want her to cry. Bad things happened in my home, and I didn't want her to know all of it. So I started to talk about other things. I talked about the babies that lived in our house.

"They are really sick. Their parents were mean to them. Like, they hit them as babies, and now they have brain damage. Their parents do drugs and have to clean up before they can get their babies back. Some of them can't breathe on their own. They need machines to help them. They have to be fed through a tube in their stomach because they can't eat food. They get sick a lot, and we have to go to the hospital. Sometimes they die and go to heaven with Jesus."

As I talked, Allison was always quietly listening. She was a thinker, I could tell. She always thought about what I said. And most times, she would bring up a question the next day or so.

"How often do they die?" she once asked.

"Oh, I don't know. My little brother Noah died last week. That's why I missed a day. I woke up, and Faye was screaming. I had to call 911, and the police, firefighters, and ambulance came to our house. Noah, he didn't look very good. Faye was just screaming though. She didn't help him breathe like she was supposed to. She just kept yelling at me. It was sad though. They couldn't save Noah. He died that morning."

"Are you sad?" Allison asked.

"Yes, of course I am. I loved Little Noah," I said, a little shocked by her question.

"Oh, well, you don't cry. I didn't know Noah, and it makes me cry," she reasoned.

"Well, it's sad, but you can't cry. They are with Jesus, and that is wonderful to be with Jesus. They are stars in heaven. I can't wait to go live with him," I assured her.

"What do you mean?" Allison asked.

"Well, when you die, you go to heaven, and it's wonderful. I think there is a lot of food there. It's very happy with music and stuff," I explained.

"You want to die?" she asked.

"Umm, yeah, I guess so. Like, heaven is *wonderful*. Everyone is so happy there, and at church, they said there is no sadness. I don't think people can hurt you there because God doesn't allow that.

The babies, they are lucky, you see. They don't have to live in this world with Jack and Faye," I answered.

"Natalie, you're not supposed to want to die. You are supposed to be happy on the earth. Life is supposed to be good," Allison reasoned with me. "Your life is not supposed to be sad."

I couldn't really respond. Life was sad. It was hard. As far as I knew, people left. The good people left, and they didn't come back. My daddy left, the sweet babies would leave, and the kind nurses. And Allison was right, I was sad. I was very sad when I was at home. And I realized that day that I wished a lot that I could live with Jesus. Was that bad?

Allison continued to talk with me at recess, but instead of listening, she asked me a lot of questions. Some of them I refused to answer. Allison had a kind heart, and I didn't want to hurt her. She got upset very easily. But she was brave with her questions. She was very…bold.

"Does Faye hit the babies?" she asked one day.

"Oh, no," I said. "She would not hit the babies 'cause they are not bad. She yells and screams at them, but she doesn't hit them. Sometimes she is a little mean to them. One time I saw her put a pillow over Timmy's face when he was crying. But I think he could still breathe. After she left the room, I moved it, to make sure."

"Natalie, that's not okay!" she raised her voice.

"Oh, I make sure they are okay, Allison. Don't worry. She doesn't hit the babies," I soothed her.

"She only hits you then," Allison asked.

"Well, yeah. But I deserve it. I break the rules," I said.

"Natalie, stop it!" she yelled. She shocked me. Alison never got mad.

"Natalie, your foster mom and dad are not good people. They don't treat you right. Babies come to your house, because their parents hurt them, and in that house your parents hurt you. You have to stop. You have to tell someone. You are sad. You have bruises. You have tears. You don't have food ever. You have to tell someone!"

I was utterly shocked. What was she saying? It made sense, yes, of course, but I couldn't tell anyone. I just couldn't! She's lost her mind!

"Allison, I can't tell. Faye doesn't give me brain damage, so it's not that bad. I can still eat and breathe. It's okay! I'm not getting hurt like the other babies did, so it's fine," I said.

"No, Natalie. Just because you don't have brain damage doesn't mean it's okay what Faye does to you. She starves you. You are the size of a kindergartener. You have marks all over you all of the time. Your clothes are dirty. You have to walk to school, even when it's freezing outside with snow and rain. You are sad, Natalie. You want to leave the earth. It's not normal, and it's not safe. If you don't tell someone, I will."

"Allison! *No!* You can't! You just can't!" I was panicking. No, I was freaking out. She promised. "You promised!"

"Natalie, calm down. It's against the law. You aren't safe. You have to be safe. You are my friend, and I care about you. My dad is a cop. He talks about this. You have to be safe. We will tell Mrs. Smith. We will tell her. I will go with you, okay? I will come with you all the way."

The bell was about to ring. Allison wasn't changing her mind, and she was right. I was sad, I was hungry, and I did want to leave the earth. She was right. I had to tell. It was time to tell, whatever the consequences. Allison was my friend. She would help me.

"Okay. Okay, but you have to come with me," I said.

"Okay, I will." She gave me a hug. "Let's go."

That afternoon turned into a really long one. When we went up to Mrs. Smith, Allison told her that we needed to tell her something important. As we did, Mrs. Smith became very upset. They took us to the office. At first, she tried to just take me, but I said I wouldn't go without Allison. She was my partner; she was going to help me. I had to go to the nurse and answer questions. Then they examined me and asked more questions. They told me not to talk about what happened when I got home. We would keep this at school. But the truth of the matter was they didn't have to relay that message to me. I knew that this was a big deal, and if Faye found out that I had talked about our private life, I was going to be in huge trouble.

Over the next few weeks, I got pulled out of class a lot. I had to go to the counselor and talk to caseworkers. They were all nice. Some of them I knew because they came to our house for the babies. I told them about the things that happened. Most of it, anyways. I was still reluctant to talk about everything. Some things I just didn't want to discuss.

They told me that I might be getting a new family. I was really excited! That would be so cool! But I really just wanted my daddy. I asked if they could help me find him, but they said they couldn't do that. But the investigation was under way. One weekend, people came in our house and asked me questions there. It made me very nervous, and I lied. I couldn't talk about these things when Faye and

Jack were in the other room! What were they thinking?

Weeks went by, and nothing really happened. I just guessed they were looking really hard for a new family for me. But my guess, it was wrong. One afternoon I came home, and Faye was sitting in the chair waiting for me. The nurses were already gone. It was just she and I. She smiled at me, but there was nothing endearing about it. The smile was…evil. Something like a villain does when their plan is working. Wicked.

She said, "Welcome home. How about you come over here and sit on my lap?" She had an underlying tone of greed.

"Yes, ma'am." I set my backpack down and walked near her. To be honest, I hated being close to her. Truthfully, she scared me so much.

"Do you have a new friend at school?" she asked.

How did she know about Allison? I thought. I hadn't said anything about her.

"No," I said.

"Are you sure? The caseworker told me you had a friend that you liked to talk to."

The caseworker? She said she would not tell anything I told her. That our conversations were our secret. She lied. I began to get very nervous. What did she tell?

"I-I-I guess I do. She's nice. We swing together," I said hesitantly.

"I see. And you tell her lies?" Faye asked.

"No, I don't lie to her," I stated.

"Oh, yes, you do." She pulled me back, her hands gripping my waist tighter. "You tell a lot of lies…to a lot of people. You know, they almost took you from me because of your lies. They almost took the babies and all of our money."

I didn't know what to say. She knew. She knew I told people about our home life. She knew! And almost… They almost took me away? *Almost?* My panic was full-fledging, and my tears they came. There was no stopping it. I was in trouble, I knew it. I was in big, big trouble.

"Do you know what you almost did? They almost took all of these babies away because you told lies about what happens in our house. And you know what I think about lying. I hate liars. Liars have to be punished." The smile on her face was gone. The glint of evil in her eyes showed through. She stood up, still gripping me. It happened before I knew it, but the next thing I knew, I was on the floor.

This time, I was in big trouble. I could tell, because she used her legs, kicking me across the floor toward my room. Then the yelling started. Screaming. Telling me I was worthless. Telling me I was a liar. Telling me that I would never leave. I was hers. It lasted longer this time. She had a lot of fury. I tried to count how many times she hit me so I could tell them. *Accuracy*, I thought. But then she noticed I was counting.

"You little b—. You think you can count? Well now, I'm going to make sure it's a number that you can't reach."

She was right; it was a number I couldn't get to. She hit and kicked so hard, numbers became obsolete. I became very dizzy and sick feeling. I threw up, and that only made things worse. I can't remember how long it lasted, but it was for a while. A long while.

After she grew tired, she made me clean up my throw up. Then it was bedtime, though it was just five o'clock. If there was something she made sure I understood, it was that I was a bad girl. I was a liar. I was going to be punished. Liars had to go to bed. Bad girls didn't get dinner or breakfast.

This regime lasted for a few weeks. I lost weight, I knew, because my clothes were falling off more than usual. At school, I didn't talk to anyone anymore. Faye told me that she would have people watching, and if she saw me talking to anyone, I would be in worse trouble. When they called me to the counselor's office, I didn't say anything. And I mean I didn't speak a word. I told Allison that we couldn't be friends. She begged me to talk to her, but I wouldn't. Faye was crazy, and I didn't want Allison in the cross fire. The next year, she moved away, and I have to say that I was relieved for her. She would be safe from Faye.

I became a hermit. I didn't speak to anyone ever again about what was happening to me. I couldn't trust people. The caseworkers, the counselors—they didn't keep their promises. They were the people who lied. You couldn't trust people. And I was not going to be brought down again for that. I was done. My life, my bruises, my sadness, my dreams were mine. Completely mine.

I kept my word to myself. Never again did I tell anyone about the abuse that went on in our home. No one believed me the first time, and nothing was going to change. I was stuck there until I turned eighteen. And that was my wish, to grow up so I could move away and never come back. I'd go to college and work on doing great things. But some days, it was all too much, and my wish was not to be eighteen. More often than not, it was to be a star. To be among the heavens, with no hurt and no more pain.

Hair Cut

As most little girls, I loved playing with hair. I would play with the babies' hair, braiding it, creating strange different new styles for them and for myself. They were always so sick. The least I could do was help them feel pretty.

I was in the fourth grade now, and style was becoming a very important thing to me. I didn't have a lot to work with, considering my appearance was not at all flattering. I still hadn't gained much weight over the past year. My mouth was entirely too big for my face. My teeth were rather large, and I had a large gap in the middle of them. To add insult to injury, they were also slightly bucked forward. My nose was small, and because my eyes were set far apart, proportion was off. But I did have my hair. It was long to the middle of my back. It was a deep red, though it seemed to get darker as I grew older.

One day, I was experimenting with beadwork. There was a Jamaican girl in my class who had tons of multicolored beads in her hair. She was so pretty, and it looked so fun. I decided that I would try and pull off the look. That evening, I remember braiding my hair into tiny little braids. It took hours, and my fingers were incredibly tired. However, I knew it was the most logical way to put the beads in. Once I was all finished, I had several necklaces that I had made in summer Bible school camps. I decided it would be much more fashionable to wear the beads in my hair rather than wear the necklaces themselves. So I snuck into the kitchen and got the scissors. I wasn't supposed to use scissors, even though I was almost nine years old. Faye said that they weren't for children. I didn't like breaking the rules, risking myself getting into trouble, but this was an important cause. Faye used to be a hairdresser, and I just knew I would impress her with my design. I was giddy with the idea, and I thought that if she liked my hair, she would forget all about my use of the scissors.

So after contemplating the patterns and such, I started to string the beads in my hair. It was a lot more difficult than I thought it would be. It was a very long, tedious process; however, it was coming along. And I had to admit, I was having a blast! Fixing my hair always made me feel like a normal girl. And sometimes, I would start to feel pretty. As I came to a close, I was very pleased. I thought it looked cool! I was sure the Jamaican girl in my class would agree. Excited, I decided to show Faye my new hair. I went to go find her, fervently hoping she would be as delighted as I.

I went to her bedroom door. *Entertainment Tonight* was just finishing. Usually, if she was in a good mood, I could get a snack at this time, which added to my excitement. I figured she would like my hair and maybe give me a few extra animal crackers. I knocked, and she said, "Come in."

As I walked in, my smile was timid. I suddenly realized that she might not like my hair. If she got upset, I'd risk getting the snack and might possibly get in trouble. I slowly walked through her door. She was looking at the TV. She said, "What?"

I was silent for a moment. Suddenly, it all seemed like a really bad idea. Then unexpectedly, she turned before I could retreat.

"What the hell is that shit in your hair!" she shouted.

"I, uh, I was trying something new. Like a girl in my class."

"Oh my god, you look like a damn nigger. Piece of trash. I can't believe you did that. What were you thinking?"

"I-I-I…thought it looked pretty," I stuttered.

A roar of laughter filled the room. "Pretty?" she said. "You thought *you* could look *pretty*?" Another spell of laughter. I could feel a lump in my throat forming. I knew better than to let my tears spill here, so I forced myself to hold them in the best I could. No matter how many times she called me ugly, it still stung.

"You are stupid if you think beads could fix that face of yours." She started to stand, and I felt the sick feeling of nervousness as she rose. I knew what was coming. Before I could even flinch, I felt the back of her hand hit me so hard I fell to the ground.

"Get that shit out of your hair right now, or I'll do it for you."

"Yes, ma'am," I whimpered as I hurried to my feet and ran out of the room. I hurried back to the bathroom.

"You got ten minutes, Natalie, and I'll be there to help."

In sheer panic, I hurried. I knew what her help would consist of, and after the blow to my face, I knew she wasn't in a good mood. I started sliding off the beads and unbraiding my hair as fast I could. I was trying to avoid tangles, but it wasn't working. Most of the beads were out, but there was one section that wouldn't budge. The rubber band I used was twisted somehow, tangling my fine hair into a matted mess. My hands were shaking; I knew I only had about three minutes before she was going to be in the bathroom. I looked down and saw the scissors. I picked them up, knowing that they were the only solution. It was a small bit of hair, one tiny braid. I decided to just cut the end. It would get rid of the beads and the matted rubber band. Slowly, I edged the scissors toward my hair, angling them in such a way that the least amount of my hair would be cut. Within a few seconds, the tiny tangle was in my hand. Problem solved. I quickly whipped away the bits of hair and put all of my beads into a little bag. I knew if she saw all of that mess, it wouldn't matter if my hair was fixed or not. I'd get it for sure. I unbraided the rest of my hair. I was just about to brush it out when Faye walked in.

"Well, damn, too bad you got 'em out. I was looking forward to getting a hold of your little ass. Get in bed," she snarled. "I don't want to see you anymore tonight."

It was just about 7:30 p.m. Another night started before the sun even went down. My stomach was growling. I didn't get to have dinner because I was in trouble for not cleaning my room two days ago. My stomach was growling viciously, but it didn't quite drown out the lump in my throat. As soon as I was in bed, I turned my head toward the wall. I could hear the babies screaming and Faye cursing at them, telling them to shut up. Even though I felt bad for them, I was thankful it wasn't me she was yelling at.

Tears slowly drenched my pillow, and the right side of my face was sore from the blow I'd received earlier. I opened my curtain to watch the birds. They were so happy, so free. I suppose it's silly to be jealous of an animal, but I was. How I wished I could fly away. But I had to be thankful, I told myself. Tonight could have been much worse. She only said a few mean things, but that wasn't out of the ordinary. I only got hit once, which was out of the ordinary. I closed my eyes and tried to sleep. I couldn't help but wonder what they were going to have for lunch at school tomorrow. Another reason I loved school was because I got free lunches. Monday through Friday, I got at least one meal. That was good. Especially when they served pizza. Finding myself calmer, I slowly drifted to sleep. My last thoughts drifting toward tomorrow was that it was going to be a much better day.

I woke, as usual, by Faye barging in, turning on the light, screaming, "Get up!" I hurried out of bed and got dressed. I went into the kitchen where breakfast awaited. My stomach was growling and demanding. A piece of buttered toast and half a glass of diluted orange juice. Faye would always put three times as much water as the instructions said so it would last longer. Mostly, our juice tasted of water with a little orange or grape flavoring, but I was too parched to care, sucking it down and swallowing my toast in all of two bites. I went to the bathroom to fix my hair. I started to comb it out when Faye walked in.

"Make sure you brush your nasty teeth."

"Yes, ma'am." I opened the drawer where my rubber bands were. I decided a ponytail would suit. But as I opened the drawer, I immediately regretted the decision. In my hurried rush last night of cleaning the bathroom, I forgot to sneak the scissors back in the kitchen. Panic filled me, and my hands started to tremble. I slowly shut the door and let go of my hair. Faye was looking at me strangely. She was usually avoiding me at all cost, so I couldn't understand what was happening. Suddenly, our front door opened, and one of the nurses walked in. I felt relieved as Faye walked out of the bathroom. I was just beginning to strategize about how to get the scissors back to the kitchen without being noticed. All of a sudden, Faye and the nurse were right outside the door.

I could hear Faye say, "Yeah, I was just getting ready to help Natalie with her hair."

I almost lost my breakfast. This could not be good. What was going on? Faye had always pretended in front of the nurses before, giving me a kiss before I headed off on my long walk to school or telling me that I looked cute when I know she didn't mean it. But this, fixing my hair? Something was up. She opened the bathroom door, and I jumped.

"Come into the living room, Natalie, so I can fix your hair like you want," she said with a smile that sent chills down my spine. "Bring the rubber bands."

"Yes, ma'am," I said. As I walked into the living room, my mind was flooded with reasons. *Why is she doing this? Maybe she felt bad about last night? Maybe she is just going out of her way to impress the nurse. Maybe she really did want to fix my hair.* I handed her the brush and the rubber bands as I sat down in front of her on the couch. She started combing my hair when all of a sudden, my head was violently jerked back.

"I saw those scissors in the bathroom. Why were they there?" She whispered the question in my ear. I didn't respond. I couldn't think. She would know I was lying. And I would get in trouble for that, I knew.

"Did you cut your hair?" She started pulling my head back.

Fear flooded me. "What?" I said, trying to gather myself. She held most of my hair in a tight grip.

"Did you *cut your hair?*" she screamed.

"Yes, ma'am, but only a few strands 'cause the rubber band

got stuck, and you said to get the beads out, and—" Pain ended my sentence. Quick as a flash, I was moving. Not by my own feet though. Faye was dragging me by the hair on my head toward her room. I was screaming in pain. I could see the nurse through the blur of my tears. I could see her shocked face. Once we were in Faye's room, she threw me down. My head hit the corner of her bed. Before I knew it, my swats had started. She was hitting me with both hands. Rage, with all the rage in the world. I simply curled up in the fetal position, protecting what I could with my hands and using the floor as my shield. I assumed she was getting tired because the swings were slowing down.

It would soon end, I thought. Then all of a sudden, she grabbed me by the hair on my head again and slung me into the bathroom. I couldn't figure out what was going on. Was she going to kill me? Drown me? Then I saw her hand. She held a pair of shear scissors. I screamed in panic, not knowing what she was going to do.

"Please, please don't! Don't cut it! I just couldn't get the rubber band out! I'm sorry, I'm so sorry!" I shouted.

But my pleas were no good. I felt my hair dropping to my feet. I heard the scissors clip close to my ear. I was numb with fear.

"Be still or I'll cut off your ear, too!" she snarled.

Pieces of my hair were everywhere, clinging to my face because it was wet with tears. All around the toilet and the floor. My hair was everywhere it shouldn't have been, no longer on my head. I was drowning in my own tears. This was horrifying. Before I knew it, the snipping had stopped. But I couldn't bear to open my eyes, so afraid of what I might find. Faye left and came back with a broom.

"Clean up your mess, you stupid brat. I bet you'll never do that again. Oh yeah, let's look in the mirror, shall we?"

She grabbed me by the arm and all but shoved my face into the mirror. After I got over the shock of my face hitting the cold surface, I looked.

The sight was something I was completely unprepared for, though I knew what it was going to entail. My hair was gone. It was chopped to pieces. Uneven and ragged. I looked like a little boy. My tears were overflowing now.

"Aw, look how ugly you are," Faye said with a vindictive smile. She started to laugh. "Clean this shit up. Come out when you're done."

I couldn't stop crying. I know it must seem foolish to be so upset about hair, but it was my hair. My favorite thing. The very feature I had that made me feel pretty. It was gone. I swept it up and put it in the trash. As I tried to look into the mirror again, I could only cry.

I was done cleaning and headed to my room. I didn't get to go to school that day. I didn't know if I was happy or sad about that. What would people say about my hair? What would I tell them? But I also knew that I'd be lucky if I got to eat anymore today. And I would have to spend the whole day in my room.

Later on, Faye came in and made me get into the car. She took me to the beauty shop, where the lady tried to salvage what I had left. That made sense though. Faye was always worried about image, and with the way my hair looked, it was sure to catch attention. When we arrived, a story was already constructed.

"Oh, Natalie was trying to have short hair like me. She wants to look like her momma, but it didn't work out." She chuckled. "Will you do what you can?"

The nurses that were at our house didn't say anything. I figured maybe that's what I deserved for cutting my hair. Maybe that's what I get.

After we left the hairdresser, Faye asked, "So what do you think?" I told her I thought I looked ugly. "Haha, nothing new, my dear," she responded. "Nothing new."

Spelling Bee

....

It's easy to let life deteriorate into making a living
instead of making a life. It's not the hours you put in, but
what you get out of the hours that count. Learn to express
rather than impress. Expressing evokes a "me too"
attitude while impressing evokes a "so what" attitude.

—Jim Rohn

....

E ven though I knew Faye hated me, I still tried to change her opinion of me. I tried to impress her, to please her and make her proud. I signed up for sports and tried to make straight A's. I figured that something would please her. And even if it didn't please her, my teachers always liked it. Some praise from someone was better than nothing at all. The spelling bee was coming up, and I thought that would be a good idea, so I decided to try out. I studied and studied, learning what seemed like a million words. I was pretty good at English, and spelling wasn't too hard if you just sounded out the words.

The first round was just in our class. The person who won in the class would get to try out in the school-wide one. And luckily enough, I came first! I was kind of excited. That afternoon, I asked

Faye to come and watch me. She said that she would.

My chance to shine! I thought. *She would have to be proud of me if I won,* I thought the night before the spelling bee. I would get first place, and my teachers, Jack, and Faye would be proud.

The next day was here before I knew it, and 3:00 p.m. came even faster. All of the contestants were called to the cafeteria. It was time to shine! First, we had a practice round where we just had to spell our names. The audience wasn't there yet, and the stage wasn't completely set up. There was going to be a microphone set up, but in the practice run, we wouldn't use it. I was near the end because my last name started with a *W*. I was thankful for that as it allowed me to see all of the others go first. As my name was called, I stepped up on the *X* and spelled my name. *Easy enough,* I thought.

Soon, people started piling in, all of the elementary students, parents, and teachers. I started to feel very nervous. I heard one of the other kids mention the term *stage fright*. I wasn't exactly sure what it was, but I was confident that I was suffering from it. Soon, I saw Faye and Jack walk in. I waved. Even though I didn't like them, they came to see me here, and I was grateful for that.

The time was drawing near. There was a panel of judges sitting in front of us, only adding to my anxiety. The line seemed to be moving fast as the sound of the "wrong answer" buzzer was frequently ringing. Before I knew it, my name was called.

"Natalie Winters," one of the judges called. I walked up and stood on the *X*. I realized that the microphone towered above my head. The judge told me to bring it down. As I turned the small knob in the middle of the pole, it suddenly dropped down, and a loud ringing noise filled the room. I was startled and completely embarrassed. I didn't know what to do! A teacher came up to fix it, but all of the students were laughing, both in the audience and from behind me. I looked at Faye and saw her just shaking her head in disapproval.

A screw up, I thought to myself. *I'm just a screw up.*

"Okay, Natalie," said the other judge. "Your word is *radio*."

"Um, radio. Uh…um, I…" Tears were starting to fill my eyes. I couldn't think; I couldn't breathe. I was overwhelmed with fear. "Radio, R-A…um. R-A…D-E-O." Then the sound of the buzzer suddenly confirmed my thoughts. I was wrong. Well, of course. I was an idiot.

I walked off the stage just crying. Faye and Jack were leaving and already had reached the door. I'd probably be in trouble for embarrassing them. I felt so worthless. So useless. I was a complete failure.

I went to the bathroom and just cried. Soon, my teacher came in to console me. I told her that I was sorry.

"I'm so sorry, Mrs. White. I'm so sorry. I'm stupid. I let you down," I sobbed.

"Natalie, look at me," she asked in the sweetest voice. "Spell *radio* for me."

"R-A-D-I-O," I said simply.

Smiling, Mrs. White said, "See, you knew how to spell it. You're not dumb, and you will never be worthless. Do you understand?"

"Yes, ma'am," I said.

"Don't ever let anyone tell you different. You are wonderful."

Her words were odd as I was sure no one had ever said anything like that to me. "Thank you," I said as we got up and joined the class. I can't say I really believed Mrs. White, but I knew that I'd like to. Faye just always told me the opposite, no matter what I did. But I hoped with all my heart that Mrs. White was right. I just wanted to be good at something, to be worthy. I wanted to excel so that maybe one day Jack and Faye would treat me nicely. Or maybe if I did something great, if I were wonderful, maybe my daddy would come back for me. If I was super smart, he would. If not him, maybe someone would. I thought about the time the caseworker told me she was looking for a new family for me. Maybe if I were good, I would get one, one day. If I worked hard.

That evening, I drilled those positive hopes into my head, even as Faye tried to beat them out. Apparently, I humiliated her and Jack. I said sorry, but it didn't matter. In her eyes, I'd always be worthless. And despite what Mrs. White said and what I wanted to believe, a part of me knew she was right. If there wasn't something wrong with me, my daddy and mommy would have wanted me.

Happy Birthday

A gift consists not in what is done or given, but in the intention of the giver or doer.

—Lucius Annaeus Seneca

Birthdays were really nothing to get too excited about. It is the day you were born. And for me, May 27 was a day I questioned a lot in regard to reasoning. I was turning ten years old. I was glad because now I was in the double digits. Life had rolled on by. There were good days, bad days, and ones worse, but that was life.

However, this year, Faye told me that I could throw a party. I was excited about it! She said I could invite anyone I wanted to. So I invited all of the kids in my class. We had a rustic swing set in the backyard donated by a local church, and I thought it would be cool to have the party there. Maybe all the kids would want to come over again after the party if they had fun.

I handmade the invitations. They took me a long time because there were twenty-two kids in my class, but I didn't want to leave anybody out. But I ended up making twenty-four invitations. There were two people that I really wanted to come, but I had to ask Faye to help, which wasn't ever an easy subject to approach.

One afternoon, I went into the kitchen to talk to her, "butter her up," if you will. Faye could be nice when she wanted to. It was rare, but she could be. We talked about my birthday party. She said she would buy me a cake and ice cream. I was excited and very grateful to her. Sometimes she was very sweet, especially if we had money in the account. I had brought all of my invitations to show her. She knew there were twenty-two kids in my class, but I made twenty-four invitations.

"Why do you have two extra?" she asked.

"Well, I was hoping to invite two extra people," I said hesitantly.

"Who?" she questioned.

"Well, I...I think that my grandma and daddy still live in Amarillo. I wanted to send them an invitation, if I could find their address," I explained with extreme timidity.

"I see. Well, I'll see if I can find the address, I'll send them the invitations," Faye said.

"Really? You will? Oh, thank you! Thank you!" I couldn't help myself; I threw my arms around her and gave her a hug. It shocked both of us, but she accepted the gesture.

My party was next Friday, and it was only Sunday. But I was so excited. My daddy might come! And my grandma, too! And Faye wasn't mad that I asked her. She wasn't mad! Usually, she became very upset when I talked about my daddy and grandmother. It was an untouchable topic, not to be brought up and not to be questioned. I knew that I had to be extra good this week. I didn't want to make her mad and have her change her mind.

For the rest of the week, I lived in a dream. I imagined about what I would say to my daddy. I imagined hugging him and him holding me. I also knew that I had to find a nice way to ask him to take me back. But it was my birthday, and I would tell him that's what I wanted for my present. It didn't cost money. He could do it. He would do it! I was doing well in school, and at least I didn't get in trouble from the teachers. Maybe he would be impressed with me and want me back.

I passed out the invitations to my classmates, and they all said they would come. That was surprising to me considering my "geek" status. No one talked to me, I sat by myself at lunch, but they said they would come! I assumed it was because of the cake and ice cream. I made a paper for the RSVP, and they all signed. It was a guarantee of their attendance. I was sure that this was going to be the best birthday I ever had or could ever dream of!

Friday afternoon was here before I knew it! That morning I paid careful attention to my appearance. I was tired because I had hardly slept the past week. I was too excited. Everything that was happening was thrilling. Things were changing. My life was changing!

I went to school, all smiles that day. The other kids didn't seem excited but said they were still coming. We were going to have fun; they'd see.

For the first time I can remember, I was ready for the school day to be over. Three o'clock couldn't get here fast enough. When the last bell rang, I ran out of the building as if it were on fire. I raced down the street and headed toward my house. I had to hang up my decorations and get everything set up. The party started at 5:00 p.m. I had made a lot of paper signs to hang in the tree house and outside of our house to direct everyone. I was racing around like a crazy person, taping everything and making sure everything was in the right place. I knew I wasn't supposed to use the babies' medical tape, but that's all we had. Regardless, it had to be perfect. And Faye, she held up her end of the bargain. She bought me a cake and a tub of ice cream. This was going to be awesome. Even my name was written on the cake. I felt… so special.

After I got done rushing around, it was 4:35 p.m. No one had showed up yet, but that was okay. I needed to catch my breath. I decided to wait by the door so people would see me and know that they had the right location.

And that's what I did. I waited. Five o'clock came soon enough, right along with five thirty and six o'clock. I started to worry. Did I put down the wrong address? The wrong time? The wrong date? I was sure I didn't, but no one had showed. Not a single one of my classmates came. But I was still hopeful. There was still time. Maybe everyone was just running late.

And I was sure because my daddy and grandma would come. They wouldn't turn down my invitation. And they would be excited to see me! So I stood by the door and kept watch.

I asked Faye if I could use the phone, and called one of the girls in my class. She gave me her number when she told me that she was coming to the party. As the phone rang, she suddenly answered.

"Hello?" her high-pitched voice peeked.

"Er, hi. This is Natalie. Are you coming to my party?" I asked urgently.

There wasn't an immediate answer, but only laughter. I could hear other kids in the background.

"Hello?" I called again.

"Natalie, you are weird. We're not coming to your party! It was a joke! Like we'd come to your house! You stink all of the time. You are gross. And ugly." She went on, as I heard other kids chuckling in the background. "None of us are coming, you dork!"

"Oh…" was all I could say, as the tears built up in my eyes. "Okay. Goodbye." I hung up. I really needed to end that phone call.

After a while, I stopped worrying about the kids and remained at the front door. Whatever. It was some joke on the nerd. I shouldn't have expected anything less. But they didn't matter. Not like my daddy and grandma. I watched and waited for my daddy's red truck to pull into the drive. And when it did, I was going to run to him. Really run. I was so hopeful that he'd show up. He wouldn't play a joke like those kids. I knew he wouldn't.

Soon, 9:00 p.m. arrived. Still nothing. Faye had already cut the cake and ate some ice cream. We had two toddlers at the time that could swallow somewhat, so she gave them some. But I was still waiting. There was time, I told myself. When 9:30 p.m. came around, Faye came to the door and said, "It's bedtime."

"But what if someone comes? Can I stay up a little longer?" I pleaded.

Laughing, Faye said, "You really are a stupid girl, aren't you? It's nine thirty, and your party started at five o'clock. No one is going to come for you."

"But my daddy. We sent him an invitation. And my grandma, they'll come," I protested.

"Natalie, they aren't going to come. You could send them an invitation every day for the rest of your life, and they aren't going to come for you. They don't love you. Your daddy, he didn't want you. That's why he left you. He didn't love you, and he never will. He's never going to ever come back for you, no matter how long you wait. He will never come. Why are you so stupid?" she questioned. "It's unbelievable how stupid one person can be."

Tears flooded my eyes, and pain struck my heart. As much as

I didn't want to believe her, I did. She was right. If she were wrong, my daddy and grandma would have shown.

My daddy didn't want me. It had been almost six years since the last time I saw him, and he hadn't come back. I hadn't even heard from him. Maybe Faye was right. Maybe he didn't love me. No one, I guess, ever really did. I knew that my real mom didn't.

That night, I cried myself to sleep, though the sleeping part didn't come for hours later. I was stuck in this place. I turned ten years old, and there were still eight more to go before I would be able to leave. My daddy was not coming. Neither was my grandma. And those facts broke my little heart. I wanted to use my birthday wish, but I knew better than to waste it on my daddy this round. I was growing up. It was time to forget about all of that. So that night, for my birthday, I wished to be eighteen. I wished that I could be all grown up. That I could be an adult. I wished for my childhood to be done with. To be over.

It wasn't till I was older that I realized that Faye probably never sent those invitations. There is cruelty and evil in the world. Faye, she mastered both. She knew how to hit a girl below the belt. She knew how to truly break my heart. And my childhood innocence fell into her trap. That night, she succeeded in taking away my hope. I believed her as my father's absence did nothing but prove her correct. And on my tenth birthday, I started to let go of the idea of my daddy ever returning. I lost part of what was helping me survive: my faith, an attribute I couldn't afford to lose.

Monsters in the Dark

Children's bodies aren't like automobiles with the assailant's fingerprints lingering on the wheel. The world of sexual abuse is quintessentially secret. It is the perfect crime.

—Beatrix Campbell

Most children are scared of the dark, scared of monsters, werewolves, or other figments of their imaginations. Usually, a nice bedtime story or a night-light takes care of the problem. Usually. Most people say they wake up from a nightmare, but the truth was, I woke up into one.

Jack Winters was considered by most to be a strange man. He was somewhat slow. I called him Daddy Jack. Daddy Jack was a truck driver. He was gone for weeks at a time but was occasionally home on the weekends. Needless to say, there were severe marital problems between Faye and Jack. In all actuality, "marital problems" was a complete understatement. They hated each other. If they weren't talking behind each other's backs, they were screaming at each other. And when screaming didn't do the job, violence was the next step. But Jack, he was definitely an odd man.

When you're a child, you are trusting of everyone and everything. This was true of how I felt about Daddy Jack. I didn't realize anything was wrong with him giving me a bath and helping my wash my pee-pee really, really well. I didn't realize that when Daddy comes to your room after the "good night kiss" when everyone else is asleep was bad. I didn't understand that our trips, our secrets, were terrible. I trusted as any child should be able to.

"Good night, Daddy Jack!"

"Good night, Natalie. I love you."

"I love you, too." I always responded, though I'm sure I never really understood what that meant. Love. And I knew, deep down, he didn't love me, and I certainly didn't love him. But sometimes, you just have to go through the motions.

I was just starting to doze off to sleep but was awakened with the creak of the door. I saw his shadow, knowing it was him. After all, that was when I saw him the most, when the darkness fell. Scared, my eyes were closed. I was supposed to be asleep, and I wasn't. So I pretended. I didn't want to get in trouble.

Still. I was absolutely still. Interestingly though, I didn't have to try to be. Fear has an interesting way of paralyzing the body. My bed would creak with his weight gradually depressing the springs. Lying there, I would feel his hands underneath my covers, trying to find their way through darkness. He would use my legs as a guide until he found the waist of my pajamas. They would start to slide downward to my knees. My panties were next. Soon, I would be bare, and the horror would begin. He would always start with one hand. Caressing me, first very slow and gentle, working his way up with more speed and pressure. My skin would start to moisten. It would always do that before it started to hurt.

Soon, my legs would be forced apart. Slowly, he would climb

atop of me. My breathing was already shallow because of the anxious and scared feeling that fluttered in my stomach. His weight not only worsened my breathing, but also the fear. I kept my eyes shut, as tightly as I could. I didn't want to see. I didn't want to know why it hurt. I just know that it did.

That's what I remember most, that it would hurt really, really bad. I always wanted to scream and shout, but I knew that I must stay quiet. As always, I didn't want to get into trouble. The pain would shoot through my nerves like a knife. It was wrenching pain, but never could I move. I had to be asleep. I would always cry though. I could never stop those quiet, traitorous tears from seeping through the armor of my emotion. But they were silent tears. Silent. Still. But stillness, I assure you, is more terrifying than any yell or threat one could muster. Quiet, yes, it was what most would consider as quiet. He was quiet. Not a word would he speak. But I could still hear him. His breathing. The racing of my own heart. It was haunting. Sometimes, a whimper would make its way out because of the pain. Because of my tenderness and because of his sting. He would stay for a while, fulfilling his needs. Sometimes it was just a little while, but other times it seemed to last forever. But even during the shortest times, the memories, I assure you, lasted for a lifetime. The nights would come to an end, but the memories… the pain…. It never did.

Some nights were worse than others in terms of how long, what was done, and what was used. I remember it at the early age of three, though my most vivid memories were when I was around six and seven. I assume he didn't think I would remember from my early age. That I would forget. But the truth is, you never forget, even if you wholeheartedly want to. Being that he was a truck driver, I was spared some nights and tortured in others.

He would take me with him in his truck sometimes, promising so much fun, telling Faye that I loved to go. Those evenings I can't describe the misery that took place. I remember seeing the truck stops and slowly pulling in with the loud diesel truck. Either the trip was about to begin or thankfully it was coming to an end. Honestly, I don't feel that any word combinations in the English language could encompass the horror I experienced. It was those nights that everything was heightened, and now I know it was because those were the times when he was sure he wouldn't be caught. His truck smelled of dirt and cigarettes. The air was heavy, as if there just wasn't enough oxygen. The very atmosphere was weighted, holding me down as soon as I stepped into the back sleeper part. Daddy Jack was relentless during those nights. It was like he never got enough. There was so much I didn't understand about what was going on, but I didn't dare to question. I would ask him to stop, but he wouldn't. He just… kept doing it. Mostly he would just touch me, but sometimes, I would have to touch him. He wanted me to kiss certain parts… Parts I didn't like to. It was nasty. All of it. And Daddy Jack was just gross. He smelled like dirt and booze. I suppose the drinking helped him live with himself. I was thankful for it, because he fell asleep faster. Daddy Jack was always dirty, too. His hands were covered in grease. He'd always tell me that it was fun for us. That what was going on was just for daddies and their little girls, like him and me.

I tried to morph what he was doing into love. Daddy Jack loved me, that's why he was doing this. That was the way I coped with it for a while. I suppose a part of me knew it wasn't right, but who was I to ask? Who was I to confide in? I had no one to talk to and no one to trust. They didn't believe me before, and I didn't expect they'd start now. Especially with this.

I just tried to make sense of it all. Once sitting in the backyard, there was a momma cat with her kittens. She had given birth in the alley, and I brought them into our backyard to live. One of the nurses was outside with me one afternoon, and we watched them together. As I surveyed the momma cat lick her kittens, I asked, "Miss Ann, why does that cat lick all over her kittens?"

"She's cleaning them, Natalie. She's giving them a bath and taking care of them," she explained.

"Oh. Is it because she loves them?" I wondered aloud.

"Yes. She takes care of them. They are her babies," she said.

"Oh," I said. As I watched her, I thought that maybe that's why Daddy Jack licked me. Because of love. As a cat licks her kittens, it's all out of love, right? But I somehow knew that something was wrong with this love of his. I never heard of anyone talk about their daddy doing these things. And my daddy John certainly didn't do those things to me, and I knew he loved me. Something wasn't right. I didn't like it. It always hurt so much. It made me cry. Isn't love supposed to make you happy? Are you supposed to want love? I didn't want Daddy Jack's love.

I wouldn't know the answers to my questions for a long time. All I could do was what he told me. Those nights were terrible. I would lie there, begging my very being that I would fall asleep. Pleading with my dreams to take me anywhere other than where I was. When he would finish, I would always sob quietly into my pillow. That's all I could do. That and wish. I would peer out the window sometimes and wish, wish with all of my might that God would make me a star. I knew I had not done anything great. I knew that I was not worthy. I had not led a country. I had done nothing grandiose. All I had to offer was an A on a math test, but I would fall asleep wishing.

"Please, God, make me a star. Take me away, and make me a star. Please, Jesus, let me be a star with you, and take me out of this world..."

Baby Bump

. . . .

Fear is the parent of cruelty.

—George Anthony Froude

. . . .

Daddy Jack took advantage of me as often as he could. He told me it was our secret. A secret between him and me, and no one could ever know. I guess a part of me knew that it was wrong, but I wasn't sure what to do. I wasn't sure what he would do. Jack never hit me as Faye did, but I couldn't put it past him. I'd seen him hit Faye before, so I'm sure he'd come at me if I made him mad enough.

So I kept our secret. No one ever knew what happened late at night or in his truck. Honestly, I'm not sure Faye even knew. At least, she never said anything about it. I figured it would be easy enough to keep my mouth shut though. I was able to when it came to everything else. And it wasn't like anyone would know, right?

I never knew exactly how babies came into the world, but I had my ideas, as any ten-year-old does. I knew that it had something to do with love though. And something to do with a boy and a girl being together. The most logical was kissing. When a boy and a girl kiss, their saliva mixes, and she swallows it. That's why the baby grows in her stomach. I mean, that made sense. However, during one lunch conversation at the table between fifth grade girls, I quickly became educated.

"I think it happens by sex," my friend Valerie said.

"Yeah, I'm pretty sure. My mom said that when a man and a woman love each other, they have sex, and that makes a baby," Riley agreed.

"Sex?" I asked. "What is that?"

The girls giggled and turned red.

"You don't know?" Valerie asked.

"No, I don't." I was confused. I didn't recall ever learning the term. I had heard of it, but I thought it was a bad word.

"When a husband and wife marry, they have sex, which makes a baby. The boy sticks his pee-pee into a girl, and a baby comes after that," Riley explained.

As she continued, I felt the blood drain from my face, and I became faint. *Oh no*, I thought. *I'm having sex with Daddy Jack.*

A few weeks later, we had a reality check, where they talked about girls having their period and abstinence. And for me, it was definitely a reality check. I hated that day for I learned that I wasn't a virgin. I felt so sad. It was bad to have sex. You were supposed to wait until you were married. Until you fell in love.

They taught us that you could get all kinds of diseases. The thought made me sick to my stomach. What if I got a disease? What if I got a blood virus? Daddy Jack never wore those condom things. Then there was pregnancy to worry about, too. There were so many complications…

A few weeks passed, but the worries lingered in my mind. I was worried about the venereal diseases they talked about, but I was more concerned about having a baby. What was I going to do if I had a baby? How would I know? And everyone would know the secret if I had a baby! I just checked myself every day. For bumps or any kind of sign. Time passed, and nothing ever showed up. I decided not to worry. I wouldn't worry about it until something happened.

However, soon after, something did happen. One afternoon, I noticed a bulge, but it wasn't on my stomach. It was lower. As I examined it, fear crept into my heart. *What is it?* I asked myself as my mind answered. The bump wasn't red like the pictures we saw. It didn't appear to be infected… The bump was on the inside. Then, it dawned on me. *It…it must be a baby coming. I'm…pregnant.* There was no other explanation. The bump wasn't a wart or anything. It was inside. Oval shaped. It was what had to be…a baby. I was going to have a baby.

Over the next few days, I worried and planned about what I would do. First things first, I wouldn't be telling a soul. I would just have to hide it. I'd wear baggy clothes as it got bigger. And then when I had the baby, I'd just have to figure out how to take care of it. Maybe I could just tell someone I found it and then beg to keep it. If it was taken into CPS, I could get Faye to request it to come back to our house. It would be extra money for her, so I didn't suppose she'd mind too much. And I'd take care of him or her. I kind of hoped it was a girl. I'd play with her and love her and dress her up pretty. I began to think of names.

If the baby was a girl, I was going to name her Jennifer. I loved that name. I thought it sounded so pretty. And that was my teacher's first name. She was so nice, kind, and gentle. Plus, she had long pretty hair and a nice smile. I hoped my little girl would be like her. If the baby was a boy, I wanted to name him Benjamin, after a boy in my class. He was really nice, and I thought he was cute.

She or he was growing, I knew. Because my bump was getting bigger. I wondered when it would migrate more toward my stomach because it was kind of uncomfortable. Sometimes it hurt really badly, but I figured that was part of having a child. It wasn't supposed to be easy. I worried though about medical care. I knew you were supposed to see a doctor, but I didn't have that luxury. I just went on about my days. I tried to eat as much as I could at school because I knew the baby would need food to grow. I was going to be a great mom, I really was. Not like Faye, though. I would love my baby and take care of her. I just had to make it through this pregnancy, but it was taking a toll on me. I was really tired. And a lot of the times, I didn't feel too good. I was worried all of the time, though. What if she was sick? What if my baby Jennifer needed tubes like the babies at our house? I lay awake at night, thinking about all of the horrible scenarios. I always was one to assume the worst.

But the bump was getting larger, almost by the day. And it hurt almost constantly.

One day at the playground, I was starting to limp. My baby bump was primarily on the left side and was causing a lot of problems. Sometimes my entire leg would go numb. I wished it would hurry up toward my stomach, but it didn't. It just kept growing right there. I tried to recall reality check. I remember them talking about the process, but that day I was so emotional and freaked out by all of the information that I didn't remember what they said would happen. I didn't know how long I had been pregnant. Or how many weeks I had left to go.

That afternoon outside, my gym teacher noticed me limping around. For the past week or so, I just wasn't my active self. She asked me what was wrong. I just told her I hurt my leg and tried to deter her, but she wasn't having it. She sent me to the nurse.

As I walked inside the building, I felt sick. The nurse would know for sure what was wrong. They were smart and trained in all of this stuff. I didn't know what to do, but I knew that I needed help. Maybe she would help me. Maybe I should just be honest with her. If I lied, she might get mad and not help me take care of my baby. I turned the corner into the nurse's office and stepped in.

"Hello, Ms. Michaels," I stammered.

"Oh, hello, Natalie! How are you today? What brings you in here?" she questioned.

"Um, well, my leg is going numb," I said.

"It's going numb?" She seemed alarmed. "When did this start?"

"A few months ago."

"A few months ago?" she repeated. "Natalie, that is not good. You should have come in sooner. Come lie down on the table." As I lay down, she asked, "Where does it hurt?"

She waited for my response, but I didn't answer. I was afraid to tell her where it hurt. Where the bump was.

"Natalie? Where does it hurt?" she asked again. I started to cry.

"Oh, Mrs. Michaels!" I said through the tears. "Something is wrong with my baby. She hasn't moved to my stomach yet." I sobbed.

Mrs. Michaels held me, though she had a confusing look on

her face. "Natalie, what on earth do you mean 'your baby'?"

I tried to calm myself to explain. "Mrs. Michaels, I have a baby. Look, I can show you." I closed the curtain and took off my pants and underwear. "See?"

"Oh!" Mrs. Michaels shrieked. "Oh, Natalie, that's not a baby. Oh my goodness, we have to call your momma Faye."

"What? What do you mean it's not a baby?" I was shocked, and surprisingly, I was angry. I had a baby. I'd had sex with Daddy Jack, and I was pregnant. Wasn't I? Though I'd never tell her how I was pregnant or by who. I just… What else could it be? "It's been growing, Mrs. Michaels. For a while now."

"Oh, darling!" She assisted me putting my clothes back on. "Honey, it's not a baby. It's some sort of tumor. We need to get you to a doctor immediately."

"It's a tumor?" I asked fearfully.

"Something of the sort, honey. But don't worry, we are going to take care of you! Okay, don't worry. I'll call your momma Faye, and she'll be here. It's going to be okay. All right?"

I didn't say anything. I had a tumor, not a baby. I didn't really know how to accept the news. I was sad though. I was looking forward to having a daughter or a son. I wanted to love her and take care of her. I wanted to be a mommy. A good one. But in some ways, I was relieved. Daddy Jack wasn't going to be my baby's daddy. I worried that if it was a girl, he might do to her what he had done to me. No. I wouldn't let that happen.

My thoughts were all over the place. I was so upset about all of it. As I waited for Faye, I hoped that Mrs. Michaels wouldn't tell her that I thought I was pregnant. I'm not sure how Faye would respond to that. I'm sure that in some way, I'd be in trouble over it.

The weeks to follow were torturous though. I had to go to the doctor and take off my clothes. It was awful. When we were in the room, I was so scared. I didn't know what this man was going to do. Was he like Daddy Jack? Faye didn't explain anything to me. And I freaked out. I didn't want him to touch me.

Oh, not again, I thought. *I don't want to have sex with him, too.* I was so worried about everything. The secret was sure to come out now. What if the doctor knew I was having sex? It wasn't going to be good. I just... It was all overwhelming.

Oddly enough though, no one asked me anything. They told me that I had a hernia and that I had to have surgery. The doctor said it was from extreme strain, but it was odd that I'd received one at my age. I kind of wondered if it came from having sex with Daddy Jack, but I didn't ask, mainly because I didn't want them to ask me any questions. He told me that when I see bumps though, I should always tell my mommy because it could be very dangerous. I agreed with him while telling myself that would never happen.

I knew though now that I really didn't want to have sex anymore. Next time Daddy Jack tried, I was going to fight him off. Or tell him, "No." I hated him for all of this. He caused me so much pain on so many different levels. And what if all of this happened again? I just couldn't let it happen again.

The following week I had surgery, which was another terrible experience. The surgery went well, but my aftercare certainly didn't. Faye dropped me off at the hospital and picked me up the next day. I heard some of the hospital staff talking about how weird it was that she didn't stay with me. But that was just Faye. I didn't bring in a paycheck to her, so she didn't really care all that much about me.

Over the next few days, I experienced pain as I never had before. Faye didn't fill my pain prescriptions. She said that I'd become a drug addict like my mom if I took them. I cried and cried. It hurt so badly, I thought that I was surely dying. I'd doze off to sleep, hoping I wouldn't wake up. But I would, to pain. I lost weight, because Faye wouldn't bring food to my room. And I'd rather starve than try to get up and walk.

The whole experience was horrid... and confusing to me. There was so much I didn't understand about all of this. I thought about what could have been my baby. I knew that I would be a good mom one day. Though, I missed my little bump. The little bulge was something for me to take care of and it took my mind off the fact that no one was taking care of me.

But, as time passed, I got better. Soon, hopefully, I'd be able to go back to school. That was the worst part of the whole situation, not going to school every day. The classroom was the only safe place I had, and I wasn't allowed to go back for two weeks. A good thing though was that Daddy Jack didn't come into my room or take me on trips for a long time after that. I guess he was kind of scared and didn't want to hurt me worse. I was thankful for that. Maybe he did love me a little bit. Maybe him stopping for a while was his way of saying sorry.

Thanksgiving

The Pilgrims made seven times more graves than huts. No Americans have been more impoverished than these who, nevertheless, set aside a day of thanksgiving.

—H. U. Westermayer

Holidays were something that I hated growing up, not because of lack of gifts or absence of joy. It was because I wouldn't get my guaranteed eight hours a day, five days a week away from the house. Even having a Friday off was pure torture. I remember finding it so strange that kids would fake sickness to miss school and do just about anything to get out of going to class. In my case, I would do anything to keep from missing school. Even when I was sick with a high-grade fever, I would insist that I felt okay. When storms would threaten our town, I would fervently hope that classes wouldn't be cancelled.

I remember one time I had pinkeye, and the nurse sent me home. Faye just told me to walk home, but I changed the plan. I left for the playground for about an hour and snuck back into class. Perhaps that seemed odd, but school was heaven compared to my home. School was my escape, it was my safety, and it was my comfort zone. Teachers were nice. I always tried to do great on everything to make sure I was making them happy. In a sense, school was my lifeline. I received all the praise, love, and attention I needed when I was there. When I was at school, I knew that I would receive a meal. I would not be hit. I would not be hurt. I was a nerd, dressed in less-than-appealing clothing, which led me to be bullied, but those kids had nothing on Faye and Jack. I was immune to their silly little remarks. No, school was a safe place. It was, for at least eight hours a day, a place where I could grow, learn, strive, and not worry about not being worthy.

But when holidays came, those times were cut short. Something that was absolutely unbearable to me. I remember one Thanksgiving that was particularly terrible, a Thanksgiving Day that I truly had nothing to be thankful for.

I was in the fifth grade, about ten years old. It was a Wednesday, and school was let out at noon. The air was cool, but the bright autumn colors seemed to give some degree of warmth. Adrianna, who was Faye's first biological daughter, and her family were coming to visit. I never liked Adrianna, and it was clear she never liked me. Every time she was around, I got into twice the amount of trouble. Though she was about twenty years older than me, she acted as though we were the same age with fierce sibling rivalry and jealousy. I suppose that it didn't help matters that her son, Shawn, and I were approximately the same age, but not at all approximate in talents.

I was a girl who tried my best at everything and usually succeeded. I had straight A's in school. I had scholarships to every Kids, Incorporated sport: basketball, track, soccer, T-ball, baseball, volleyball, you name it. Faye didn't mind my participation, as long as she didn't have to pay for anything, take me anywhere, and I wasn't bothering her. Honestly, the feeling was absolutely mutual. As long as I didn't have to talk to her, be around her, or be involved with her or Jack, I was thrilled. I was definitely an achiever. If there was something to be accomplished, I was going to give my all trying to accomplish it.

Needless to say, I wasn't a big fan of their company: her, her husband, son, or daughter. They didn't like me, and I didn't care for them. But they were in town for the next few days and would be staying in my room. And there was nothing I could do about it.

When I arrived at the house, it was chaos. Her children were much less disciplined. They did whatever they wanted, whenever and however they wanted it—something that was very foreign to me. I basically tried to stay out of the way and blend into the background as much as possible. I thoroughly tried not to be noticed by any of them. But as we know, you can try to fly, but gravity is a powerful force.

Wednesday evening passed by. I woke up early Thursday morning to study my spelling. Even if it was Thanksgiving, I was going to get my words memorized, because I had made 100s on all of my tests so far that semester. Ever since I lost that spelling bee, I was adamant about making a perfect score. I couldn't let this one be the black bird. After I finished, I went to the park. No one noticed I had left, and for that I was thankful.

I came back home around 1:00 p.m. I slipped in and got a plate full of food. Another thing to be grateful for was that I was going to at least get to eat this weekend. Faye and Jack were very poor, not because we didn't have money, but because they would spend it before it could be put to good use. I was extremely underweight as a child. At this time, I only weighed about forty-five pounds. Faye would tell the doctors that it was simply because I refused to eat. In all reality, it was simply because there was nothing to eat. Oftentimes, our food was rationed to the most extreme of circumstances. I was not allowed into the cabinets or fridge without the threat of a thrashing. Most of the time, she had locks on the cabinets. And if they weren't locked, she would hide the food so that you couldn't find it. If you ate something without permission, you were in trouble, which was another factor. When I was in trouble, I wasn't allowed food. And I was always in trouble. If I complained that I didn't have enough or was still hungry, she'd make sure I really didn't have enough by giving me nothing at all. I remember meals consisting of half a piece of bread with mustard and one-fourths of a slice of cheese. That was dinner, if you were obedient.

At least during the holidays, the food wasn't so bad. We would get donations from the local churches. Faye would often apply to several so we would get tons of food. She loved the charity the holidays presented and would always take full advantage of all the local food drives. I suppose it bothered her too at times, not having much to eat.

But Thanksgiving was a feast. And on Thanksgiving, I could get seconds, possibly thirds, if I made sure to behave myself. It was definitely thrilling to my stomach. So that afternoon, I ate as much as my small tummy would allow me, and then I slipped back out. I preferred to stay away. As far as I could tell, they never noticed when I was gone. I had checked out several books from the library over the break. I enjoyed going to the park, swinging, or losing myself in the fictional world the book offered. I'd do anything to escape the reality I was in. Especially when Adrianna was here.

The days went by quickly. Friday evening had arrived with the quickness of a flash. Everyone went shopping that day. I wasn't allowed to come because there was toothpaste left in the sink, and

I was the scapegoat for Shawn and Ellie. Faye had such a pet peeve for that. A sink should be spotless at all times, in her opinion. I never understood why it was a big deal. I mean, it was not like it was on the floor. But whatever. I'd suffered through worse things than being told to stay here when they left. But for my punishment, I had to spend the rest of the day cleaning the bathroom with a toothbrush. When I finished, the kitchen was next. I didn't really mind; scrubbing in little circles was mind-numbing, and it wasn't a beating. I was by myself and away from all of them. Again, it could have been much worse.

They got back around six o'clock. Adrianna kept ranting and raving about all the wonderful gifts she got everyone. I knew better than to expect anything, but I was still hopeful, as any child would be. But that's the thing about Adrianna; she loved to shoot down my hopes and spirits. She made a display of the gifts she bought for her children; she even let them have some of the gifts she had bought for Christmas early. But for me, I was bad. I was a bad girl, and Santa didn't like bad girls, and bad girls didn't get gifts from him or anyone else. Same old rant. I never got caught up in the whole materialism of it all, though. The only thing I ever wanted was my daddy, and neither Santa nor Adrianna would be able to pull that one off.

Adrianna explained she had worked up an appetite and wanted potato soup. I had never heard of anything like that in my entire life. It sounded strange. Why would anyone make a soup out of potatoes? But then again, it was food, so I don't suppose I really cared.

Dinner was ready. Everyone sat around the table ready to feast. I remember looking into the bowl and being a little grossed out. It was white and lumpy, with huge chunks of potatoes emerging like glaciers in the arctic. The smell was awful. It smelled as if it were rotting by the second. But who knew? Maybe it was good.

It took me a long time to take the courage to find out though. As Shawn and Ellie sampled the slop, they shouted with disgust, which further discouraged me.

"This is disgusting!" Shawn shouted. "I'm not eating this crappy food."

Ellie mimicked his complaints. "Ew, this is gross," she complained while throwing her spoon across the room.

At that point, I was even more frightened by the lumpy mess. This stuff, whatever it was, was not appealing. But I had to try it. I took my spoon and sampled it, and before I could prevent it, my throat repulsed and gagged. I didn't know what was in it, but it was terrible. Absolutely terrible. It was sour and sticky somehow. Everything about it violated the human senses. But I knew if I didn't eat, I would be in trouble. And I hated to be in trouble. So I tried again but couldn't stomach it. I spat it back out in my bowl, and much to my bad luck, I was spotted by Adrianna.

The next thing I knew, she was screaming. "I can't believe you don't like my soup! You little *brat*! Do you think you're too good? Do you think that *you* are too good for *my soup*?"

"No, ma'am!" I shrieked. "I'm sorry. It just…"

But neither an apology nor an explanation was enough to fix my actions; not nearly enough. Adrianna started to yell at Faye, telling her that I was an ungrateful brat for spitting out my food. I tried to correct her and plead with Faye, but it was too late. Faye had that look in her eye. I was in trouble. Once again. But this time, I could tell there would be a physical element.

Even though I expected the hits to some degree, they still always seemed to catch me off guard somehow. My reflexes could never respond that quickly. Upon the blow, I flipped out of my chair and landed on the floor. The kicks, those were always much worse than the hits. A slap from a hand was nothing compared to the blow of a leg. I just shriveled, as I always did. Usually in the fetal position, covering my face, waiting for Faye to get tired, waiting for it to pass. But this time was worse because I had an audience, and Faye had fans.

They were all laughing, yelling, and chanting, and it riled her up. Instead of the strikes weakening, they were growing stronger, and soon, there was more than one person delivering them. The kids joined in; it was a game. Who could hit the hardest? I was a living, breathing punching bag. But the breathing part was dwindling. Every breath taken in was forced out by another strike against my back. Shawn and Ellie were going at it, beating me like a Columbian does the bongo drums, smacking my head, face, whatever part of me they could reach. I started to get lightheaded, then my vision was going in and out. I didn't know when they would stop, but I prayed for it to be soon. Or to at least lose consciousness. At this point I was crying, not because of sadness, but because of the pain. I felt so weak. Maybe they'd just kill me, knock out a vital organ. That was the last thought I consciously remembered. *Death, I'd be thankful for that.*

I don't know how long I was out, but I awoke on the side of my chair. My head was pounding, and I felt incredibly weak. I looked around to find everyone on the couch watching a Christmas movie. It was my plan to crawl to my bed and sleep it off. I tried to move, but it was much harder than I expected. My muscles were incredibly sore. They were bruised, and it felt that they were also broken somehow. The soreness was almost worse than the initial strikes. I was doing all I could to gain distance but was doing nothing more than moving like a snake without its head, squirming. And unfortunately, I caught the attention of Ellie.

"Natalie is awake now! Look!" she screamed.

They all rose and approached me. Faye grabbed me by the hair, her favorite method of holding me. I was on my feet but was barely standing. The quick motion had blood rushing to my head and left me in a dizzy haze. Faye pulled me toward the table and said, "You know, it looks like you could use something to eat. How about some potato soup? Won't you like that?" She said that with a hiss.

Before I could stop her, she grabbed the bowl and shoved it into my face. Once again, I couldn't breath. I was gagging, choking, and trying everything I could to get air. But my efforts were dismissed. She kept pouring the soup down my throat until the bowl was empty. I started throwing up; I couldn't help it. I was nauseous before it began, and the soup sent me over the edge. Faye stepped back.

"I hope you know you're cleaning that up," she snarled. She always made me clean up my own puke. I hated that most of all. It was nauseating.

All I could manage was a shake of the head. I was hunched over, trying to breath, but no matter how hard I tried, I couldn't get air. My lungs were screaming at me, and I was doing everything possible to answer their demands. But I couldn't. I fell to my knees, gasping, choking up everything within my body, it seemed: blood, saliva, and potato soup. It was all there. And so were they. Jack, Faye, Cole, Adrianna, Ellie, and Shawn. They watched me, just like they were watching the Christmas movie. My suffering was their motion picture.

"That's what you get. See if you ever disrespect my cooking again," Adrianna warned.

After some time, I was finally able to catch my breath. I cleaned up my mess, trying not to think about it, trying not to become sick. It was better to hold my breath, but I was having an unusually hard time doing that. After I was finished, I limped off to bed. I felt like a semi truck had hit me. When I reached my room, it was a relief to close my eyes and drift back into the safety of unconsciousness.

For the next two days, I don't think I moved more than a few feet, and only to use the bathroom. Fortunately, Adrianna and everyone left me alone. My body was bruised, and it ached. But that wasn't the worst of it. Ever since I lost my breath Friday night, it seemed as though I never got it back. I sounded raspy, and the air itself seemed to be tainted as it entered, burning my throat and my lungs. I couldn't stop coughing up crap. I was sweaty and extremely hot. I didn't know what was wrong, but I'd never had symptoms such as these. And they were only getting worse. I just know that I felt awful. I had to sleep on the floor, because the others were using my bed. The hardness of the ground made things worse. All I could do was lay there and listen to the others.

Adrianna and her motley crew left Saturday evening. But, that morning, I heard Adrianna talking to Faye. "I think I know why my potato soup was so god awful."

"Did you figure it out? It tasted terrible," Faye said.

"Yeah, I went to throw something in the trash. I spotted the milk gallon. I looked at the expiration date. Apparently, the milk had gone sour, and so did my potato soup," she spoke through a howling laugh.

They both echoed each other in laughter. I couldn't believe it. The soup had been made with rotten milk? It was legitimately disgusting, and I got in trouble? Fury ran through my veins. How I hated all of them. Such fools! Here I was, feeling as though I were dying, and they laugh at the fact that soup was made from sour milk. The same soup that was shoved down my throat. I was completely outraged but quickly contained myself. What exactly could I do? Nothing. Absolutely nothing.

After they left, I went to the bathroom to take a shower, trying anything to recover and get things back to normal, but I was weak. I hadn't eaten anything, and I'd hardly even had a glass of water. When Monday morning came around, I knew I wasn't going to school. I looked like the angel of death and felt much worse. Even Faye knew herself that I needed a doctor. This holiday was never going to end.

My appointment was at 11:00 a.m. I heard Faye on the phone talking to a receptionist earlier that morning.

"Yes, Natalie has come down with something terrible. She can't stop coughing. Her niece and nephew came into town for Thanksgiving, and they played nonstop. And rough too. She has bruises all over her. I keep telling those kids not to climb and jump out of trees, but you know children. They never listen to Momma." Chuckling, she continued, "And you know, they did so much running around, and I think she just might have the flu because of it. I can never get her to keep her jacket on. But anyways, I really need to bring her in. I'm worried about my little girl."

The nausea was back. She made me sick all over again. Lies. I could never understand how anyone could be so good at them.

She could come up with infallible stories that no one would ever think to question. And why would they? Jack and Faye were loving foster parents who took in children that no one else would. They cared for the sick kids that had the most terrible problems. They were wonderful people. Like I said, lies.

I was looking forward to the doctor's visit. I was hoping that they would see the bruises and question me. I planned on telling them what happened. I had worked up a little courage with the help of the anger I had from this morning. Stupid idiots, they were. But my pediatrician didn't ask.

I was eager that they would see how pale I was, but they didn't seem to notice, just kept blaming it on the sickness. When I went to the doctor, the symptoms of my illness would hide the abuse. That's how it was for all of us.

I was praying they would hear my lungs and see the pain was not from infection but from the affliction of a beating. I was in the room, but it was like I was invisible. It's like the doctor was just oblivious to it all. My diagnosis was a severe case of bronchitis. I was sent home with antibiotics and respiratory breathing treatments that I had to take for the next two weeks. But the worst part was that I had to stay home for two more days. They were worried about it being contagious.

This Thanksgiving was taking over the year! I was sad and defeated. Two more days without school. I felt so alone. I felt worthless, knowing that no one truly made an effort to notice me and to notice my pain. Again, I failed. When would I ever find the courage to stand up against Faye? But then again, how come no one would look into my eyes and see the hurt that was more prominent than color? Why, why did no one care to see what was really going on? I felt bad to complain and to question. I knew that there were worse scenarios. I saw the babies each day, living in wheelchairs, hooked up to machines. At the end of the day, I suppose I didn't really have reason to complain. Faye never damaged me like that. But I couldn't help it. I just wanted someone to notice and to do something about it. But they wouldn't this time. And probably not the time after that. This Thanksgiving had offered nothing to be thankful for.

Upon reference of my condition years later, I suppose the diagnosis of bronchitis was accurate. Never would the doctors have guessed that I was really suffering from aspiration pneumonia from being force-fed and the soup entering my lungs. The following year, I was diagnosed with asthma. My lungs never recovered from that weekend. Neither did my heart. Holidays were horrendous. And the thought of being thankful about anything, well, it was just silly.

Eleven Years

Crimes sometimes shock us too much; vices almost always too little.

—Augustus Hare

About two years had passed since my last birthday. I was twelve years old and in the eighth grade. We had moved out into the country, kind of close to the Thomas' house. Times were harder than ever before. Our house was a run-down, double-wide trailer, almost as unstable as the family moving into it. We had a lot less money, though I didn't really know why. There was so much work to be done to ensure it would pass the state inspection. But Faye, she knew exactly how to navigate around those requirements. Persuading the fire chief was first on the list. And she succeeded. Faye always managed to bend the boundaries and revise the rules.

We were located about twenty miles outside of town. Absolutely isolated. Faye relished the control. She liked to be able to plan when people would come and when they would go. So the distance made things convenient for both Faye and Jack. It was so far out of town that the caseworkers probably wouldn't stop by as much. And with no one being around us, it was easy to do whatever they wanted without the fear of neighbors seeing or hearing.

Lately, Faye and Jack were getting reported to Child Protective Services on a number of accounts. Though nothing was done other than a quick meeting, I suppose they became a little nervous. After all, the children were their livelihood, and they would take every measure to ensure that they didn't lose that monthly income.

But even though the distance may have taken us away from the city, away from the fear of being reported, the move added significantly more problems. It was extremely expensive on gas. Even when we lived in town, we couldn't afford to fill the tank. Now, those problems were exacerbated. Money was…well, there wasn't any. Our electricity went out a lot. Fortunately, we had generators provided by the state in case of emergency to keep the babies' machines working when we couldn't pay the bill. And food became scarcer than it ever had been. We had a water well, which prevented us from getting the water cut off, but the hot-water heater was out. So taking a cold shower was the only option you had. In the summer, it wasn't so bad. But in the winter, it was miserable.

Times were very hard, and it seemed as though they were constantly getting worse. Next year, I was going to be in the sixth grade. Fortunately, the school district provided bus transportation. I hated the bus, but if it were up to Faye to have to take me to school, I would have never gone. And the thought of that was horrifying.

Weekends were rough though. Once the bus dropped me off on Friday afternoon, there was no going back to civilization until Monday morning. And because we lived so far out in the country, there was nowhere to go—no park, no convenience store or gas station. The only option was the open fields. It was lonely out there. I didn't have any friends. And even if I did, asking them over was not an option. I didn't know if Jack would take advantage of a new girl being in the house, and I would never subject one of my friends to that. Plus, I didn't want anyone to know how we lived. I couldn't let anyone know what my life really consisted of. School was a place I could get away from all of it. People at school knowing would only add to my troubles, and I didn't need anything else to deal with.

Once a month though, near the first, the various checks would come, and we would get to go to town on a Saturday. Faye was pleasant these weekends. She always was in a great mood when she had money in her pocket.

It was a Saturday afternoon, and our WIC card was just renewed and one of the Medicaid checks came in. Faye asked one of the nurses if she could come in to watch the children because Jack was out of town, fortunately. The weekends when he was away were wonderful. But Faye hated getting the kids out, and I agreed. She made me do all of the work, and it was extremely difficult. Most of the time there were at least two who needed wheelchairs. Lifting the babies was really hard for me. Most of them weighed more than I did. Carrying them honestly scared me. If I dropped them, it could be life threatening to both of us. So I was glad when the nurse agreed.

Since Faye was in a good mood, I decided to ask if I could accompany her. Much to my surprise, she said yes. I couldn't help but be excited. The grocery store was an adventure. We didn't get to go to many places. More than that, we didn't get to go to a store often, so it was almost like a field trip. And, as an additional bonus, I knew we'd have some food this weekend, which was thrilling.

The store was extremely crowded. Faye didn't mind if I wandered around, just as long as I found her before she left. So I asked, "Mom, may I go look in the arts and crafts?"

"Yeah, I guess," she said. "Just meet me at the front of the store in thirty minutes."

"Yes, ma'am," I said as I excitedly turned and headed to the aisle. Gosh, I loved when we got checks in the mail. Faye was so pleasant then. I went over to the markers. I loved looking at all of the colors. I knew there was no way that I could buy them, but I loved to look and think of ideas for art class at school.

Rummaging through the coloring books, I heard my name.

"Natalie?" It was an old, frail voice, one that sparked memories. I turned toward the direction, and there was my grandmother. She was older but still completely recognizable. Her long white hair was twisted up, and she was wearing a blouse.

I was stunned. Was it really her? As I walked closer, I could detect her floral smell, shifting my mind back to times when I was absolutely happy.

"Grandma?" I asked in disbelief. "Is that you?"

"Oh, Natalie. Look at you. You're all grown up," she said.

Before I could register what was going on, I ran to her and gave her a big hug. "Grandma!" I was so excited to see her. She was still here! I couldn't help the tears of joy that stung my eyes or the lump in my throat. She was really right in front of me. I thought back to my birthday party for a millisecond, but quickly deterred my thoughts. It didn't matter. I wasn't mad anymore. Here she was, my grandma.

We were caught in our embrace when a voice startled us both. "Beth," Faye said in a cool tone as she was standing behind us.

"Oh, hello, Faye," my grandma nervously stuttered. "I just saw Natalie, and I said hello."

She seemed scared and immediately let me go, though I resisted. I had missed her so much, and in the back of my mind, I wished I could go home with her. But before I could think of what to do, Faye was grabbing my arm and pulling me away. I knew better than to resist, though I longed to.

"I see," Faye icily said. "Well, that's nice of you, but we better be going."

"Wait, Grandma. Where's Daddy?" I asked. I had to know where he was. "Where is my daddy?" As soon as the question escaped me, Faye's grip tightened.

"Ow," I whimpered, but I was distracted by my grandmother. Her face was solemn and all of a sudden became extremely pale. Her normal smile quickly faded in a sharp, stern line. And she slowly shifted to Faye.

"You didn't tell her?" she demanded. "You didn't tell her about her own father?" She was angry. I don't think I'd ever remember hearing her speak in that tone.

"That's none of your damn business. She's mine. That was the deal," Faye said in a cold voice.

What was going on? What where they talking about? Fear and panic washed over me.

"Wait, what? Tell me what? Where is my daddy? Tell me!" I started screaming. What were they talking about? What was going on?

"Go ahead, Beth. Tell her," Faye stated.

My grandmother looked at me with tears in her eyes. "Natalie…" A long pause created an indescribable bout of suspension—a suspense that spoke louder than words ever could.

"No! No! Where is he?" I screamed. "Oh, where is my daddy?" But my voice was losing all force as I felt my heart sink within my chest.

"Your daddy… He…" My grandmother could hardly speak as she was becoming choked up.

"Go on, Beth! Tell her!" Faye shouted.

"Natalie, honey… Your daddy died. He went to live with Jesus about a year ago. He had cirrhosis of the liver, and he's…he's gone home." Her voice was low and wrenched with pain and hurt.

I stood there in shock, trying to digest her words. That had struck me like a dagger in the heart. And as I replayed them, the dagger just turned, twisting me into a whirlwind of emotion. I couldn't respond. I didn't know what to say. I couldn't say anything. I couldn't comprehend. My daddy… My daddy, he was gone? No… It couldn't be.

"Come on, Natalie. It's time to go." Faye pulled me by the arm, but I couldn't move.

"Natalie! Move your ass! Let's go!" she screamed, her voice startling me back into reality. As we turned, I looked back at my grandmother. Begging her. Questioning her. Pleading with her through my eyes.

But Faye just dragged me along and continued grocery shopping like nothing had happened, even though my world had just been crushed. I had told myself for so long that my daddy would come back, even if I knew it wasn't likely to happen. But that was just the thing; there was a chance, the hope of it. Maybe the odds didn't look good, but the possibility was there. And now, it was gone.

That dream of seeing my father again was destroyed. All that I had left of him was my faded memories. I fought back the tears. Now was not the time to let them fall, even though they kept threatening. For the rest of the day, I didn't speak a word, and fortunately, there was no need to.

On the drive home, Faye said, "You know, there is no reason for you to pout and be upset. He wasn't your daddy anyway. Jack is. John didn't love you. He didn't care. And you shouldn't have feelings for him. Get over your attitude about it, or I'll bust your ass and really give you something to be upset about."

I didn't respond to the warning. I didn't care. I didn't have it in me to worry about what she would do. She may bust my ass, but it couldn't compare to my broken heart. To be honest, I didn't have anything in me anymore. I was tired. Sick and tired. This life was, well, it just wasn't worth anything anymore. Everything was gone. My daddy, he was gone forever.

That night I went to bed, but I didn't sleep. I finally let my tears fall into the privacy of my pillow. The final threads of my heart were severed and cauterized with the words of my grandmother. The tears of my heart mixed with all the dirt that had accumulated over the years in my soul. And with that mixture, I began to form bricks, and I began to build my walls.

Not only to keep people out, but to ensure that I was kept in. I felt unworthy of everything, everyone good. I changed that night. My hope was erased. Everything was over. My daddy, he was gone. He had been gone for over a year, and I didn't even know it. And the thing was, he could have been dead for three or four years, and I wouldn't have known because no one would have said anything. Perhaps he had always been dead, in a way. As he was never really there. I lost him long before the heavens gained him.

Yes, my daddy, he died when I was four. He died the day he left me, and I… Well, slowly, I had been dying ever since. And my mom, well, she was good as dead, too. I never even knew the lady. I had no memory of her. It wasn't rocket science to know that she didn't care. And my grandmother certainly wasn't making any overt actions to get me back. There was no one left to care for me, and that night, I made up my mind that I was done caring for everyone else… except the children. Someone had to care about the children.

A Child's Life

Death, in itself, is nothing; but we fear, to be we know
not what, we know not where.

—John Dryden

. . . .

The days came and the days went; weekdays consisted of school, and weekends consisted of schoolwork. Friday nights I planned out the assignments that I needed to complete before Monday and watched an episode of *Grey's Anatomy*. Not your typical teenage eventful evening, but it was all there really was to do. Saturdays, I'd do all of my reading for the week just to get ahead. The nurses usually didn't come on Saturday or Sundays, except under special circumstances, so I had to take care of the children. Most of the time, I'd wake up around seven, and Faye would be preparing to leave. I could never figure out where she went or what she did. But she would leave, and the house and children were in my care.

As she headed out the door, she would scream, "Don't screw anything up!"

"Yes, ma'am," I muttered. *Whatever*, I thought. She was such a nag. As usual, I had no idea where she was going, and honestly, I didn't care where it was, just because it was a place that I didn't have to deal with her. That sufficed.

The typical routines fell into place. I went to the kitchen to make sure all of the formulas were mixed and medications were drawn. Most of the time the nurses were nice and prepared everything for the weekend, providing labels and notifying me of any changes in medications that might have occurred the previous week. It was a courtesy, because though I could draw up the medications for all the children myself, it was a little nerve-racking. I mean, they were on some pretty potent drugs. One wrong mistake, and it could be fatal. I was thankful for their help. I suspected that some of them knew that I was the one who would care for the children, so it was just the safest method.

Everything seemed to be in order, except one of the doses was missing for Sabrina. Sabrina had several medical complications, the foremost a severe seizure disorder along with being extremely irritable and very hard to console. Medications and feedings usually went together because the medication was very hard on the stomach, but for her, I gave her medication about fifteen minutes early. It was better to let the drugs kick in and calm her down before I ventured to feed her. If not, she wouldn't keep the formula down.

However, today, her morning dose was missing. I didn't think anything of it. The nurses had to draw a total of eight sets of medications for the weekend. It was very easy to miss one, and it happened now and then. Fortunately, I knew what medications she needed and the proper dosage. Most of the time, I had them memorized for the kids that were in our house. It was easier that way. I didn't have to keep track of papers and notes.

I drew up her doses and checked the time. About 7:50 a.m.

Just five minutes behind. Not too bad. I gave the other kids their doses then Sabrina hers. I decided that I'd feed her last because of the delay. About 8:20 a.m., I went to her crib. She was very calm, which was strange for her. She was rarely calm.

I picked her up, and we went to the rocking chair. That usually helped soothe her, and I preferred to rock the children. There was just something comforting about it. She took her bottle very well, which was a rarity. She usually fought with me over it, spitting out the milk, tossing and turning. Though toward the end, she started to drift asleep. I began to think that maybe she was coming down with something. Sabrina wasn't a sleeper, by any means. And regardless, it was eight forty in the morning, nowhere near naptime.

I took her temperature, and it was normal. Still concerned, I decided just to rock her. Maybe she was just tired.

As I rocked her, I thought about all the children. I loved them and I cared for them, some even as my own. I always tried not to though. I hated that I cared so much because when they left, it was hard for me to deal. I'd lost so many people in my life, and when one of the babies went to another home, it reminded me of just that: losing loved ones. I tried not to be emotional, but they were babies, and they needed love. I could never truly keep my distance.

It was hard to be their caregiver. There was so much work and so much responsibility. Some times were easier than others, but I missed out on a lot of sleep, especially when someone was sick.

But I loved them and thought of them as my children and tried to take care of them as if they were. Sometimes, when Jack and Faye had an opening, they would take a normal child, without any medical conditions. Oh, how I loved when that happened. I mean, I loved the sick babies, but it was nice to have a normal child to take care of and teach. Watching them grow and develop, reaching the standard development goals, was exciting. Kids are so curious. Their little minds just growing, absorbing language and skills. I was so happy to be with them. There is nothing more wonderful than a little child's laugh.

Often, I thought about having my own children one day and how I thought I'd almost had one before, wincing at the memory, from only a few years back. How horrible it would have been to become pregnant by Jack. Fortunately, during the nights he'd visited my room, I was not yet mature and not yet menstruating. I understood that now. And Jack rarely made any more visits to my room, but I can't say I was relieved. What he wasn't getting from me, he was getting from someone else.

I tried to keep him away from the children. At least, not letting him be alone with them on the weekends, but there were times when I had to be away. It pained me, the thought of these innocent children having to go through what I was. They were just babies.

However, my power and control over what Faye and Jack had was next to nothing. But when I was able to protect and love the babies, I did. Rocking Sabrina, I watched her sleep. It's a beautiful thing watching a child dream. There is innocence about them. And you just want to keep them there, in that place where there is no fear. Let them know not of this cruel world.

Checking the clock, it was almost eleven. I had so much work to do today, especially for my Texas Government class. There was a lot of memorization there. As I was putting Sabrina back into her crib, I noticed that she just looked…off somehow.

Her coloring was different. She was pale, and her breathing was very shallow. I quickly became alarmed. As I checked her pulse, I found that it was irregular and not very strong. Something was wrong. I wasn't supposed to call Faye unless there was an emergency.

She would get so mad at me, and I'd be in trouble when I got home, but I didn't have a good feeling. So I picked up the phone and dialed her cell, praying it would be turned on.

"What!" she answered. Though her tone was fierce, I was glad to hear it.

"Mom, Sabrina doesn't look well. I think something is wrong," I said quickly.

"What do you mean something is wrong?" she asked in a hateful tone.

"Well, I'm not sure. I was just rocking her, and her color seems off, and her breathing isn't good. I didn't notice it until now. I mean, I gave her, her medicine this morning, then I—"

All of a sudden, I was interrupted. "You gave her what?" Faye screamed.

"Her medicine," I responded in a confused tone.

"Well, *f*—! You idiot! I gave her, her medications this morning! I already gave them! Damn you!" She was yelling, but it didn't matter. A sick feeling entered my gut. *Oh my god*, I thought. *Oh my god*.

"I'm on my way back. Stupid idiot. She's probably going to die." Faye hung up.

Her words sent me into a panic. Die? I didn't know what to do. I felt so sick to my stomach. I just gave this child another dose of her medicine, so now she was overdosing. But how was I supposed to know? I mean, Faye never gave the kids their medications. Never! There was no way I could have known. I just thought there was a missing dose. I didn't know. I didn't know!

Tears started streaming down my face. I felt light-headed as I kept replaying Faye's words. But more so, I felt a fear, as I'd never felt before. We had to get her to the doctor. I needed to call 911, but

I knew better than to do that when Faye wasn't here. If the police showed up and there wasn't an adult with the kids, Faye and Jack would get reported.

When Faye gets here, she'll take her to the doctor. I soothed myself, keeping my hands on Sabrina's pulse.

About thirty minutes later, Faye came strolling through the door idly, without a care in the world. It was a confusing sight. She wasn't mad or angry. Just… Well, she looked like she was in a daydream.

"Okay, do we take her to the hospital? Have you called the doctor yet?" I rushed to her, not caring if she got upset.

"What on earth are you talking about?" Faye said. "Why would we take her to the doctor?" she questioned me.

"Because I gave her an extra dose. It's lethal. She could die! Like you said!" I shouted.

Laughing, Faye answered, "Yep, she damn sure could. And you know what, it'll be your fault. I'm going to tell the police what you did, and you're going to go to prison. That's where child killers go, you know."

Her words were foreign. What the hell did she mean? Before I knew it, I was screaming.

"What? I… I… I didn't know you gave her medication! You can't let her die!" My voice was full of fear but sharp with rage.

"Oh, f— you! I was trying to help you by giving her meds, and this is the thanks I get!" she yelled back.

"She could die if we don't get help! She could die! We have to take her!" What the hell was wrong with her? How could she not understand this? Why would she throw this against me?

"Oh, Natalie, I guess you better say your prayers then. And

anyways, I can't call the police. That would get CPS involved, and they could take away the kids. My money. Death is much easier to hide than this. I'll work it out, for me, I mean. But I suggest you start praying. If she dies, it's on you. I'm going to make sure of it. And you're going to prison for the rest of your miserable life. Great job! Way to kill a baby!" As she walked out of the room, she looked smug. "Oh, and don't bother me unless she's dead. I'm going to take a nap."

I was trying to digest what was going on, but I couldn't wrap my head around what she said. I was appalled, but mostly, I was scared. I sat down with Sabrina, holding her, not taking my fingers away from her pulse. Oh God. This poor baby.

I didn't know what to do. Faye took the phone with her, probably to ensure I didn't call the nurse or police. Lost and in a panic, I began to pray harder than I'd ever prayed before.

"Please, God, I'm so sorry. Please don't let her die. Please, I beg of you. Punish me for the rest of my life, but please, please save her." I was sobbing while checking Sabrina's pulse. It was growing weaker, and her color was getting worse.

But I just kept praying, "Please, God, please don't let her die. Please. I'm so sorry." That phrase. I prayed it over and over again. There was nothing else I could think to say. I needed this baby to be okay. Not because I didn't want to go to prison, but because I couldn't live with myself knowing that I killed a child.

"Oh God, please. If you're there, please save her." I was begging him. "Please, save her. I'm so sorry."

I held her for the rest of the day. I didn't move and couldn't, even if I wanted to. Faye took up the feedings and medications for the others, surprisingly. I guess even she understood I was in no condition to care for anyone.

Around one thirty in the afternoon, Sabrina's pulse was so

weak, and she lost consciousness. I tried to arouse her, but nothing would do. I just knew she wasn't going to make it. Her skin was pale, and she looked like she was on the brink of death. I kept my fingers on her neck, ensuring her pulse was still there. I knew CPR, though I prayed I wouldn't have to use it.

Fortunately, we had spare oxygen tanks and tubes. One thing Faye did make sure that we never ran out of was medical supplies. I put her on oxygen and continuously checked her saturation levels.

As time passed though, her oxygen levels slowly increased along with her heart rate. Soon, evening had arrived, and thankfully, Sabrina was still alive and was coming in and out of consciousness, though she was very groggy. That night, I held her close. I wouldn't, I couldn't, let her go. As I grew tired, I started to sing, both to keep myself awake and because I knew Sabrina enjoyed it.

Song after song I sang to her. Rocking her. Praying silently in my head. Hours had gone by, but I still couldn't put her down. I was so scared.

I was singing, "Twinkle, twinkle, little star, how I wonder what you are. Up above the world so high, like a diamond in the sky." I stopped as the reality of the hymn struck me.

"Oh God. Please don't let her die. We don't need another star in the sky tonight. Please, please." My prayers were desperate. "Let her be okay. Just let her be okay."

Around two in the morning, her pulse was mostly back to normal, and she was becoming very irritable—something, for the first time, I welcomed. She was okay, I thought. Most of the medication had passed through her system at this point, and she hadn't had any since the previous morning. She was going to be okay. Oh, she was going to be okay.

"Thank you, God. Oh, thank you, God!" I felt so relieved. Over those hours, I couldn't escape my thoughts. I had almost killed a child, a little baby. I tormented myself over what had happened. What I did and how Faye acted. I knew she hated me. And I knew she was a mean, manipulative person, but just to let a child die?

The worst part is, if little Sabrina would have died, I have no doubt the police would have believed Faye's story. No one ever doubted her. And if they did, she found a way to persuade them. Everyone always believed in Faye and Jack. They'd gotten off on murder before, and they'd do it again. And they would throw anyone under the bus before their welfare checks were taken away. I loathed the both of them. They were despicable, horrible beings. I questioned how God could let them live. How could people like Jack and Faye get away with so much, always going unpunished? It wasn't a question that I'd be able to answer.

I fell asleep with Sabrina in my arms. Waking up around 6:00 a.m. to her squirming, I went and placed her in her bed. That was the first time I'd let her go since it all happened. I watched her fall back asleep, reminding me of my thoughts from just a few hours before. What a day. I knew that she was probably hungry, but I was too scared to give her anything. Tomorrow was going to be a hard day for the both of us. The side effects of the events today weren't going to be pretty.

As I went to my room, I found myself so exhausted. Today was probably one of the worst days of my life, and I'd seen my fair share of bad days. I was so tired, emotionally and physically. But before I fell back asleep, I let all the tears and frustrations from the previous day escape. As I cried, I thanked God. He saved that child today for me. I was so thankful for that. And, that night, I promised that I wouldn't ever let it happen again. No matter what Faye said, I would never take that risk. I'd never sit by idly and watch the life of a child slip through my hands.

Faye was right. It was my fault. Today, if Sabrina had died, it would have been my fault. Not because of the medication error, but because I didn't get Sabrina help. Because I didn't stop Faye from letting her die. No, not ever again would I let that happen. Never, ever again would a child face death because of my ignorance and fear of Faye and Jack Winters.

Packing for Travel

"**G**et the f— up!" Faye yelled as she barged in my room, startling me out of my sleep. Trying to arise out of my unconsciousness, I realized it was a Sunday.

"I just can't take this anymore. You are too much!" Faye was screaming frantically. "You are just… Ugh, I can't stand you. You're ugly. You're stupid and worthless. Don't you see that, Natalie? Don't you see?" She was questioning me now, pleading with her eyes for me to agree.

"Yes, ma'am," I answered, knowing that her question was not rhetorical and that it was more trouble than it was worth not to answer.

Faye was frantic, running around my room and throwing random pieces of clothing into a bag. It was a scene that I'd witnessed before, and it happened every few years.

"Get up and get dressed. I'm taking you away. I can't bear to look at you." She explained, not to me, but almost to herself.

She did this sometimes. Her emotions were always up and down, but sometimes she would just break, and it was usually in regard to not wanting me around anymore. She was sporadic and schizophrenic with her emotions. Her eyes were weary from no sleep, but dilated from not taking her meds.

"Come on! Let's go! We have to get you out of here!" she frantically said.

"Yes, ma'am." That was the best answer in these times. Actually, it was the best answer at all times. I wondered where I was going this round. Last time she decided she didn't want me, she took me to another foster home. I stayed with them for two weeks before she came and took me back. It was nice, actually, to get away from her, and the other family was nice, but they had a lot of kids.

"Get in the car," she ordered. Jack was at home with the kids, leaving me with a pit in my stomach.

"Where are you taking me?" I asked as she backed out of the driveway.

"To the children's home, Natalie. I can't have you in my house anymore. You are just worthless, you know? I made that deal with your dad, and I hate myself for it." Sighing, she continued, "You were just not worth it. I didn't bargain for this. I don't love you, you know. I don't. I mean, how could anyone ever? That should have been my warning sign. I mean, when your own mother doesn't want you. When your mother didn't want you, I should have known you were no good."

She was talking a mile a minute and driving just as fast down the highway. Faye was in some sort of manic breakdown again. I hated these. I mean, she always said horrible things, but in this state she was so mean. Her words, no matter how hard I tried not to listen, not to absorb, hurt.

"You, you're just f—ing ugly!" Swerving, she reached over and pulled the visor down so I could see myself in the mirror.

"Look at you!" Disgusted, she ordered, "Say 'I'm ugly.'"

Gosh, I hated this. I hated these moods. This was going to be a long ride, too, because it didn't seem like she knew where she was going.

"*Say it*, g-dd—nit!" she screamed.

"I'm ugly," I muttered.

"Again, say it again. Look at yourself," she ordered as she swerved back on the road again.

"I'm ugly," I stated again.

"Yes, you are. Keep saying it, Natalie. Keep saying it! So you know!"

"I'm ugly… I'm ugly… I'm ugly…. I'm ugly… I'm ugly," I stated in the same voice over and over as she ordered.

"Yes. You're ugly and stupid! Keep saying it!" She was screaming at the top of her lungs now in a crazed voice. "Say it!"

"I'm ugly and stupid… I'm ugly and stupid." I chanted in a soft monotone for a while, just staring at myself in the mirror. "I'm ugly and stupid… I'm ugly and stupid." Maybe I was ugly and stupid. Tears were forming in my eyes as my words were becoming belief.

All of a sudden, the sound of Faye's scream startled me. Ugh, the noise was worse than nails on a chalkboard. She swerved and pulled over on the side of the road again. Putting the car in park, she put her hands on her head and started pulling her hair.

"Shut up! Shut the f— up! I can't stand the sound of your voice!" she screamed.

I stilled. This was bad. She was crazier than normal. Fear slowly crept into my throat, and I started to shake, trying to prepare myself for a beating. But she just started rocking back and forth, pulling her hair.

Suddenly, she peeled out, hitting the gas, on the road once again. We were probably going ninety miles an hour in that huge van. She stopped saying anything and now looked completely calm. Too calm.

"I should have never taken you from your dad. You two deserved each other. Both worthless and useless," she simply stated.

My fear was slowly replaced by anger. I didn't care that she said bad things about me. I was used to it but not about my father. I fought back the urge to respond.

"But it's okay, it's all about to be over," she consoled herself.

And just like that, the fear was back. What was she talking about? What was she going to do? I started to become panicked. Over?

"You know, I'd rather receive a beating from my mother than to call you my child," she said, agreeing with something deep inside herself. But the statement caught me off guard.

"Your mother beat you?" I asked before I knew the words had slipped out of my mouth.

"Yes, you f—er!" she screamed, her crazed eyes almost bulging out of her head. Immediately, I silenced and regretted my words. But she just kept driving, not saying anything else. I started to gaze out the window, wondering where she was going to take me.

I must have dozed off during the drive. We left at about eight that morning, and I awoke to the sun beating on my face through the car window. I looked at the clock, and it was noon. We were pulling up a driveway with a sign. As we got closer, I read, "Panhandle Assessment Center and Children's Home."

I quickly recognized the place. I had been here before at the foster parent meetings. It was like a children's home. Like an orphanage.

"Get out," Faye said as she came to a stop. "Here's your s—. I don't want it or you anymore."

"Yes, ma'am," I answered as I got out of the car.

"Maybe someone else will want you someday. But don't hold your breath!" Faye shouted while bursting into laughter. I shut the door, and she whipped around and drove out of the parking lot, leaving me standing in the dust.

"Idiot," I muttered. Part of me was very thankful not to be in her presence, though I had no idea what I was supposed to do. I mean, do you just check yourself into an orphanage or what?

I took my bag and walked over to where some kids were sitting.

"Uh, hi. Umm… Where do we check in?" I asked, not really sure what to do.

"Check in?" this boy with fiery red hair asked. "What the f— do you mean check in?"

"Er, my, uh…mom just dropped me off," I tried to explain. I hated calling her my mom. "My foster mom, I mean. Where do I go?" I asked.

"You get the f— away from me, you little b—!" The boy came

and pushed me down before I could even realize what was happening. I stood slowly, trying to get my balance back. While I was gathering myself from the ground, I started to reach for my bag. But before I could get it, the boy grabbed it, dumped out all of my clothes, and kicked them in the dirt.

"There! Now they are dirty just like you! You little c—!" the grungy boy yelled. Laughing, they all walked away. I hurried and picked them all up. I didn't have much, but I wanted to hold on to what I did have.

What the hell is wrong with him? I thought. *And what is a c—?* I wandered over to the swing. I didn't care what I was supposed to do. I'd figure it out later. This was a crappy day.

I sat down on the swing and started to sway. I hated Faye. I really did. She was insane. No, more than insane. Jack was a disgusting creep. I hated being around the both of them, but still, they were all I knew. Being abandoned into unknown territory is a scary thing, no matter what hell you might be living. The fear of the unknown is almost paralyzing.

I probably swung for hours, losing myself in my thinking, letting go of the tears that had accumulated throughout this morning's event. Oh, how I wished my daddy was still alive. My stomach, screaming for food, was continuously interrupting my thoughts. I was so hungry. I looked around and saw a group of children. I picked up my bag and walked toward them.

They were walking into a building. Upon my entrance, I realized it was a cafeteria. Oh, thank goodness. Food.

I just followed behind the others. It was a cafeteria-style buffet.

"Corn or green beans?" the lady asked me as I stepped in line.

"Um, green beans, please," I said hesitantly. Would this lady notice me? It didn't appear so. She just slopped a huge scoop on my plate and went on to the next kid. They weren't shy with their food here, and that was very much appreciated. We had spaghetti and meatballs with some garlic toast and green beans.

I sat down at a table and annihilated my food. I was famished. And it was really good. Once I finished, I sat and observed the others. There were so many children with hungry tummies, but more so, starving hearts. Looking at them, there was brokenness, an emptiness in all of them. A longing for someone to care. I recognized the look in their eyes readily, as it was the same look in mine. Needless to say, I fit right in.

Soon after everyone finished, an adult came in and blew a whistle. Everyone stood up and brought their trays and looked like they were heading back outside. In the rustle of moving, I bumped into a girl.

"Ouch!" she exclaimed.

"Oh, I'm so sorry," I apologized quickly. I didn't want another encounter like earlier.

"Oh, it's okay. I'm Maggie. What's your name?" she asked.

"Um, Natalie," I said meekly.

"Are you new here?" she quizzed.

"Uh, I think so." I didn't really know what to say. I didn't really know where I was or what I was doing.

"Oh, cool. Your parents gone?"

I was shocked by her question. How ordinarily she asked, as if it were no big deal. "Yeah. They're gone," I said. That's the honest truth. They were.

We walked outside. The afternoon was cooling down from the heat from earlier today. And I felt a lot better after eating.

"My parents are gone, too. Want to swing?" she asked as she

followed my eyes to the swings.

"Yeah, sure," I agreed. She seemed nice enough.

We went to the swings. Maggie was very talkative. Honestly, I wasn't really keeping up. I was too distracted. What was I doing here? How would I get to school? Should I tell someone I was here? I questioned myself frantically. This was all just so new.

"Um, where do we sleep?" I suddenly asked, startling the both of us.

"Over there, in the far cabins. Did they assign you a number?"

"Uh…" I stammered. "No."

"Oh, that's weird. Well, there is an empty cot next to me. You can sleep there if you want," she offered kindly.

"Okay, thank you." I smiled shyly.

"So what's your story?"

"Uh… I don't really want to talk about it." I said. I didn't know what my story was. I didn't know what I was doing here. Faye just dropped me off. I was fearful to tell someone because I didn't want her to get mad. I mean, she said she wasn't coming back, but she was emotional. With the chance that she would, I didn't want to make her angry.

"All right. That's cool. None of us really have parents. Well, I do, but they are drug addicts," she explained. "I grew up in a crack house, but I've been here for two years now. It's nice."

She went on and on about all kinds of things. I wanted to listen, I really did, but this day was just too much. After a while of swinging, we heard the whistle. Maggie walked with me to the cabin. It was only about 7:30 p.m., but I just wanted to get in bed and read. I managed to grab my backpack before Faye went all crazy this morning, dragging me out of the house. Maggie said she wanted to read, too, so I loaned her one of my books. I kept an eye on her though. That wasn't something I did, loaning out my books. They were precious to me, but she seemed harmless. And I had become pretty good at reading people for their true intentions.

For the next few hours, I lost myself in a world of fiction. Oddly enough, it was refreshing. Soon, a counselor came in, looked around, then turned out the lights. It was odd. No adult had even noticed I was there. Some organization. Jeez, you could run away, and no one would even know about it. And even if they found out, it'd take a while.

I had thought about running away from the Winters a lot, but I was always scared of what Faye and Jack would do if I didn't run fast enough. Part of me thought they wouldn't care if I just disappeared, but the other part of me knew that I would be in huge trouble if I did. This place wasn't so bad though. I mean, Maggie said they got three meals a day, and for the rest of the time, you could pretty much do whatever you wanted as long as you didn't misbehave.

I quickly became educated on exactly what "trouble" meant here. She talked about the discipline plan. It seemed like a complex system, but for the most part, it just consisted of grounding in a particular building, something like that.

I wasn't planning to find out though. She said a bus came on the weekdays for school around 7:00 a.m. and drops us off at close to 5:00 p.m. We were still pretty far out of town, so it took a while. But overall, it seemed like a pretty decent place. I mean, it could have been worse.

"Thank you, Maggie," I said before I went to sleep. I was grateful for her help.

"Welcome, chick!" she said happily. Chick? That's strange. She was kind of odd but really perky. Maybe we'd be friends.

I dozed off thinking about this new life. Honestly, I felt safe, and the fear of the situation was wearing away. It was going to be okay. Right? *Sure, yes. It'll be fine.* I coached myself. I worried about the babies though. I hoped they were okay. Leaving them alone with Daddy Jack was horrifying, but hopefully, Faye made it back quickly. He never did stuff around Faye. I was really going to miss them, but I was kind of relieved to be away from Faye and Jack. I thought of the whole thing like a vacation.

A new start this Sunday brought. Maybe it wasn't so bad.

Monday morning, we were awoken by the counselor lady again barging in and turning on the lights. Ugh, what is it with people and just flicking on the lights and screaming to wake people up? Faye did the same thing. I couldn't help but think that there were better ways. I took a set of clothes out of my bag and headed to the cafeteria. They were still a little dusty from the day before, but they'd have to do.

They served oatmeal. It looked kind of odd, but I was hungry. Afterward, Maggie showed me where to wait for the bus. Soon, it arrived, and we were off to school. I took my bag of clothes with me. I wasn't keen on leaving them behind. I didn't trust the people there. At least, not yet anyways.

We arrived before I knew it. And the day passed quickly. School went as it normally did, but during math, I got a note saying I was needed in the office. Who knew what that was about?

I gathered my things. I was hoping it wouldn't take long. I was missing math, and this class was my favorite. When I turned the hallway, I could see Faye through the window, and I couldn't help but be a little disappointed. I suppose she decided she wanted to keep me after all.

I walked through the doors and was greeted by her over-the-top fake smile.

"There's my girl! How are you! Ready to go?" she asked.

No, I thought, wishing I had the guts to actually say it to her. But I didn't. "Yes, ma'am," I said. Again, the safest response.

"Okeydoke!" she chuckled. "I'll have her bring a note from the dentist tomorrow, okay, ladies?" she cooed at the secretaries.

"Oh, all right, Mrs. Winters! Don't worry too much, we trust you! And we know Natalie is a good girl and doesn't skip!" one of them responded.

Laughing, Faye replied, "Oh yes, isn't she? Well, we'll see y'all tomorrow! Bye!" She waved. "Say bye, Natalie," She ordered me under her breath.

"Bye," I said solemnly. *Stupid. The lot of them*, I thought. *Ugh.*

As we walked to the car, Faye grabbed my hand like I was a little child, swinging it back and forth like it was freaking red rover. I got into the passenger's side of the van. The thoughts of yesterday were immediately coming back.

"So how are you, honey? Good? Missed you yesterday! We got a check in the mail today! I was going to go get some new shirts! Do you want one? Pink? I think you should get pink! You look so pretty in pink!" Faye exclaimed.

I looked at her in disbelief. Yesterday, she dropped me off at a freaking orphanage, telling me she didn't want me anymore. Yesterday, the very sight of me infuriated her. This lady, yesterday, was having me chant in this very seat that I was ugly and stupid, and today I was pretty in pink? What the hell? This just couldn't be normal. Nothing about it was.

I didn't dare say one word though. I just smiled the best I could manage. She was crazy. No, she was utterly, completely, and irrevocably insane...

Birdsong

. . . .

*A winner is someone who recognizes his God-given
talents, works his tail off to develop them into skills,
and uses these skills to accomplish his goals.*

— Larry Bird

. . . .

Faye never abandoned me like that again. Oddly enough, I was thankful. Even though I didn't enjoy being with her, I didn't like being dropped off at some random place. I'd been through that before, and it was a chilling reminder of losing my daddy all over again. Even though I didn't like Faye and Jack, the feeling of not being wanted and left alone surpassed anything they could do. And oddly enough, I found comfort in being with them in that I woke up each day knowing a range of behaviors to expect. There is comfort in routine, even if it's horribly constructed. People, after all, are creatures of habit and schedule. I found hope in what I could, and waking up each *day in relatively the same surroundings, knowing what the day would most likely consist of, was reassuring to me. There wasn't much to take comfort in, but I definitely used what was available to me.*

I knew I had a talent, but I was always very reluctant to say anything. I didn't know how Faye would respond or what she would do if she knew. But that is just the thing about a gift… It's not easily hidden…

I really loved to sing. I sang all the time to the babies while rocking them to sleep and along with the country radio. I don't suppose I could ever say who my favorite artist was, because for me, it would be like picking out which snowflake was the prettiest. I loved them all, and I just really loved the twang of country music. Honestly, it reminded me of my daddy and our late nights out at the bar dancing. There was homeliness there for me in a sense; singing along with Straight and Chesney helped me escape just a bit from the home I was actually in. Plus, I really loved it and I knew that I was good at singing. I can't say how I knew, I just did.

One morning we went to visit this little church outside of town, and they talked about how they had what was called "Sunday night singing" where anyone who wanted to come and sing, could. I really wanted try it in front of a crowd, but I was a bit scared. As, the week went by, I debated it. But when Saturday night rolled around, I decided I would practice and maybe give it a shot.

I went into our van and found just the cassette I was looking for, with just the song… "Angels Among Us," by Alabama. It was one of my favorites. I always thought the babies in our house were angels, scattered among us. I was always bothered when people would say, "they had no life because of their illnesses." That just wasn't true. They were made exactly how God wanted them. Special. Perfect. I sang this song to them all of the time, just as a reminder of that very thing.

I went to my room and pulled out a little portable player, praying silently that I could get it to work. One of the nurses had given it to me when I explained how much I loved music, but it was a little unreliable. As I slipped the tape in, I attempted to fast-forward to the beginning of the song. With the earphones on my ears, I sang loudly. I usually sang very quietly, but this time I knew I needed to practice singing with exertion.

I knew the words and melody by heart. I repeated the song a good fifteen times, before I just made my decision. I was going to "Sunday night singing" and I was going to sing this song. We would always go, because there was a lot of food after the service. They called it "pot-luck." Strange name, if you ask me, but I really liked it. Someone always brought cookies and that was my favorite part. And fortunately, it was Faye's favorite part too. I'd made up my mind that I was going to perform, but first... I'd have to ask Faye...

I eased into the living room slowly and with caution. I didn't know what kind of mood Faye was in. I waited for the evening to roll around, just in case I got sent to bed. If so, at least it would be close to dark time. As I peaked around the couch, she noticed me.

"What are you doing?" she asked.

"Ummm, I.... I wanted to ask you a question." I said meekly.

"Okay. What?" She bargained.

"Well, I.... I...." I stammered.

"Spit it out!" She raised her voice. At that sound, I almost chickened out, but decided to push forward.

"I'd like to sing at Sunday night singing tomorrow." I said quickly.

"What? Why?" Faye asked.

"Well, I really like singing, and I think it'd be fun." I reasoned.

"You can't sing!! You know how embarrassing that would be!!" She said in a disgusted tone.

"Yes ma'am." I agreed with her. I knew not to fight her on the insult. "But, I think it would be fun. And it's a church... I don't think anyone would laugh there."

"Oh, you'd be surprised..." I waited there for a moment, but she didn't say anything.

"Battle lost." I thought, but before I turned away, she said, "Fine. You can sing. And when they make fun of you, don't you dare cry about it!"

"Oh, yes ma'am. Yes ma'am! Thank you! Thank you!!" I ran off to my room, before she had the opportunity to take it back.

That night, I lay in bed so excited. I was going to sing! It was going to be like a concert! Hopefully they would all clap for me! And maybe, they would ask me to do it again!! I dreamed wide-awake that night, just anticipating the following evening.

That morning, I woke up and practiced. I really wished I had a tape without voices, so it would be just me, but I figured singing with Alabama would be good too. Plus, if I got scared, he'd be there to back me up.

The evening was soon here. I wore my nicest dress, and did my best to curl my hair. I just wasn't very good at it, but again... we were going to be at church. These people would surly excuse my appearance.

When we arrived, I went up and put my name on the list. Since I did it right before, I was the very last one…. Oh, the anticipation. I sat on the pew, twirling my fingers around and around. I was so nervous. There were twenty people set to go before me, but as the time slowly passed, I became more nervous. Panicky.

"Oh no", I thought. "What if I forget the words? What if I get sick?" But, before I could back out, the sweet lady called my name.

"Natalie," she said with a smile, "It's your turn." I stood slowly and walked up the isle. Very slowly, almost like a bridal march. I was so cautions; my pace almost absent, reflecting my hesitation. At any time, I could turn around…

But soon, I arrived at the stage. They handed me a microphone. I'd never held one before. It was really heavy, but exciting to hold. I stood up there on the stage with everyone watching. I had to wait for them to put the cassette I'd given them earlier into the sound system. My anticipation was rising, but I just glanced across the crowd. They were sweet old people, just smiling at me. Surely, they'd be nice if I did badly. Soon, the music began and slowly, my nerves were calmed by the melody. And I sang… better than I ever had before.

I poured out my heart and soul into that song. I meant every word, and didn't miss a beat. Before I knew it, I had finished, and everyone had stood up and they were clapping… I guess that meant I was good?

As I handed back the mic to the lady, everyone was coming up to me and hugging me. I was a little freaked out by it… Why was everyone so excited? Maybe it was because I sang a country song instead of a hymn.

"Oh, you sing like a beautiful bird honey!" One lady said. She was nice and there were so many compliments just like it to me, and Faye. Of course she adored it. That lady just loved attention in any form.

"I know she is wonderful," Faye told one man. "I encouraged her to do it. You just can't hide a voice like that!"

"Whatever" I thought but dismissed it. I was too busy talking with all of these people. Later on that night, I was educated on what a "standing ovation" was and what it meant. I was flattered. I did well, and that was a relief. Surely there was an angel among us and one that decided to help me out.

After that night, singing became routine for me. I sang everywhere I went, and Faye was eating it up. She got so many compliments from it and I started to get a lot of requests.

There was a music teacher that also took interest. He said that I had a great talent, and that I needed to be trained professionally. He gave the lessons for free, and I began to see him every week.

I also started entering competitions. My very first job was at the Big Texan Steakhouse at their opry. I tried out, and they took me on. I sang every Tuesday night, and well, I made a lot of money. People would give me flowers and candy. It really made me feel loved.

One night, I made a lot in what they said was "tips." Over eight hundred dollars. I didn't care for the money. I knew Faye would keep it anyway. I just preferred the roses and applause. Plus, I had a lot of fun… And, if you sang, you got a free meal! And they had really good food. It was a win, win. Plus, if I did well, Faye was really nice to me.

By the time I reached middle school, I was very good and confident with singing. I readily signed up for choir, though it wasn't my kind of style. They didn't say their words like Garth Brooks did, and that was frustrating to me. But, no less, singing was singing.

Near the end of the year, there was a school wide talent show and I entered. I sang what had become my favorite song, "I hope you dance" by Lee Ann Wolmack. There were many contestants, but I won. And weirdly enough, after that talent show, I started to make friends.

Everyone thought I was cool, and said I was going to be famous. Kids started sitting by me at lunch and asking me to hang out. A few weeks' later, cheerleading tryouts came about, and people insisted I tried out. When I asked Faye, she agreed.

Besides, what did I have to lose? I mean, it wouldn't hurt to try. I knew nothing about cheerleading, but I was always a quick study and a hard worker. I wasn't very outgoing, but singing had helped with that. It also helped with my popularity. Since that talent show, everyone knew my name.

Tryouts were a long, enduring process... and very intense. Girls were crying and just freaking out over all of it. I wasn't. I didn't suppose it was that big of a deal.

When Friday rolled around, they made the announcements of who made the squad. "Natalie Winters" was the first name called. I was shocked, but thrilled. Faye was excited because she got glory and praise because of it. Plus, with practice, I could be home a lot less.

Everything seemed to be taking a turn. In sixth grade, no one talked to me. I believed that I was stupid and ugly... But now, just a year later I had friends, people were nice to me, I was a cheerleader and a singer. The next year I made the squad again, and because I was so small, I became the flyer.... Who would have thought that I would have ever been the girl on top of the pyramid? School was a better place than it ever could have been. And as high school came around, I couldn't help but think that maybe, somehow I'd be able to leave the Winters' home... Maybe my being a cheerleader would help me some way... Maybe someone would notice the bruises now... But then again, I knew I could never initiate the questioning. They'd have to figure it out on their own. But, I still kept intact the possibility that no one ever would. I knew better than to put my hope in what people might do.

So I sang and cheered with the secret hope that maybe things were going to change... maybe, there was a chance for everything to get better. And it was just strange to think, that it all started with a song...

Doctor's Office

*The greatest mistake in the treatment of diseases is
that there are physicians for the body and physicians
for the soul, although the two cannot be separated.*

— Plato

. . . .

The season was late fall. The temperature was cool, and the wind was always at a constant breeze. I was a freshman in high school. Faye had let me try out for cheerleader, and I made the team. I was ecstatic! There was something to keep me away from home at least a few hours a day to forget about my unhappiness.

It was Friday night, but we didn't have a game, which was good, because one of the babies, Kelsey, was in the hospital. Medical complications. It was always because of medical complications. However, I felt particularly close to Kelsey. I begged Faye to let me go spend the night at the hospital with her.

We were going to have nursing care all weekend, and I couldn't help but be thankful. I wouldn't have to worry about the other babies, and I couldn't help my feeling of relief. I needed a little bit of rest, and I hoped to get ahead in all of my classes. When I was ahead, life was just easier.

When we arrived at the pediatric ICU, the doctor was in Kelsey's room. I had known Dr. Schlock my whole life. He was my doctor, and we were in his office often with the other kids. He was doing a checkup on the baby and said she was improving. I was asking him many questions about her condition. I think he found it peculiar that I knew so much about the child's condition.

"You sure know quite a lot, Miss Natalie. Do you help your momma take care of the babies?"

Trying to force my crimson smile into a genuine one, I said, "Yes, I do."

Ugh, if he only knew. Faye had left the room for a moment, so it gave me some time to talk with him. Faye hated when I talked to the doctors. I was just supposed to "keep my mouth shut at all times."

Part of me thought it made her feel inferior. As it should. Of course I knew more about the children. I was the one taking care of them! On that note, no one was taking care of me, and I had something that I needed to run by him.

I had a severe blister on my right foot that had become pretty infected, accompanied by some sort of problem with my toenail. I assumed it was from working out in shoes that were too small. Just putting them on was super painful, but I had no choice. They were all I had.

The infection had been progressing for a few weeks now. It smelled horrible and wasn't getting better. I told Faye, but she told me not to worry about it. But the pain was getting to me, and last week, I walked with a limp.

"Um, Dr. Schlock, may I ask you something? Well, show you something? I think there is a problem with my foot." I stammered over my words nervously. I needed to hurry and show him before

Faye got back.

"Sure, Natalie. What is it?" He seemed curious. I winced as I took my shoe and sock off. As soon as he caught a glance, he gasped.

"Natalie! Oh, how long has your foot been like this?" he demanded.

"Um, it started like two months ago. Is it bad?" I questioned.

"Did you tell your mother about this?" His voice was slightly raised and very demanding. I grew very uncomfortable.

"Yes, sir. But she's busy." I tried to cover the truth. If she got in trouble, I would, too.

He seemed very upset and called a nurse into the room. He was rambling off orders of medications that I had not heard of. I was confused. I didn't really understand why he was so upset over it. I mean, it looked pretty gross, but I didn't think it was that big of a deal.

Shortly after that, Faye came into the room. Dr. Schlock started to raise his voice at her about my foot.

Oh no! I thought. *This can't be good.*

"Why have you not brought her into the office for this, Faye? This is severely infected and could cause her to lose her foot!" he said in his most stern voice, laced with authority and disapproval.

I saw the look on Faye's face. Fear. She apologized incessantly to the doctor and assured him that she didn't know. Dr. Schlock explained that he needed to put me on emergency antibiotics and demanded that I come in Monday after the antibiotics had some time to clear up the infection.

He came over and took a swab of my foot, getting some of the pus off, then put it into a tube. It was disgusting.

"This is going to hurt a little, Natalie, okay? Just be super still," he said as he slightly opened the wound with a small knife and squeezed.

I winced. It hurt much more than a little bit.

"Sorry, Natalie. I have to get some of this infection out."

I couldn't watch anymore. The smell, the sight—it was all just a little too much for me. I waited as he then put some sort of cream on it and then bandaged it up.

"Keep this on, and try not to get your foot wet. You'll need to come back Monday morning. Okay?"

He was talking to me, but also directing Faye.

"Yes, Dr. Schlock. That won't be a problem," Faye assured him.

When he left the room, Faye looked at me. I could see the rage in her eyes. I was in trouble. I knew it. But she didn't say a word to me. But then again, she didn't have to. Her eyes told me everything. It would only be a matter of time before punishment came, most likely tomorrow after our departure.

The nurse got me a cot so I could stay in the same room with my little sister. The antibiotics were upsetting my stomach. She got me some soup and told me to get some sleep. She was so nice.

Faye just sat in the corner, not saying a word, but with a look of pure malevolence in her eyes, making me very uncomfortable. But I didn't say anything.

I ate my soup and settled in the cot. I dozed off before I was suddenly awoken.

"Get up, Natalie," Faye said. "Come on, honey, let's go."

I wasn't sure what time it was, but I knew it was late.

"Come, we have to go! Hurry, we have to get you to the doctor's office, Natalie. Hurry." Reading my confused sleepy look, she tried to explain.

"The doctor's office?" I asked in disbelief. Why were we going to the doctor's office? We're at the hospital. What?

We left the room in a rush. There were only two nurses on the unit, and I'm not sure if they noticed us leaving. Faye was scuttling me out of the room, all conspicuous-like. I was confused. Faye seemed really worried about me, but her tone and behavior was… weird. But she seemed so concerned.

But something just seemed weird about it. Dr. Schlock said that he would see me Monday, but I dared not question Faye. I was already in danger from the transgression earlier and didn't want to make matters worse.

Soon, we exited the hospital. It was really cold outside. The wind had turned icy. I hurried into my light jacket as the goose bumps all but attacked my body. Faye hurried me to the car. I got in wearily. Something was not right. But there was nothing I could do. We pulled out and headed down the street to where Dr. Schlock's office was located.

Slowly, she pulled into the parking lot. As I looked around, I noticed that it was completely empty. There wasn't a car or truck in sight. The realization made me very uneasy.

I asked Faye, "What are we doing here?" I noticed the time. It was almost one in the morning. Why would we come here at this time? *Oh gosh, this isn't good at all.* I began to squirm in my seat. As she pulled into a parking space, panic rushed down my spine. *What on earth is she doing?* I thought.

Nervously, I asked again, "Why are we here?" Faye looked at me with a glare that morphed my panic into pure fear and had every nerve in my body on end. This was bad.

"Why, honey, I brought you to the doctor's office just like you asked," Faye said in the coldest tone.

Before I could respond, she reached out and put her hand behind my head. Before I could stop her, she slammed my head against the dashboard. And before I could recover, she slammed it again. I tried to get out of the car, but the doors were locked. My right side was affected mostly, but I was instantly dizzy and disoriented.

Get out of the van! my subconscious hissed at me. But as I tried to open the door, Faye slammed my head against the dashboard again. Harder this time. The wooziness was traumatic, and I was disoriented. My head was throbbing. The next thing I knew, she had me out of my seat belt. I was fighting her the best I could, thrashing my arms at her with all my strength. But I was just barely ninety pounds, and after the three big blows to my head, I was incredibly weak. I was no match for her, and we both knew it.

But I had to get out of the van. I knew I did. So I just started screaming, "Please, please, someone help me! Please, please, *help*!"

I was yelling at the top of my lungs with every ounce of vigor I had. There was no one around, but on the off chance there was, I was going to make sure they heard me. "Help! Help!" I shouted while Faye continued striking me.

"No one is going to help you!" Faye sneered. "Not now, not ever! You little b—! You got me in trouble with Dr. Schlock!"

Before I knew it, she had my foot in her hand, ripping off my shoe. I panicked. *Oh God, not my hurt foot!* I thought.

The mere idea of her touching my infected foot gave new resound potency to my strength. I started flailing and kicking with all my might. I tried everything in my power to get my foot away from her, but her grip was too strong.

The next thing that happened issued a pain that was indescribable. As she started to squeeze my foot, I screamed bloody murder. Every nerve in my body was on end; it felt like a thousand knives were inserted into an already-bleeding wound. The sound that emanated from me was shrill as I didn't even recognize it was my own.

Her grip tightened. I knew pain. I did. But this, this was not just pain. This was excruciating torture. I tried to shake her off, but she just kept squeezing. It was like a python's grip. Unshakable. I couldn't get out of her grip.

I would do anything to make it stop. *Just kill me*, I thought. I could deal with that, but not this. I kept screaming, but my body was becoming weak. I was light-headed and nauseous. I felt so powerless, and I could hardly move out of even my own volition. I continued to screech and yell, but soon the pain became so severe that my sound escaped me. I became nauseous and faint. Then there was no pain. There was just darkness.

When I woke up, we were back at the hospital parking lot. I was in the backseat of the van. I sat up slowly, but even that was too quick. Immediately, I began to vomit. I leaned over onto the floorboard. I couldn't see what I was throwing up—it was too dark— but it tasted like blood. Every part of my body ached. I felt as if I had died a thousand deaths. My vision was coming and going, which was only adding to the nausea.

What was happening? I didn't know. But I knew I'd never felt this way. As everything started to go black, I wished for it all to end. Death would be much simpler, much faster, and not as drawn out. *Death is peaceful*, I thought as the darkness greeted me again.

When I awoke again, Faye was sitting next to me. She had her hand on my wrist, and she was looking at me with deep concern. She put her hand up to my face. As much as I wanted to flinch, I couldn't muster the strength, and even if I could have, my nerves were too shot to respond. When I looked at my hands, they were covered in blood; I wasn't quite sure where I was bleeding.

"How are you feeling?" Faye asked.

Startled by her voice, I said, "I'm...okay," even though I knew I wasn't. My voice was raspy and was barely audible. I ached everywhere but my foot. Oddly enough, I couldn't feel it at all. When I looked down, I saw my sock. I wasn't one to be queasy, but the sight of it made me want to throw up again. It was drenched in blood and pus. The smell was intoxicating in the most severe of ways. I could see the swelling through my sock, and I knew that underneath, it was probably much worse. As I tried to move it, fire shot up my leg. I cried out involuntarily. I couldn't help it. This kind of pain was something I had never felt before.

As I tried to move it, I noticed that I could hardly flex my ankle, but I didn't know if this was because of the severe throbbing that it caused or if something else was wrong.

Faye just sat there, staring at me. I wondered what she was thinking. I couldn't help but see a trace of worry on her face. Suddenly, she grabbed some wet wipes from the back. As she reached toward me, every muscle in my body tightened.

Oh, please. No more! I thought. I couldn't tolerate another round.

"It's okay," she soothed. "I'm just going to wipe you down."

The wipes were like ice against my skin, maybe because they were cold, but possibly because my head was burning hot. But at this point, it didn't matter whether or not I was all right; it just mattered that I looked all right. I knew we had to go back into the hospital.

As Faye moved to my arms, I couldn't help but notice that she was going through the box quickly. Though I couldn't see myself, the residue from the wipes made me imagine the worst.

"Here, put this on," Faye said. It was a sweatshirt, about three sizes too big, but I took it. My shirt was streaked with blood and would surely cause attention when we walked back in.

After a few more wipe downs, Faye said, "Okay, let's go."

I suppose I looked decent enough at least to walk in without looking like I belonged in the emergency room. After all, though, this was a hospital. I figured that most people wouldn't be too shocked to see a beat-up being walking around?

"Put your shoes back on," Faye ordered.

Oh God, no, I thought as horror swept through my body. I couldn't bear to touch my foot, much less move it or walk on it.

"Now! Here's your shoes!" Faye said sternly.

"Yes, ma'am," I agreed. I didn't want to upset her again. I pulled the shoelaces completely out of my shoe. I needed it to be as loose as possible. They were already small, so there was no hope of it just sliding on, but I tried.

As I did, I couldn't help the tears from streaming down my face. The pain was almost intolerable. I eased the shoe on as softly as I could, using as much care as I could muster.

"Hurry up! We need to get back in and see how the baby is doing."

"Yes, ma'am." I finally got the shoe on my foot. But standing was going to be a difficult task, much less walking. She opened the door, and I maneuvered myself, mostly sliding off the seat and onto the ground. I put all of the weight on my left foot.

"Come on!" Faye ordered, hurrying me. I had to suck it up,

though every part of me deterred my own actions of setting my right foot on the ground. But I knew I must ignore them. As I set my right foot down, I immediately started to yelp like some sick animal. I couldn't help it. The pain shot up my leg, and tears started to fall again.

"Shut *up*, Natalie! Get your ass a-moving! Now!" she ordered in a hushed voice.

I couldn't respond. Gosh, it hurt so much. I slowly eased more weight down as the pain gradually increased. I had never felt anything like this before. I tried to take a baby step, but I almost fell down. It hurt so much, but I had to push through. Faye was still irritated, and I couldn't risk getting in trouble again tonight.

Seeing I was in desperate need for aid in balance, Faye grabbed my hand. "Hold on to me while we walk in for balance. Don't you dare cause a scene, Natalie," she warned.

I grasped her arm, trying to hold all of my weight by my upper-body strength. Unfortunately, I was so sore, tired, and achy, this wasn't as beneficial as I would have hoped. Faye grabbed my arm in return, helping to hold me up, and we started to move.

Faye was moving slowly, but I was still struggling. I had to concentrate solely on directing my body to move as my subconscious scolded me not to. The pain was distracting me to a point beyond comprehension. It was excruciating.

We made it to the elevator, and we rode up to the third floor. But before we entered the pediatric ICU, Faye directed me into the bathroom.

"Go wash yourself up better. I'll be waiting out here. Hurry," Faye said.

I walked in and locked the door behind me. Immediately, I took all the weight off my right foot and felt instant relief. As the light flickered on, I peered into the mirror. My reflection was barely recognizable. I looked ragged and tired. My face was pale but somehow red and bruised. Dry tearstains looked as though they were etched in my skin. Even though Faye wiped me down, there were still smears of blood along my cheeks and at the top of my head. My eyes were weary, and my vision was blurred.

As I looked closer, I could see where the blood was oozing from. I had a three-inch gash on the left side of my forehead, with most of it extending into my hairline. Fortunately, most of it wasn't visible. I gently dabbed it with water and applied as much pressure to stop the bleeding as I could handle.

I hobbled over to the toilet and finished wiping down my arms. I eased the shoe back off my aching foot. Quickly, the nausea came back as I caught sight of it. Disgusting. I slowly peeled off my sock. Underneath, my foot was unrecognizable. The blister thing was gashed open, oozing blood and pus, and the bandage that once covered it was now located at my heel. My big toe was swollen to almost beyond identification. My foot itself was starting to bruise severely. Easing a wet paper towel, I gently tried to wash it off. It hurt so much. I winced, as every little touch stung.

When I finished, I just sat there for a moment, trying to muster the strength to put my sock and shoe back on.

"Hurry up, Natalie!" Faye's knock on the door startled me.

"Yes, ma'am," I said quietly as I slowly eased my sock and shoe back on. When I stood back up, I couldn't help but notice how light-headed I was. I just wanted to go to sleep.

I opened the door and found Faye waiting. I couldn't quite read her expression, but I wondered whether or not she was worried. This was the first time she had ever beaten me in a public setting; she was bound to have some anxiety about someone noticing.

She took my arm, helping me walk. When I looked down, I couldn't help but notice a few claw marks on her arms along with slight bruising on her right forearm. They were from me, and a smile slowly crept onto my face. I fought back. It was a pinprick compared to what she did to me, but nonetheless, it was an injury to the opponent.

We rushed back into the room, and Faye eased me onto the cot. My body was demanding rest. I settled in and closed my eyes and dozed to sleep. A deep, deep sleep.

I awoke the next morning to the sound of people. There were nurses everywhere attending to Kelsey. She wasn't doing very well. Their attention was on her, which was convenient for Faye. I wasn't dying; my mediocre injuries were nothing compared to intubation, ventilators, and all that jazz. I could easily be dismissed.

Faye caught my eye and motioned for me to get up. I nodded and slowly pulled myself off the cot, but I could not escape the abrupt opposition of my muscles. I felt as though everything was injured in some way. My head was pounding, and every part of me seemed to ache.

"I'm going to take little Natalie home. I don't want her to see this," Faye told one of the nurses as she came over and helped me off the cot, knowing full well that I would need some assistance walking. As we were walking out of the room, I ran into one of the nurses running in.

"Oh, I'm sorry, miss. Excuse me," I apologized.

"Oh, it's okay, honey. It's okay. Oh my goodness! What happened to your darling head?"

"Oh, I…" I stuttered

"Oh, last night, our little Natalie rolled off her cot and smacked her head on the corner end table. She is just the wildest little sleeper you've ever seen. It about scared me half to death, and she got that nasty little gash and a horrible knot on her forehead! It looks so horrible, I know, but we are going to see Dr. Schlock Monday. I'll have him look at it then," explained Faye conveniently.

"Oh, honey." She looked at me sympathetically, turning to Faye. "Well, all right. You guys take care. Faye, I'll call you as soon as we have an update on Kelsey. I think Dr. Schlock is concerned with a few things that don't seem to be improving."

"Yes, yes, of course. I'll be calling you, too," she said with a sheer, polite smile, perfectly coated with that veneer of evil shine.

As we stepped into the elevator, I became tangled in my thoughts. I couldn't help but to be impressed with Faye, for as stupid as she was, sometimes she sure was brilliant. I mean, the woman could barely read but could whip up a story like it was composed by a brilliant author—flawless, unquestionable, and perfectly reasonable. She was an artist and a very talented one.

Once in the car, Faye asked, "How are you feeling?"

"Okay," I muttered, knowing better than to give an honest response.

"Well, you look like s—," Faye ventured. "But that serves you right. Go talking behind my back to Dr. Schlock again, and I'll make sure you have your own room in the Pediatric ICU. Understand?"

"Yes, ma'am." I knew after last night's happenings that I was to believe her and to do exactly what she said.

When we arrived home, Faye no longer cared about me not being able to walk. Fortunately, I didn't care about appearances. So

I crawled, hands and knees, to the door, into the house, and into my bedroom. I'm sure I looked like a moron, but truth be told, I just couldn't bear to stand. Once in my room, I went straight to bed. I really wanted to shower, but I was impossibly tired, and my head was throbbing. I was so thankful I didn't have any mandatory homework. The thought of having to read and concentrate was insurmountable; there was no way that I could have done anything with the shape I was in. Quickly, I became exceedingly thankful for the fact that we had nurses this weekend. Taking care of others was just not within my capabilities at the moment.

I was also thankful for the ability just to go to sleep. It's like my whole body was just begging me to do so. My head felt as though it was swollen somehow, and I became aware that my thinking seemed…distorted. I closed my eyes and didn't wake until Sunday morning.

When I woke up, I quickly became aware of my body and its needs. I was starving; I needed the restroom and some Tylenol. I rolled to the edge of my bed and sat up slowly. My head felt as though it were swollen somehow and like it was too big for my body. As I tried to stand and put weight on my foot, tears stung my eyes. It hurt so much, but I could at least walk a little better than I could yesterday.

I went to the bathroom and started to run water in the tub. As I undressed, I examined my body. I had bruises everywhere, and I'd lost some weight. My skin was lucid and pale. When I took off my sock, my foot looked horrible. There was pus and everything else oozing from the wound. I hadn't been taking the antibiotics Dr. Schlock prescribed. I idly wondered how he was going to react to this, but I'm sure Faye would have a story by then.

I eased myself into the cool water, hating severely that we didn't have a hot-water heater; the cold made my senses more aware and everything else more painful. I washed myself as quickly as I could.

I went back to my bedroom and dressed then headed to the kitchen, limping, well, hopping really. I knew we didn't have much, but I was sure there were some cornflakes.

As I hobbled into the kitchen, I was met by Faye and Jack.

"Oh, hi, Natalie. I was just telling Jack how badly you misbehaved at the hospital," she said all cheery-like. I didn't respond but continued to the cereal cabinet, thankful she no longer kept the locks on them. She did that for the longest time so no one would eat what they weren't supposed to; it helped her ration the food. Now, there wasn't food to ration, so there was really no point to having them.

I caught Jack's eye, and he looked at me with pity. I just glared at him. He was such a coward.

"And what do you think you're doing?" Faye said as she saw me pulling down the cornflakes.

"Getting some cereal," I answered dully.

"Well, don't you think you ought to ask first?" Faye questioned me.

"May I have some cornflakes?" I asked drearily.

"You may. See, how hard was that? You should be thankful for the food and know to ask for it," Faye counseled.

Screw you, was my mental response. "Yes, ma'am," was my verbal one. Gosh, I hated that woman. I sat down to eat. We were out of milk, so I ate the cereal dry. It didn't matter. I was too hungry to care. When I finished my second bowl, I felt better. Looking around, I wondered where the nurse was. Part of me was hoping she would see me, maybe ask what happened. Maybe I'd have the courage to tell her.

As I went back to my room, I peered out the front window. There weren't any cars other than our van in the driveway. I guessed the nurse went home. *So much for that idea*, I thought as I climbed in my bed and dozed back into a deep, deep sleep.

I awoke the next day to the morning light, realizing suddenly it was Monday.

"Crap!" I mumbled. I was late. I turned over and realized it was past ten in the morning. Great, I was more than late. Why didn't Faye come and wake me up? I eased myself up and headed to the bathroom, but as I opened my door, Faye met me.

"Morning, Natalie. As you can see, you're not going to school today. You don't look well enough. And I canceled your appointment with Dr. Schlock and rescheduled it for Friday. That'll give us some time to get these antibiotics he gave you in your system.

But don't worry, I told him that you had a game and practice all this week, and Friday was the only time we had available. Now, I want you to get up and moving today. You can't stay cooped up in your room. I've made eggs and toast for you. They are on the table."

I was stunned. She never ceased to amaze me, always knowing how to cover for her actions. "Yes, ma'am," I muttered and detoured to the kitchen, wondering when she got eggs and toast for breakfast...

I spent the day reading. I truly did feel much better, but I was concerned that I had missed a day at school. I hated being absent, but I kind of agreed with Faye in that I did look like crap.

But Tuesday was here before I knew it. I still had bruises, but I just made sure to wear long sleeves and jeans. The gash on my forehead had healed quite a bit since Saturday morning and could be covered with makeup to an appreciable extent. I guess that's why they call it Cover Girl; you can cover the girl and all the pain.

The school day passed by without my recollection of it doing so. I was still very tired, and class couldn't overrule the sleepiness I still felt. Cheerleading was my last class of the day. We were stunting today, something I usually loved, but today I dreaded it. The thought of people touching me made me wince. But I couldn't let anyone know that. I'd have to suck it up. It would surely raise suspicions if I didn't want to participate.

I wore sweatpants and a sweatshirt to practice. I knew I was going to die from heat, but I had to keep myself covered. I just told everyone that I was cold and still not feeling too well from yesterday.

We were working on liberties, where you stand on one leg while others hold you. Usually it was one of my favorites, but today it was a loathsome task, especially since I was right footed.

As we set for the stunt, my bases tightened their grip on my foot; it was unbearable. There was no way I was going to be able to fake this.

"Hey, guys, I was thinking that we should try left-foot liberties. Just to switch things up," I suggested forcefully.

"Yeah, that's a good idea! That way we could have an opposite in a pyramid or something," one of the girls agreed, much to my fortune.

But it was difficult. I kept falling, and it was getting frustrating. I was getting extremely hot and light-headed from the heat of the sweatshirt. I just had to take it off. The bruises on my arms weren't too bad, and at that moment, I was willing to risk it. My T-shirt would have to suffice. I just had to make sure it didn't come up.

But cheerleading was a contact sport, and hiding much of anything never really worked out. As our stunt group tossed me up, I lost balance and quickly came back down again, but when one of the girls reached to catch me, my shirt rose up my back.

"Natalie! Look at this bruise on your back! What happened?"

she asked.

Crap. I hurried out of their hands and pulled my shirt down. What was I going to say? Before I knew it, my coach was at my side, gasping. "Natalie, this is awful. Come here." She pulled me away from the rest of the girls.

Oh no. What was I going to say? She couldn't know the truth.

"Natalie. Is there something you need to tell me?" she asked solemnly.

"No, ma'am," I answered too quickly.

She stared at me in disbelief before asking, "Natalie. Where did you get that huge bruise on your back? And that gash on your head? And you are limping on your right foot. What's going on? Is there something I need to know about?"

Immediately, I froze. I didn't know what to say. I guess my makeup had worn off, and I didn't realize I was limping still. I was trying so hard to hide everything. I didn't want to lie, but she couldn't know. She just couldn't.

"I...I...I was practicing on the trampoline this weekend. Um, backflips and stuff. And...and I fell. I banged myself up pretty bad. I'm sorry," I stammered.

"You're sure? You fell?" she questioned my answer with much suspicion.

"Yes, ma'am. I was trying back tucks and fulls and lost my spotting and fell off the trampoline," I assured her.

"Uh-huh. And you got all of these injuries then?" she ventured.

"Well, after a few falls. You know me, I don't give up very easily." I faked a chuckle to lighten her mood while also trying to release her of the doubts she had.

"Okay," she said in what seemed to be a semi believable tone.

"Well, Natalie, you need to stop practicing so much. We'll get it down at practice. You can't be perfect all of the time. Okay? No more trampoline stunting. Understood? I don't like seeing you hurt like this. It's not good for the team or for you. We need you healthy." She pushed me to agree.

"Yes, ma'am. No more trampoline stunting." I smiled and headed back to the group. That. Was. Close.

After practice was over, I grabbed my stuff and went to meet the bus. On the drive, I thought about practice, what I said, and how quickly I said it. I recalled what I thought of Faye the morning we were leaving the hospital and how I was so shocked that she could come up with a story so fast, one that was completely believable at the drop of a dime. I thought it was part of her evil nature. I looked down on her for it. It was disgraceful. But during that bus ride home, I realized that I had done exactly the same thing with my coach earlier. The same evil, manipulative, vindictive thing. A perfect story at the drop of a dime...

Head to Toes

Our hearts are drunk with a
beauty our eyes could never see.

—George W. Russell

For most, freshman year of high school is often a struggle. You're new and have no idea what's going on or what's expected. The stress of a new environment exacerbates the fears of the unknown. Most are dealing with a new ideology of themselves. Hormones are raging. Feelings are changing. Everything is just chaotic.

My freshman year was difficult, but not in the way that I suppose an average newbie faces. Times were getting rough at the Winters' home. Faye was agitated most of the time. She was angry and irritable and sometimes just down right mean. Well, meaner than usual.

Everything in our house seemed to be slowly getting worse, especially our financial condition. Jack was always withdrawing most of his check, so we never knew if there was going to be income for food, gas, or any other necessities that were needed. Every two weeks, when the mail came, it was like a gamble, a horrible waiting game that ultimately made Faye a ticking time bomb. More often than not, there was no money. And that made Faye ferociously irate, and I was the target of her fury.

Unfortunately, the trauma with my foot didn't end that night at the doctor's office. My ankle just wasn't the same. The tendons just couldn't recover as I was constantly working on it, either at home with the children or at school for cheerleading workout. The shoes I wore were two sizes too small, which further complicated matters.

I kept getting infections around my two big toes, primarily because of ingrown toenails. Faye was irritated by it because I complained. But honestly, I couldn't help it. My walking was becoming impaired, and I worried that the infection would get into my blood stream. I couldn't help but echo the words of Dr. Schlock: "She could lose her foot!" So I bugged Faye about it constantly.

She bought me triple antibiotic cream and band-aids, but nothing was doing the trick. I asked for new shoes, knowing that was a big part of the problem, but she refused.

"You should be thankful for what you have!" she'd always yell when I asked.

I was thankful, but the annoyance of the situation was hard to deal with. One afternoon, I came home and Faye greeted me happily.

"I made an appointment with a podiatrist today for your feet and toes. We're going to see him tomorrow. It'll make you feel all better," she said sweetly.

I was always concerned when she used that tone, but I was really happy about the appointment. Maybe all my griping had paid off.

The next morning we headed to the office. It was empty when we arrived, and I became panicky. Empty parking lots and doctor's offices had a way of conjuring memories.

But from the back, a girl in bright blue scrubs appeared. I was instantly relieved.

"You must be Natalie Winters. Come on back."

I walked back with her, and she instructed me to take off my shoes. She shrieked when she saw my toes.

"Oh honey, that's awful. But don't worry. Dr. Cohen will take a look at you. He'll fix you up," she stated.

I couldn't help but notice she flushed when she mentioned his name.

Soon enough, he arrived. And he was... weird. Just a quirky fellow.

"Well, Natalie, I'm Dr. Cohen. Let's look at your feet."

"Yes sir," I responded.

"Well, they look horrible," he said.

What? I thought. *Did he just say that out loud?*

"Tell me if this hurts," he said as he reached down and squeezed my foot.

I responded in a yelp, before I could in words. "Ahhh, it hurts."

"Alright. What do you do?"

"Excuse me?" I asked.

"Sports. Track. Athletics. What are you involved in?"

"Oh," I realized. "I'm a cheerleader. I am president of the art club, a member of student council, key club, and the National Honor Society, I coach at a local cheerleading gym. And I..."

"Geez," he interrupted. "I hope you make time for school with all that. Are you even passing your classes?"

His question quickened my heart rate. The audacity of this man.

"I make straight A's, you pompous arse," I responded coolly. If there was one thing to get me going, it was to insult my intelligence. Faye did it, but no one else would.

He smiled and responded, "Okay then. Excuse me. I have to go talk to your Mommy."

After twenty minutes, he came back. "You can go, Natalie. See you next week!"

"Okay… what about my feet?" I asked him.

"I'm going to take care of it. Your mom, Faye, will inform you. And we'll talk more next week."

The next week I returned, even though I really didn't want to. It was a holiday, so thankfully I wasn't missing school. I had a bad feeling about the whole thing. I asked Faye what he was going to do, but she just gave me illusive, uninformative answers.

When we arrived, the same nurse was there, but she led me to a different room. The doctor was in there waiting. He was so odd and seemed really antsy.

"Natalie, you ready to be fixed?"

"I didn't realize I was broken," I said in a snarky tone, not forgetting his comment about my intelligence.

"Yes, yes." He chuckled. "Let's get those shoes off, so I can fix these toenails of yours."

"What are you going to do?" I asked him.

"Well, I thought you'd be so smart to figure it out!" he responded rudely.

I just stared at him in disbelief.

"Oh, don't worry. I've talked this over with Faye, your mommy." he said in a sarcastic tone. "It'll be over in a jiffy. But first, I'm going to numb your toes, okay?"

"Yes, sir," I responded politely. I quickly became aware that it probably wasn't good to make angry a guy who was about to do a procedure on me.

I felt the needles go into both of my toes. It hurt, but I had felt worse pain. But when I heard the drill, I panicked.

"What are you doing?" I sat up quickly.

"Calm down, Natalie. I'm removing the infected toenail, as your mother requested. But if you're not still, I'll cut off your toe," he warned.

I laid back down, slowly and cautiously. The sick feeling in my stomach slowly crept up. I wondered what was going on.

I tried to reason in my head, taking note of every sound, every move he was making, everything I felt. Thirty minutes later, it was all over.

"Here is a prescription for numbing cream. You'll need that. And try not to work out too much. You don't want an infection. I'll see you in a month to check the results."

"Yes, sir." I walked out to the waiting room to find Faye, but not before I looked down. Thankfully, my two big toes were intact. I was scared to death that he'd cut them off. But they were both covered in bandages.

When I got into the van, Faye was smiling to herself. I wondered what for, but I didn't ask. I preferred silence along the drive. No need to talk, as it would only leave room for me to say something wrong and get in trouble.

As we arrived home, I hurried to my room. I was really curious and decided to take off the bandages. As I did, there was a lot of blood and pus. And well, honestly, a lot of pain, too. But, as I looked closer, I realized that the nail was completely gone. On both toes! He removed all of it.

I was bewildered at the sight of my own feet! I thought, *What the hell did he do! And Faye, what did she do! The idiots. Oh well,* I thought. *Nails grow…*

Weeks went by. The wounds were healing, but the nail on either toe had not come back yet. I made light of the situation, and just figured I'd wait to ask Dr. Cohen.

The day of my follow up I was anxious to see him. Well, not *him* necessarily, but to get some answers.

As soon as he entered the room, I demanded, "Why aren't my toenails growing back?"

He looked at me shocked. "Because I removed them. Permanently. That way you won't get any more infection. They won't ever grow back," he said in an angry tone.

"You what? Permanently?" I was yelling now. "Why in the hell would you do that? You didn't tell me! You idiot!"

"You calm your little self down. Don't throw a tantrum at me. You had a problem, I fixed it, per request of your mother. If you have a problem, take it up with her. I informed her of other solutions, but she insisted on this one. It's not my problem."

I was infuriated and crying now. I couldn't believe what I was hearing. Or maybe I could and was angry at myself for not being more proactive about the situation.

"Why are you crying?" he asked, confused.

"My feet— they're ruined," I mumbled between my sobs.

"Oh, it's just a nail. No one cares," he said in what was probably as close to compassion as he could get.

I just continued to cry.

"Well, let me know if you need anything else. Good luck in school."

Before he left, I followed up on his statement. "You're right about that… No one cares." Then I walked out of the room.

Faye was waiting in the car. I was so enraged over all of it. I got in and just looked at her, mustering all the hatred I could through my eyes.

"Why are you looking at me like that?" she asked.

"You. You had him remove my toenails." The very words brought tears to my eyes once more. "Permanently."

Chuckling, she said, "Yes. That way you won't bother me about them any more."

I was crying again. I just couldn't help it.

As she drove off, Faye scolded me. "Oh, shut the hell up, Natalie. It's just feet."

"But now they are hideous," I reasoned aloud.

Laughing, she said, "Yes. They are hideous. You are hideous. From your head, now all the way to your toes!" She laughed and laughed. I cried and cried.

I was hideous… from my head… to my toes…

Terrible, Torturous Tonsils

Unfortunately, my medical problems didn't end with my toes. Lately, I had been getting a sore throat a lot—a whole lot. It seemed it was always there. I tried to tough it out, but one afternoon, I passed out in class and was sent to the nurse.

When I arrived, they realized my temperature was 104 and sent me home immediately. Fortunately, the nurse called Faye and explained that I would not be able to return without a physician's note. Though Faye was annoyed, this time she complied.

Results showed that I had strep throat, so I got a shot of penicillin and was able to return to school. The one thing I didn't budge on was going to school. I didn't care if I felt horrible, because being at home was definitely worse.

A few months later, I had the same symptoms. And on a trip back to the doctor's office, they diagnosed me with strep once again.

And so another shot of penicillin for me. Fortunately, Faye had me on Medicaid, so she wasn't required to pay for my medical care. If it wasn't for that, I'm sure I would have never received treatment.

Only a few weeks later, the strep was back, and my doctor told Faye that I was a carrier of it and that I would need a tonsillectomy.

They were going to schedule my tonsillectomy in November, but I refused to miss school for that long. I preferred to do it over Christmas break. For whatever reason, Faye backed me up on this, and it was scheduled in December, shortly after Christmas.

The day arrived before I knew it. I was a little bit excited about it. I really liked the hospital. It seemed so safe. I also liked the idea of being a doctor... It seemed so heroic. I noticed that the people in the white coats were listened to and respected. That was a profession I admired, for I wanted to be treated like that.

Faye dropped me off at 7:00 a.m. after we checked in and I got a bracelet. She informed me that they'd call me back and said she'd come to pick me up later that night when it was over. She also made sure I knew to keep my mouth shut.

Part of me was nervous that I was going to be alone, but another part of me was glad she wasn't going to be around. When they called my name, the nurse asked where my mom was.

"She had to go take care of the babies," I informed as Faye told me to do.

"Oh, honey? You're here by yourself?" she questioned.

"Yes ma'am, but it's okay. I don't mind." I assured her with a smile.

She helped me get undressed, but she let me keep my panties and socks on. The two things I insisted. I was so embarrassed by my feet that I didn't ever dare to be without socks.

I was sitting in the bed, thinking about how thirsty I was, when the doctor walked in.

Dr. Davis was the surgeon. He was a huge, burly man that was always making jokes I didn't care for. He seemed somewhat oblivious to his environment. And he sure was faked out by Faye. He came into my room after I was in a gown. I hated it, but I was still able to wear underwear and socks, so I was complacent about it.

"Well, hey there, Kiddo! Are you ready to take a nap?" he almost shouted.

"Er, I thought I was going to have surgery with anesthesia?" I asked, confused.

Laughing now, he said, "Oh, I forget how intelligent you are, Natalie! Yes, then. Are you ready for surgery?"

"Yes sir, I would like to examine my tonsils afterwards please. If I may?" I asked. I knew it was weird, but I wanted to see them. They were mine after all.

He looked at me with amused surprise. "You know, I think I can do that. Hopefully." Looking around, becoming confused, he asked, "Where is your mother, Natalie?"

"Faye," I always corrected. I hated having her referred to as my mother. "Faye is taking care of the babies. I'll be on my own today."

He didn't say anything for a moment, but just stared at me. "Do you want someone with you, Natalie? Aren't you scared?"

Was I scared? I almost chuckled. No, I wasn't scared. This wasn't something to be scared of. It was just surgery. I didn't figure he'd be beating me, or… well, I knew I was safe. Anesthesia was nothing to fear. Nothing at all. And I didn't need anyone.

"No sir, I'll be fine. Medicine is efficient, and this surgery has a low risk rate. You have great credentials. I looked them up,"

I informed him. Since my past medical procedure, I was anal about knowing what was going to happen to me at the hands of a doctor. I researched everything.

He smiled, "You did, did you? And you're impressed?"

I smiled politely. "Yes sir. And well, I also have God. I believe He will look out for me. No worries. No fears. Let's proceed." I was ready to get this show on the road. I was really excited about seeing my tonsils!

"Well, normally, I would require someone with you, but I'll let it slide for Faye. She's such a great lady. Taking care of all the sick babies like she does. Truly an angel, that woman. You're lucky to have such a wonderful mother."

He waited for my response, but I refused to say anything to comments like that. I just smiled politely.

Realizing I wasn't going to say anything, he continued. "Well, Kiddo! I'll see ya in there!"

Ugh, about time! I thought as he was leaving the room.

Soon, the nurse came in and talked to me about what all was going to happen. I was ready for it.

The anesthesiologist told me to count to ten but said I wouldn't finish.

"Okay. But I'll get to ten," I stated confidently.

Laughing, he said, "Okay sweetheart, here we go."

I could feel the cold liquid entering my veins as I started counting down. "Ten, nine... I got to ten, see?" And before I closed my eyes, I caught him smiling at me. Then, there was darkness.

Water was all I could think when I woke. I was thirsty, and hungry. And I needed the bathroom. I started to get up.

"Hi, Honey!" The bright-eyed nurse said. "How are you feeling?"

I looked at her quizzically. I just had surgery, how did she think I was feeling?

"I need the bathroom. And water. And food," I whispered. My throat hurt exceedingly badly.

"Okay, which first?" she asked sweetly.

"Water. Then bathroom. Then food." I quickly reorganized the arrangement according to need.

She took me to the bathroom. And made me pee in a bowl. That was weird. Then she gave me a small cup of water and told me to drink it slowly. *Yeah right!* I thought, as I gulped it down. I was parched.

"What would you like to eat, honey?"

"Onion rings," I told her.

"Oh, sweetheart, you can't have onion rings. You can have Jell-O or soup… Or ice cream? Only soft foods."

"Oh, I'll take ice cream," I said excitedly.

"Alright, I'll be right back."

Quickly, she returned holding a bowl of vanilla. Perfection.

"Eat it slow, or you'll get sick," she ordered kindly.

Again, yeah right. I was starving. But the coldness was making it hard to swallow.

"How does your throat feel? Do you have any pain?" She interrupted my eating.

I hadn't even thought about my throat. When I did, I realized I couldn't really feel anything at all.

"I don't feel anything?" I told her, confused.

"Oh, well you still have the numbing medicine. In a little bit, it will hurt. Ring the red button when it does, and I'll get you some medicine."

"Okay. I mean, yes, ma'am."

"Alright, I'll be back in a bit."

"Wait!" I stopped her as I suddenly remembered. "Dr. Davis is supposed to bring me my tonsils."

She looked shocked by the statement and, from what I could tell, didn't really know how to respond. "Errr. Okay, I'll tell him."

"Okay. Make sure he doesn't dispose of them!" I would be infuriated if that happened. When else would I get the chance to see tonsils in a jar?

I finished the ice cream and watched the Disney channel. I liked Disney. And I appreciated how all of the princesses were always without a parent or parents... Cinderella was my favorite. I suppose I could relate to her the most.

They were at the ball, right before Cinderella was about to meet the prince, when Dr. Davis walked in.

"Hey Natalie. How are you feeling?" he asked, far too loudly.

"Well, thank you," I said softly.

"I have something for you..." he offered.

Immediately excited, "My tonsils! You have them!?"

"Shh, calm down, Sweetie. You'll rip your stitches."

"Can I see them?" I shouted, all hush, whisper-like.

He slowly pulled a jar from his pocket and held it up.

And there they were. Red, white lumps in a jar of fluid. Awesome.

I reached for them, and Dr. Davis handed them over, amused by my reaction.

I looked at them in the jar, turning it around, looking at every angle. I started to open it when Dr. Davis stopped me.

"No, Natalie. You can't open them. You have to keep them in a jar. And in the freezer, if your mom allows it."

I immediately stopped, but looked up more thrilled than ever. "You mean I can keep them? Forever?"

He was laughing now. "Yes, I suppose you can."

"Awesome." Perhaps I didn't care for Dr. Davis before, but I did now. "Thank you, Dr. Davis," I said shyly.

"You are quite welcome, Natalie. I only hope Faye doesn't get upset with me for letting you take them home."

I never thought of what Faye would do. But I didn't care. They were my tonsils. Not hers.

"It's okay," I assured him, still holding and examining the contents of the little jar.

"You know, with this much curiosity in tonsils, you might be good for medicine. You could be a doctor like me," he offered. I had never really thought about what I was going to college for, but he had a good point. This was so cool.

"Is it hard? To become a doctor?" I asked.

"Well, all good things are hard, Natalie. At least a little bit. But you are smart and talented. You can do it." He was smiling, and immediately, I blushed. Compliments always made me so uncomfortable.

"Thank you. That's very kind." He was a good doctor.

"It's the truth... Well, Natalie, I better get going. I'll call your mom and let her know that you can go home."

"Oh, can I please spend the night here? Please! I love the hospital!" I was shouting again, neglecting the slight sting starting to arise out of my throat.

He chuckled, "Well, if you love staying the night at the hospital, surely you'll be a physician." He continued to laugh. "But, I'm sorry. I can't keep you here. It's against insurance policy. However, with day surgery you may stay all day. How about until eight-o-clock tonight?"

That was fair enough. "Okay! Thank you so much, Dr. Davis. You're the best!"

"Natalie, easy with your throat!" he said impatiently.

"Oh… sorry," I said wistfully.

The nurse walked in, and Dr. Davis turned to her. "Debbie, we are going to discharge this young lady at eight-o-clock, and not a minute before."

"Yes, Doctor," she said, confused.

"Bye, Natalie. I'll see you next week at your follow up."

"Yes, Dr. Davis. Thanks! See you!" I said, remembering to whisper this time. Truth be told, my throat was starting to hurt.

The nurse caught my wince. "I'll go get those pain meds."

"Thank you," I said, quickly becoming aware of the fire starting to build in my throat.

Eight-o-clock came far too fast. I didn't want to leave, but I knew I must. I didn't feel well, and honestly I just wanted to go to sleep. The pain medication made me feel weird. I didn't like it.

Soon enough, Faye walked in.

"Get dressed so we can go. I've had to wait around all day for your ass," she said, tossing my clothes.

"Yes ma'am." I slowly got out of bed and got dressed.

The nurse came in and took out my IV.

"Let me go get a wheelchair, and I'll take you out." She smiled at me.

"She doesn't need that. She can walk," Faye said.

"I'm aware she can walk, Mrs. Winters, but it's our policy. She'll be leaving our hospital the way we require."

I liked Debbie, but after that statement, I loved her. I had so much respect for people who put Faye in her place.

Faye didn't respond but just stared in amazement. Soon, Debbie returned and helped me into the chair. And honestly, I was glad... I really wasn't feeling well.

We got into the elevator and quickly I became dizzy.

"You okay?" Debbie asked.

"I... I... I don't think so," I muttered.

"Oh, Natalie. Stop being so dramatic," Faye said in a tone that was kind but was also a threat.

I didn't say anything. I was really hot and I started to sweat. My breathing quickened. Soon, we were out in the cold December air and I felt better.

"Okay, honey, stand up slow," Debbie said, but Faye all but pushed her out of the way and pulled me out of the chair. The quick jolt threw me into a whirlwind. As she pulled me up, I could feel it coming. And before, I could stop it, my puke flew all over Faye.

"Oh, Sweetheart!" Debbie exclaimed. "Maybe we should go

back. I'll page Dr. Davis."

"No. You won't. We are going home. Natalie needs her rest," Faye said, with a chilling smile. I knew it then, that I was going to be in trouble.

"Mrs. Winters, she could be having a reaction…" Debbie started to say, but Faye cut her off.

"She's had surgery before. I'll call Dr. Davis myself if she's not better by tomorrow. Thank you. Good night."

Faye shoved me into the back seat and shut the door. As soon as we were on the road Faye looked back.

"You little b—. I hope you know you'll be washing your puke off my shirt tonight. And while I'd love to beat the s— out of you, I might just save it for tomorrow. Give you something to look forward to."

I couldn't respond. I felt too sick.

"Answer me!! Or I'll pull over and give it to you now!" Faye screamed.

"Ye…. Ye…. Yes ma'am…" I stammered, pushing through the burn in my throat.

When we arrived, I realized Faye wasn't kidding about the shirt. She took me to the kitchen and handed me a toothbrush and soap.

"I want it spotless. You won't go to bed, until it is!" she ordered.

"Yes…… Yes ma'am." I felt so bad… The fire in my throat was raging, and my stomach was constantly threatening to eject itself. The smell of my throw up was making me nauseated, but I couldn't mess it up again. And I couldn't make Faye mad. There was no way I could handle getting in trouble tonight.

Around 1:00 in the morning, I finished. It took me so long…

And I was so tired. Faye had already gone to bed, so I just sat the shirt on top of the washing machine. I had to crawl, because my body refused to stand.

I crawled all the way to my room and used the rest of my strength to get up on my bed before I fell into a deep sleep.

The next day, I awoke, but barely. It was hard to breath. My body ached, but nothing touched the pain that I was feeling in my throat. I looked over at the clock. It was 5:00, but from the sun, I knew it was in the evening. I wanted to get up but I couldn't stand.

I crawled to the bathroom, used the facilities, and pulled myself up to the sink to get a drink of water. I crawled back to my room, hoping Faye wouldn't see me. I needed her to forget her threat of beating me today. I knew there was no way I could handle it.

I crawled back to bed and slept. I repeated this process to the bathroom only for the next three days. I was so hungry, but Faye only kept bringing me crackers and everything else I couldn't eat because of the pain.

I grew weaker and weaker. New Year's Eve was here before I knew it. I had been sleeping mainly. Even in my consciousness,

I was barely conscious. However, the smell from the kitchen was arousing my stomach.

Faye suddenly entered my room. "Hi, Natalie. Are you hungry, sweetheart? You need to eat."

She helped me up and took me to the kitchen. There was food all over. My favorite— Wolf Chili with bread and cheese. But the spices in it made it unbearable to get down.

The feast looked scrumptious, but not for someone who had an insane sore throat. If it wasn't spicy, it was crunchy and hard. But I was literally starving to death. I didn't know what hurt more. My stomach or my throat.

"You better eat, you little s—!" Faye demanded.

The fire from the food was battling the fire in my throat. I tried the chips and salsa, the chili, the carrots. I tired to force the food down, but as I did the tears were falling from my eyes. All of the pain was too much.

"What are you crying about?!?" Faye demanded.

I didn't answer.

"Answer me!!!" she screamed.

"It hurts. This food. It hurts my throat. I'm not supposed to eat this."

"You ungrateful b—!" she screamed, and before I could duck, the back of her hand knocked me out of my chair. "Get the f— out of my sight."

The blow made me so dizzy. Crawling was a struggle. On my way to my room, I stopped to the bathroom, knowing that I was going to puke.

I made it to the toilet and let go… When I opened my eyes, the toilet was filled with blood.

My follow up was today. And I couldn't even move. But I was thankful. One of the nurses, Michael, had been sneaking into my room when Faye left to give me ice cream and medicine. He was so nice and I knew he felt sorry for me.

Faye was irritated when he carried me to the car, but she didn't resist him. Michael was a large man. And he didn't take to disrespect.

"Faye, she is not doing well. I think they might put her back in the hospital."

"They won't. I know how to take care of my own daughter."

She shut the door and headed to Dr. Davis' office. We pulled up and Faye helped me out of the van. She put her arm around me, helping me walk into the building.

"Natalie… Are you okay?" she asked, seemingly concerned.

"I don't think so," I whispered.

When I walked into the lobby, I could feel everyone looking at me. I knew I must have smelled awful. I hadn't showered since the night before my surgery. My hair was greasy, and I was sure I had lost weight.

One of the nurses hurried around the counter, grabbed a wheelchair, and took me back immediately.

"Natalie, we need to get your weight. Do you think you can stand?"

"I… try" was all I could say.

And I did try, but I couldn't. It was too demanding on my body. But, still, they needed my weight. So, the nurse weighed herself and then picked me up and reweighed.

Before my surgery I was ninety-two pounds. I was now eighty-two. I'd lost ten pounds in a week. I had a fever of 103. I was dehydrated. And at that moment, I figured death wouldn't be so bad.

Dr. Davis came rushing into my room.

"Natalie?" he asked. All I could do was meet his eyes. And when I did, mine were filled with tears.

"Get an IV and a bag of fluids. Now!" he yelled at the nurse.

"Mrs. Winters, I need to speak with you outside, please," he said in a voice that made me scared.

"Yes, sir," Faye said meekly.

As they stepped outside, I struggled to listen.

"Mrs. Winters! Why have you not called me? Natalie has lost ten pounds! She is terribly ill!"

"I know. I'm sorry, Dr. Davis. She just refuses to eat or drink. I've been trying, but she's so difficult."

"Don't give me that bulls—. She's a child! And right now, she's almost damn near a dead one!" Dr. Davis yelled.

His words struck though... Was I almost dead?

"I'm sorry, Dr. Davis. I'm so sorry." Faye was crying now. "I thought she would get better. I'm so sorry."

There was a long moment of silence before Dr. Davis said, "I'm sorry for yelling at you, Faye. I just... I care about Natalie, and as her doctor, I have to make sure she's okay. I'm going to have to put her back in the hospital."

"Oh, Dr. Davis. Please don't. She'll only get sicker there. Let her come home. I have an IV pump and nurses. She'll get better care there. I promise. There are infections all over the hospital. Please."

"Faye. Clearly, your house is not the hospital or she wouldn't be in this condition," he said in a stern tone.

"It isn't true, Dr. Davis. Please let her come home. I'll bring her for a follow up in two days, and I swear that I'll call you if there is any problem. Please, please. Let me be at home with my baby."

Faye was pleading. Why did she want me home so badly?

"Faye," Dr. Davis sighed. "I'll allow it because you have an intensive care unit at your house. But if she loses so much as an ounce, I'm admitting her, and I'll have your care questioned. And I'll see her in two days. No questions."

"Yes, yes, Doctor. Of course. We'll get her better," Faye said. I could hear the relief in her tone.

Dr. Davis came back into the room. "Hey, how are you, Honey?"

I didn't answer but just looked at him.

"I'm so sorry you are so sick, Natalie. But I'm going to get you better, okay? But you have to eat and drink for me. Understand?"

I nodded.

"Okay. I'll get you some more medicine to help."

Again, I just nodded.

He smiled wryly. "You know, you forgot something at the hospital. I'll go and get it. Be right back."

Faye smiled, confused. She looked at me, and I could detect what I thought was sympathy.

When Dr. Davis returned, he was smiling ear to ear. He sat down beside me and pulled the little jar from his pocket. The one with my tonsils. They were frozen now.

I immediately broke out in a smile. I had forgotten all about them! I reached up and took the jar.

"Thank you," I whispered.

"Of course, Sweetie."

Faye didn't say anything but just stared, confused.

They put me in a wheelchair and then into our van. On the drive home, Faye asked me what I would like to eat.

"Grilled cheese," I told her. Saying the words made my mouth water.

She stopped at Wal-Mart and went in to get the ingredients. When we arrived home, Michael came out and carried me into the kitchen. I handed him my jar of tonsils and told him to put them in the freezer. He just smiled and did so.

"You can go home now, Michael. Take the rest of the afternoon," Faye said to him.

"Oh, that's alright Mrs. Winters… I…."

Faye cut him off. "It's not a request. I would like to be alone with my children."

While Faye was cooking the sandwich, Michael gathered his things and left.

"He's never coming back to this home. I don't like his attitude. And he was more tuned to taking care of you than the babies."

I didn't respond, for I was too concentrated on the smell of the food. Soon, the sandwich sat before me. It was really soft, and I could swallow it fairly easily.

I had finished about half when Faye set out another. I knew I wanted to eat it, but even with only half of the first one down, I didn't think I could eat two.

Then, she sat another one down. Then another. Then another.

"You wanted grilled cheese, you got it. And you're going to eat a whole loaf's worth. You're not getting up from that table until you do."

My eyes widened with shock. There was no way I could eat all of these.

"You need to gain weight, like your Dr. Davis said. I saw you sucking up to him. Trying to get me in trouble. Consider this your punishment." She finished the loaf and set the last grilled cheese sandwich in front of me. There were fourteen sandwiches in front of me. Well, fourteen and a half. I still hadn't finished the first.

But, I knew better than to refuse. There could be worse punishment, I knew. It was only three in the afternoon... I sat there all night eating those sandwiches. Finally, around two thirty in the morning, Faye came in, and gave me permission to go to sleep. There were still ten left. I just couldn't get them down. We'll save these for tomorrow.

And that's what she did. I ate those grilled cheese sandwiches for the next two days.

I felt better but I had to miss another week of school. Dr. Davis didn't release me to go back. I was very angry. I hated missing school, and I missed the first week of the semester.

The tonsil experience was almost over though. I had gained a little weight back, and I did feel better. But it wasn't an experience I'd ever forget. But, regardless, I did get something out of it. My tonsils. In a jar. Still, after all of this, it was awesome.

After I started school, I had told my friends about it and agreed to bring them to school so they could see. When I went home, I looked for them but couldn't find them.

"What are you looking for?" Faye asked.

"Er, my tonsils from Dr. Davis. I'm going to show them in my science class."

"No, you're not, because I threw them away. I'm not having that s— in my freezer. That's disgusting, Natalie."

"You threw them away??" I asked, outraged. "It was for biology! And you knew how much I wanted them!"

"Exactly. And that's why I threw them away. Get the f— over it." Faye walked off.

And I couldn't help but cry. Maybe it was weird, but I wanted them. They were the only part of the experience that made it all worth it. Oddly enough, my tonsils had become a part of my heart. And now they were gone. Faye was just hateful. Mean. Wicked. Yes, maybe I was just like Cinderella... with an evil stepmother.

Ticktock Goes the Clock

. . . .

Time is free, but it's priceless. You can't own it, but
you can use it. You can't keep it, but you can spend it.
Once you've lost it, you can never get it back.

—Harvey Mackay

. . . .

Time. It's one of the most powerful forces created. It cannot be stopped, doesn't dare slow. It brings about our future, whether we are prepared or not. As humans, we do our best to encompass it. We try to control it by keeping track of all the minutes and hours. But we fail. With every second, it proves to be stronger. Proves to be inexorable.

Hope is powerful, too. I believe that when people have something to believe in, no matter what it is, it helps them through the hardest of times. I knew that my daddy wouldn't come back for me. He was in heaven, and unless God wanted to cause a whole lot of commotion, he was going to stay there. So my hope shifted. I knew I had a mom, and I hoped she remembered that she had me.

I didn't know much about her. I never was able to recall her from my memory. I only knew what Faye had offhandedly said about her, that she was an ugly, fat, stupid drug addict. She was bipolar and manic-depressive, and I was just like her. Worthless.

"You have the ugly and fat down. Let me know when you start doing drugs," Faye would say. She was such an idiot. I had no use for drugs. People say they could help take you away from reality; well, no level of high could take me away from where I was. I was a logical person, I saw what drugs did. I witnessed what it did to the children's development. I saw how they affected families and destroyed lives. I remembered how they altered my parents' ability to be there for me. Drugs had already horribly altered my life, yet I had never touched them. No, I had no use for drugs.

They were a short-term solution, and I needed something much better than that. Though, I have to say, I had plenty of access. The babies were on some of the most potent medications that could be given. If I wanted to be a drug addict, I very well could have been.

But who knew who my mom was? Faye wasn't exactly good at giving facts, and I didn't trust her. Her actions never matched her words, and her words never aligned with reason. I began to learn to doubt her. I didn't listen, because whatever she said was probably just a lie or at least a manipulation of the truth. One thing I could count on was that Faye was constantly lying.

I had hope, though, in my mom. I knew her name was Charlotte, but I didn't know anything else. However, I wished that one day she would come looking for me. That she would find me and take me with her. I didn't know who she was, but I knew there was a good chance that she was better than Faye. She was my mom. There had to be some love there somewhere for me. She had love for me, I knew, because I was born. She could have aborted me, but she didn't. She kept me in her womb, and that was a gift I could never repay her for. I had been given an opportunity to live, and though life was not picturesque, I had faith it would get better. I just had to grow up first. It was just a question of time moving fast enough to ensure I'd get the chance.

It was a sunny spring day at school. Freshman classes were hard, and I looked forward to the noon break. Lunch had just started, and I started making rounds to all the different tables to say hello to people I knew. Visitation was always something I enjoyed. People have always been very interesting to me. Everyone has a story and a perspective. It was nice to learn about other people's thoughts and beliefs. And in doing that, I often learned a lot about myself. And a lot about normalcy.

I was talking to one of my friends about the upcoming varsity game. We were going to carpool, but first, I had to get permission to go. We were planning things out when I felt a tap on my shoulder. As I turned, I recognized the girl. Her name was Kellie. She was in the grade above me. We had been going to school together since I was in the seventh grade. She was nice, but it seemed she was troubled. I knew she had a drug problem, but I was still kind to her. I wondered what caused her to use in the first place.

"Hi, Natalie. Can I talk to you for a minute?" she asked.

"Hi, Kellie! Yeah, no problem. What's up?" I asked.

As we walked over to a quieter place, she seemed nervous. I wasn't really sure what was going on, but I got an eerie feeling. It probably wasn't good. When we reached the corner of the commons area, she turned around and just looked at me. I was a bit creeped out.

"Kellie, what's wrong?" I questioned. She looked down for a moment before meeting my eyes.

"I'm your sister," she said in a calm but shaky voice.

I stood there in silence, trying to comprehend what she said.

"Did you hear me?" she asked, interrupting my thoughts. "We're sisters."

"W-w-what?" was all I could muster out. *She is my what?* I thought. *Did she just say* sister?

"Well, we are half sisters. I have a different dad, but we have the same mom," she said.

"H-h-h-how do you know that? Or how do you think you know that?" I questioned, trying to hide the hysteria in my voice.

"I know it's a shock, but I thought you should know. I talked to your grandmother the other day. She and my grandma, well, our grandma, are really good friends. I'm sorry about your dad, John." She went on, but I couldn't digest what she was saying. She knew about my daddy; she talked to my grandma. I had another grandma? Where were these people? They knew about me?

She must have seen the perplexed look on my face. "It's okay. I don't want to scare you. But you have two sisters. Another named Megan and a brother named Robert."

All of this information was overwhelming. I just stood there for a moment, feeling dazed and confused.

"Are you okay? Do you need to sit down?" Kellie asked.

"Yeah," I agreed as she motioned me over to the nearest chair.

"I know this is a lot. I'm sorry. I just thought you should know. I mean, I would want to know. And it's kind of cool, you know?" she went on. "Like, we are sisters! We've been going to the same school forever, and we didn't even know it!"

"Yeah," was all I could think to say. My mind was racing. This wasn't happening, was it? I mean, how? When? Why?

"How do you know all of this?" I interrupted her ranting.

"Well, I was talking to my grandma, our mom's mom. That's who we live with. Me, Megan, and Robert. I had a yearbook, and we were looking at it. Then Grandma, all of a sudden, stopped and was staring at your picture. You look just like mom. She started crying, and then she started talking. She told us that you went into foster care because Mom couldn't take care of you, and our mom was dangerous at the time because of drugs. But she thought John, your dad, had you. So she called your grandma, and they just talked. Afterward, she just told us that you were adopted by some people and that we were sisters."

I tried to digest her story. It was all just...a lot.

"Do they go to school here? My other brother and sister?" I asked.

"No. Robert has graduated, and Megan goes to another high school."

"Oh." I was dumbfounded. What was I supposed to say to all of this? We sat quietly for a moment. Kellie was letting me digest, I think, before she interrupted my chaotic thoughts.

"Our mom, Charlotte, she wants to talk to you," Kellie stated.

"What? My mom? Charlotte? She knows me?" I questioned.

"Yes, Charlotte. I told her that I was going to talk to you, and she wanted me to tell you that she would like to talk to you. She is living in Tennessee right now, but she said that I could give you her phone number."

I couldn't respond. My mom wanted to speak to me? My actual mother? What would she say? What was I supposed to say? I had a brother. And two sisters. And a mom now? Which all have been revealed in less than five minutes. I was in an emotional upheaval. Was this really happening?

"I…I…uh…I'm sorry, Kellie, but I need some…some time. I… This is a lot," I responded. I was besieged by all of this information.

"I know. I'm sorry, but I thought you should know. You can take your time. I'll give you her number when you are ready, and you can call her. She loves you, Natalie. She wanted me to tell you that, too."

Tears flooded my eyes. I wasn't sure what was going on, but the word *love* caught me off guard. I had a mom who wanted to talk to me, and she…loved me? I had sisters and a brother… another grandmother…a family? It was a lot to take in. I was, well, absolutely dumbfounded by it all.

"Take your time, Natalie. I'll talk to you later, okay?" Kellie assured me and slowly walked away. I tried to register my thoughts, but they were all over the place. How? What? I…I just couldn't wrap my head around what just happened. My muddled thoughts were interrupted by the bell and by my friend, Nicole.

"What's wrong, Natalie?" she asked.

"Kellie is my sister, and I have a mom that wants to talk to me."

The rest of the day—well, the rest of the week—confusion pretty much defined my mind's state. Everything that I had learned was shocking. I mean, I had never even thought about having siblings, and here I was, presented with two sisters and a brother. And my

mom? My actual mom wanted to speak with me? This was crazy. Like Jerry Springer kind of stuff.

I was lost. And even seeing Kellie was disorienting. She was my sister. It was just a strange situation. And I wanted to talk to my mom, but what was I supposed to say? What would she say?

What would I ask? I didn't know. I was bombarded with fear about the whole situation. What if I talked to her, and she didn't like me? What if she said that she was glad she gave me up? And Faye. I had Jack and Faye to deal with. Faye had me on a short leash. I couldn't do anything without her knowing about it. Every day at lunch, I was required to call her. To let her know what I was doing. She knew everything. She would call my friends' parents and talk to them about what I was up to, just to ensure I wasn't lying to her. Luckily, my friend Nicole knew a little about Faye and didn't say anything. She always had my back. Lord only knows how Faye would react to this news. I couldn't let her know any of this.

I could half expect her to enroll me into a different school and forbid me to ever speak to Kellie again. I wanted to talk to her though. I wanted to talk to my mom. The hope in me was blossoming somehow. The hope that she would want to come get me, to take me away with her. I didn't know her, but she couldn't be any worse than Faye and Jack. She just couldn't.

The next Monday arrived before I knew it. I had spent the last week running through scenarios in my head about all of the best-and worst-case outcomes. Best case, my mom would come and rescue me. Worst, Faye would find out about all of this.

At lunch, I found Kellie and told her that I wanted to talk to Charlotte, but that I needed some time to figure out how. I explained that my mom, well, foster mom, was strict about my phone usage and that I didn't really want her to know about all of this.

"Take your time, Natalie. This is a lot, I know," she assured me. "Charlotte, our mom, she understands that you might be confused and need time. No worries."

And that's what I did. I took my time, trying to figure out the best method as to how to approach this without jeopardizing myself.

Nicole helped me devise a plan. If I was going to talk to my mom, I had to be away from the school and away from Faye.

We both agreed that me spending the night with her would be the best option. I was going to see if I could stay with her Friday night, and then after the game, I would call my mom.

Wednesday night, I asked Faye for permission, and after talking to Nicole's mom, she agreed. I had to do some extra chores, but I was okay with it. I was just excited that the "plan" was working.

Thursday morning, I looked for Kellie to tell her and ask for my mom's number, but I couldn't find her. I just figured she was running late. I decided to just find her at lunch. I was so excited! I wondered how Kellie felt about all of this. I mean, it had to be shocking for her to know that she had another sister. I then thought about our mom. How did she feel about that? How did Megan and Robert feel? Well, I couldn't stress about that now. I just needed to take it one step at a time.

Noon rolled around . I searched the cafeteria for Kellie, but I couldn't find her anywhere. I was super anxious to get the number. I had ten different kinds of excitement and apprehension about all this, and I needed one less thing to worry about it.

As I scanned the cafeteria again for Kellie, I spotted one of her friends and decided to ask her if she knew where I could find her.

"Hey, Lacy, do you know where Kellie is? I need to talk to her," I said.

"Oh, you don't know..."

"Know what?" I asked.

"Kellie isn't here today. Her mom died last night, and she is at home with her family. They are having a hard time. I think the funeral is Saturday or something."

I'm sure the look on my face was nothing but sheer shock. I couldn't comprehend what Lacy had just said. It couldn't be... "You mean, her mom, Charlotte?" I mumbled out the question as best as I could.

"Yeah. I feel so bad for her. She and her mom were just talking about the summer. Charlotte was going to come down and bring the family together or something like that. Kellie was really excited. I guess she'll never make it now. It's really sad. But I'll tell her you want to talk to her when I see her."

I tried to comprehend. I tried to keep my composure. "No, don't bother her. Thanks, Lacy," I said in a shaky voice as I turned and quickly darted toward the bathroom.

When I arrived, I thanked God that no one was there. That no one could hear the sobs that were escaping from me, that no one could witness me falling apart. My mother...my mom...had died. She was gone. Part of me wanted to tell myself that Lacy was wrong, but I knew better than to present that false hope.

I wouldn't get to speak with her, and my dreams of seeing her, of perhaps living with her, were crushed. I had so much regret. I took my time when I didn't have the time to take. I should have called her the day I found out. Now, it was too late.

I skipped my next class, because I was just too upset. The past few days I had worked myself into a frenzy about getting away... getting to meet my mother. I dreamed up what she would look like and talk like. I had visions of her telling Faye that she was "taking her daughter back." I had images of the two of us hugging, and her telling me that she was sorry that she left, but that everything was now okay. I had dreams of her saying, "I love you, Natalie." But, all of it was just that. A fantasy that now was utterly destroyed.

The weeks went by, and I recovered to the best of my abilities. I never saw Kellie again. I figured she moved or something because of the circumstance. I had to move on, too. That was the only way to survive. I had to find a new dream. At this point in my life, the dream was to get away from Faye and Jack. I would have done anything to get out of that house. To have a mom and dad who truly loved me. A family. Now that my parents were gone, I just didn't know if that would ever happen. I considered perhaps living with my grandparents. Maybe my grandma would want me back? But I just didn't know. Faye would never let me go back with them. If there was one thing I learned while growing up in a foster home, it was that the only people who had exclusive rights to their child, no matter what, were the parents, and mine were gone. Plus, my grandparents knew about me, they knew where I was. If they wanted me, even to see me, they knew how. But part of me knew they wouldn't. They knew I was in a home, and I guess they only assumed it was a good one. And why wouldn't they? I was a cheerleader, on the honor roll, president of the art club, and a member of student council, the National Honors Society, and the key club. Anyone looking at me wouldn't dare think that I lived in a horrendous home. They wouldn't dare dream that Faye and Jack Winters were appalling individuals. And that was a part of the problem. At the surface, no one could see. The truth is that people do judge a book by its cover, and the presentation that Jack and Faye had was flawless. And if people did find out the truth, they didn't do anything about it. No, there was no way out. All I could do was grow up. Turning eighteen was the only option I had left. That was the safest and most feasible idea.

But, no matter how hard I tried, I couldn't stop thinking about my parents. The last time I saw my daddy, I was four years old. I met him again in the obituaries. Now, I was thirteen, and the first time I met my mom was such a distant memory that it couldn't be remembered. Now, I would meet her again in the same way I'd seen my daddy for the last time… the obituaries. My parents were gone, and my hope, all of it, was lost for another five years—what seemed like an eternity. There was no escape from this hell I was in.

Yes, time is a curious thing. In some instances, I begged for more. In others, I all but pleaded for less. Time. There would be no pushing it forward, no way to put it to a stop. I just had to wait… ticktock goes the clock.

Anatomy Assessment

. . . .

Fear of a name increases fear of the thing itself.

—J.K. Rowling,

Harry Potter and the Sorcerer's Stone

. . . .

My body was changing. I was still awkwardly skinny, though working out and building muscle seemed to help a little. But it was short lived because I would go days without food, and you just can't maintain physique with that kind of lifestyle. I weighed, on and off, about one hundred pounds and was about five foot even. I was still very petite. I wore clothes from Wal-Mart and the Salvation Army, which usually hung off of my lanky body, but I did my best to have some sort of style.

My hair, for whatever reason, turned unbelievable curly. Well, frizzy is probably a better description. And my auburn tint transformed into a hazelnut brown. My skin was porcelain, oddly white. But fortunately, in the summers I could obtain a bit of a tan. I had somewhat grown into my teeth. They were perfectly straight, however, my mouth was just kind of big… Horse-like for sure.

I was nerdy, wearing cheap glasses and always with some sort of book in my hand, except when it was replaced by my pom-poms. Fortunately though, I had grown into my face. People complimented me, though I didn't really believe them. I always figured they were being nice. Faye made sure I knew that I was ugly. When I looked in the mirror, I didn't see pretty. Honestly, all I saw was sadness… a broken girl. But, when in public, I hid all of the emptiness with a smile… the best, most believable one I could offer.

I wasn't keen on being popular, but my skill in cheerleading had provided me with a platform for it. I was always just nice to people; polite, but distant. I had good friends, though I kept them in the dark on most things. We would talk about normal teenage, girly things…

I noticed however, that I had become more irritable and more moody than usual. Most of my friends had started their periods, but I had not. I was grateful for that. Now that I knew the full process of pregnancy, I was fearful for a period. Jack had, for the most part, stopped coming into my room late at night, but I never knew when he'd try again. And more so, I was not confident in my abilities to stop him if he did.

The whole subject matter of sexual activity was dreadful for me to think about. I knew now that what was happening was terrible. But I dared not say a word. Deep down in my heart, I knew what Daddy Jack did was wrong, but for some reason, I felt responsible. I thought it was my fault, and I didn't want to get in trouble over it. I felt so dirty, so bad. I felt that I was damaged goods, and no man would ever want anything to do with me. I wasn't a virgin. I was used up, and no boy would want me now. But the thing is, I didn't want them either. I didn't want anyone to know. I'd never tell a soul.

Once high school started, girls wanted to date boys, but I avoided guys altogether. I wanted them to be attracted to me, but nothing more. It was enough for me to know that they thought I was pretty. I needed or wanted nothing else. Every date I was asked out on was shot down. Those terrible nights had affected me in so many ways.

I was scared of men, fearing that it would always hurt. The pain of what "love" was seemed unbearable to me. And I knew that with any relationship, I would have to explain my fears, and I was in no position to do that. Ever. It was my dirty secret. Mine to keep. And that's exactly what I did.

But I knew it would happen, sooner or later... a menstrual cycle. The art of "becoming a woman," they say. I knew mostly about it from knowledge gained from friends, my previous bout of reality check, and research by my own hand. Honestly, the more I learned, the more I hated all of it and the more I wished the whole thing could be prolonged.

At one point, my pediatrician was concerned with the fact that I hadn't started yet, as I was a sophomore in high school. She sent me to a gynecologist. I had no idea what that entailed, as we left straight from my appointment to the new doctor. I asked Faye on the ride what it was, but she told me not to worry about it.

The office was nicely decorated. Flowers, with pink décor. Very feminine. I suppose that should have been my clue. My name was called, and I followed the nurse with Faye right behind.

I walked into the exam room. It was much different from the one I was used to. Actually, the whole process was. As I stepped in, the nurse asked Faye to wait outside the door. I was pleased. I didn't like her around. Most of the time she answered the questions for me. Most of the time her answers were incorrect. I was pleased with the opportunity to speak for myself.

When the nurse sat down, she quickly ran over my chart and then started with the questioning.

"Hello, Natalie. I see that you are here for an exam, because your pediatrician has some concerns" she stated rather than asked.

"Yes, ma'am," I answered.

"Okay. Well, I have a few questions. These are very private, but I need your honest answers. I will not tell Faye what you say, alright?"

What? I thought. *Private?*

I suppose she read my puzzled look, as she responded, "You won't be in any trouble for how you answer, okay? It's alright."

"Er, okay," I stumbled. This was strange.

"Okay. Are you currently sexually active?"

There was a long pause. Her question caught me off guard. How was I supposed to answer that? If she knew about Jack…. Well, she couldn't know.

"Natalie?" she offered again.

"No… Not currently," I answered.

"Okay. Have you ever been sexually active?" she questioned.

"Ugh. Umm…" My pulse quickened. *Oh gosh!* I thought.

"Natalie, it's okay if you say yes. We just have to know," she assured me.

"No," I answered quietly. They couldn't know about this. No one could.

"Okay. You've never had oral or vaginal sex?" she asked.

I felt as though I was going to pass out. I hated to lie, but I had to…

"No! No!" My voice was laced with anger and fear.

"Okay. All right. It's okay, Sweetheart. Calm down," the nurse soothed.

"We'll stop there. Just slip into the gown. Take all of your clothes off. Including your panties. The doctor will be in, in just a second."

I just nodded my head, as if I understood. Why did I have to get into a gown? And *why* did I have to take off my underwear?

I hesitantly did as she instructed. I hated not having panties on. I grew so uneasy. My nerves were becoming erratic, and my heart was pounding.

The knock at the door startled me, as it opened slowly.

"Can we come in?" a deep voice asked.

"Uh, yes," I said quietly.

A large man with a white coat stepped in alongside the nurse. He held out his hand to shake mine, but I didn't take it because I was shaking with fear.

What is this? I thought. *Oh gosh.* My mind was racing.

As he put down his hand, he said, "Natalie, I'm Dr. Williams. I know this is scary, but I need to do an exam on you to make sure everything is okay. I will do my best not to cause you any pain. Please hop up on the bed for me."

I did as he said without verbally responding.

"Okay. I'm going to pull down the gown, but I'll leave your waist covered. I'm going to examine your breasts."

He started to pull my gown, and before I could consciously react, I stopped him, holding my hands firmly against the material so it would not move, but I said nothing.

"Natalie. It's all right. I'm not going to hurt you. I just need to see if you have lumps or any abnormalities. It will just be a second and it won't hurt at all. I promise," he assured me.

He was a kind man, I could tell. His blue eyes had a certain twinkle about them. He was grandfatherly type. I knew I should trust him, but this was just a little too much.

"It's okay," he said as he pulled my hand down and continued to pull down my gown.

Soon I was naked from the waist up. He started massaging my breasts. During the process, I started to cry as memories began to resurface.

My sniffle caught his attention, and he immediately stopped.

"Natalie? Are you okay? Does that hurt?" He seemed worried.

"No. I just don't.... I don't like it" was all I could say. My emotions were overcoming.

"I know... I'm sorry. I'm almost done, okay? May I check one more time? The left one?" He was asking my permission.

I just nodded yes... Even though everything within me was shouting *No.*

He started the caressing again, causing my tears to spill over rapidly. But no more than thirty seconds later, he stopped. He reached over and grabbed a tissue for me.

"I'm sorry, Natalie. I didn't mean to upset you. This is just part of the exam, okay?" His faced was etched with concern.

"Yes sir," I responded as I pulled the gown back up to cover me.

"Okay sweetheart," the nurse said. "Now we need you to lie back and put your feet in these little stirrups."

If I was anxious before, I was in sheer panic now.

"But I don't have any underwear on!" was the only reasoning that I could offer.

The nurse and Dr. Williams looked quizzically at each other

before Dr. Williams said, "Natalie, I have to do a pelvic exam on you. So you can't have underwear on for that. I need to check your female parts to make sure everything is alright."

"Why? Why do you have to do this?" My voice was so shaky.

"We just want to make sure everything is alright. Okay? We need to make sure you are developing like a normal, healthy, young woman," he answered.

"Just lie down flat. It will be over before you know it!" The nurse rubbed my shoulder, easing me backward.

I was looking at the ceiling, trying to take myself away as the air hit my most private parts. There was noise that was only adding to my heart… metal clicking. My tears were freefalling now. My breathing was sporadic. Soon, I felt his hands on me. I closed my eyes, but that was a mistake.

As soon as I saw the back of my eyelids, it all came back to me. My old bedroom… the creaky bed. The truck stops. The smell of the dirt and cigarettes. Jack's breathing.

"Stop!" I screamed suddenly, jerking my legs back together. "Get away from me! Leave me alone!" My voice was enriched with emotion.

Dr. Williams immediately stepped back, while the nurse quickly grabbed my hand. Neither said anything for a moment. They just watched me sob.

After a minute, Dr. Williams said, "Natalie, we'll stop there. Get dressed, and then we'll talk about some things. Don't cry. It's over."

I nodded my head in agreement, thanking the good Lord above. I hurried and put my clothes back on, thankful for the security of my panties and jeans.

I moved the curtain, and Dr. Williams motioned for me to come sit on the chair. I was thankful for that. I couldn't bear the thought of that table.

He just looked at me for a moment, not really saying anything. The nurse grabbed me a bottle of water. I appreciated that. I hoped they weren't upset with me.

"Natalie," Dr. Williams said suddenly, "I have a question for you, and I want you to be honest. Can you do that?"

Oh, not this again, I thought. But I nodded *yes* nonetheless.

"Has…. Has anyone ever hurt you? Sexually? Has someone forced themselves on you?"

Before he had even ended the sentence, the blood drained from my face. *How does he know?* I thought. *Oh no… He can't know. Not that! No one can!* My thoughts were frantic but not as frantic as my tears recklessly streaming down my face.

"It's okay, Natalie. You can tell me," he assured.

I could almost sense the hurt in his voice. Part of me wanted to tell him. I wanted to trust him. But I knew I couldn't. *If Faye…. what would she do? What would Jack do?* I didn't know. I couldn't trust anyone. I had to lie.

"No, Dr. Williams," I said, making sure I was not looking in his eyes.

"Natalie. If you have, you can tell me. Okay? I will protect you," he stated.

"No. Never ha… never happened," I stuttered. I was a horrible liar.

"You're sure?" he prodded. I knew that he knew.

"I'm sure. May I go now?" I wanted to get out of that place. Immediately.

"Yes, but just give me a minute, okay?" he asked.

Again, I nodded. My voice was too insecure to be heard.

Dr. Williams and his nurse stepped out into the hallway. I could hear them talking to Faye.

"Mrs. Winters. I'm Dr. Williams. I have a few questions for you regarding Natalie."

"Oh, yes, of course," I heard her respond in her fake voice.

"Well, we had some trouble with the exam. Natalie became very upset. The behavior she displayed is typical of individuals who have been sexually abused. To your knowledge, has this ever happened to Natalie?"

"Of course not!" she shouted at him. "What kind of mother do you think I am?"

"Mrs. Winters," Dr. Williams said firmly, "I am not assessing your parenting here. I'm just concerned, and I need to know if it is even possible. A relative. A teacher. Anyone. Natalie was panicked in there. Most girls her age exhibit some fear, but she was petrified," he explained.

"Oh, she has never been abused. She's just doing that for attention. She is dramatic. She's fifteen years old. A teenager!" Faye reasoned to him.

"Well, I understand that. But..."

Faye cut him off, "Did she say she had been *sexually abused?*" Her tone completely changed now.

"No. She did not," Dr. Williams answered coarsely in response.

"Good then. There's your answer. We'll be leaving now," she said as she flung open the door. "Let's go!" she yelled.

"Yes ma'am." I hurried out. As much as I hated when she was irritated, I had grown to hate that room.

As we were in the elevator, I could tell that Faye was antsy. She was itching to get out of the building, almost more than I was. On the way home, she didn't say a word, and neither did I. I couldn't help but wonder if she was worried…

Part of me didn't want anyone to know, but I suppose part of me wanted help. I wanted an escape. Not just from Jack, but from Faye, too. I wanted away from all of them. But I wasn't brave. I wasn't strong enough to seek one for myself.

A few weeks later, I started my menstrual cycle at school. I was freaked out about it. Faye refused to buy supplies until I had actually started. She said it was a waste to buy them early.

I told my friend about it, and she offered me a tampon. But I didn't accept it. It was just… too much. Too close.

I called Faye at lunch and asked if I could just come home, but she said no and that she'd bring me some new underwear and supplies. I was thankful for her response. The toilet paper wasn't holding up very well.

An hour or so later, I got a note to come to the office. I hurried down, anticipating a solution to all of this. I walked in and the two student office aids were laughing.

"Ummm, I got a note," I interrupted, immediately embarrassed as it was Kyle Smith, the senior quarterback (and probably the cutest boy I'd ever seen), alongside Jerry Mills, his football bud. They were extremely popular… obviously.

"Natalie Winters?" Jerry was laughing a lot harder now.

"Yes," I responded. *He knows my name?* I quickly became excited.

"Special delivery!" Kyle said breathlessly between laughs as he pulled a package of pads and a pair of my underwear from underneath the desk.

Everything in me stiffened. This couldn't be happening.

"Better take that!" Jerry said, laughing louder than before.

I quickly grabbed them off the counter, my embarrassment turning into anger.

"Where is the bag it was in?" I asked, enraged that they had the audacity to give them to me like this.

"No bag. Your grandma… mom… whatever, gave them to us like this." He chuckled. "Said we boys looked like we could handle a girl's underwear."

Jerry was breathless at this point from the laughter. I quickly turned and headed out of there. The tears stinging my eyes. I ran to the bathroom and shut the stall. I was weeping. This was the most embarrassing, humiliating thing ever. Why would Faye do that? She could have at least put them in a plastic bag!!

Now the whole school would know. The two most popular boys knew I had… an accident. Mortifying. I just cried and cried while trying to change, wishing that I could change a lot more than undergarments. Wishing I could change everything in my life.

Cheerleader Natalie

We know what we are, but not what we may be.

—William Shakespeare

M asks are on the faces of everyone. Personally, I think it is truly hard to really see who a person is, especially if they don't want you to.

In my life, I had two parts: my school life and my home life. And in living those lives, I made sure they never intersected. I went to school, and I was Cheerleader Natalie, a girl who made great grades, who always had a smile. I was the nice cheerleader who talked to everyone. I was a little quirky, I suppose, but most didn't mind. I was the teacher's pet in most of my classes. I had friends, and most would have assumed that I had the perfect life.

But when I made it home after school, my smile would vanish. I wasn't perky, I wasn't happy. As soon as I got home, my mask would come off, because of reality; it hits hard. There is no way to fake happiness when you are in the midst of misery. Every day was the same. I would get home and go to my room. When the nurses were gone, I would come out and check on the children. Most had six o'clock feedings that would have to be done. Usually, I would get a lecture from Faye about how pathetic I was. How I was going to end up being a loser just like my mom and dad. Same old rant. Then I'd finish my homework and go to bed. Some nights I had cheerleading games or other activities to attend. I was thankful for the escape, but ultimately, they just inhibited how much I would sleep. Sometimes, it was truly hard to keep up with everything—school, the babies, and extracurriculars. There were times when I was absolutely exhausted, but I just pushed through. Nothing could really go. I mean, the extracurriculars were just that, extra, but that extra dose of sanity aided more than additional sleep ever could.

Some times were better than others. Most times, I just tried to please Faye and Jack; it made everything so much easier. I would get straight A's, I would do extra chores, cook what food we had for dinner, but at the end of the day, nothing mattered. No matter what I did, Faye would find something wrong with it. I was horrible in her eyes no matter what I accomplished. The most accurate description of our relationship is to say that I was her pet. She treated me just like a dog—certain duties, precise obligations—but at the end of the day, I was just a variable, something easily disposed of.

It's interesting though, because no one ever knew about the duplicity in my life. I was able to play both sides. In most cases I just made acquaintances with people rather than allowing them to really know me. Another reason I didn't date was because I knew that was a type of relationship that would have the potential to merge the two sections of my life, and that just couldn't happen. How I lived was the way I could deal with it. One world, my school life, helped me cope with the other, my home life. And I did everything in my power to keep the two separate. Faye could always fake a smile. I suppose I learned from the best because so could I. To my knowledge, no one ever truly knew what was happening. Sure, some of my closest friends had their suspicions, but no one ever truly knew.

But it was hard living in two worlds. Sometimes, I felt really guilty because I knew the babies were at home, trapped. But in order for me to take care of them, I had to have a little escape time for me. In all honesty, I was numb. I walked through life just trying to hold up the weight, and I didn't know how much weight I was holding until something else was added or taken away. Most times, things were added, and I was getting close to the breaking point.

When I turned sixteen, Faye got an extra car donated to her for my use. When we had gas, I would drive myself to all of my various activities and obligations. But sometimes, Faye didn't like that I was needed at other places. Mainly because that meant she would have to change a diaper or do a feeding, and my activities were making her have to do her job. Well, that just wouldn't work.

It was five o'clock, and I was just pulling in the drive. It was Thursday, and I was exhausted. I had a huge AP history test tomorrow, and I had cheerleading practice later that evening. I grabbed my book bag and headed inside.

Our house, it was as sturdy as a trailer house can be. We had a ramp that helped get the children out, but it was really wobbly. When you walked in, the smell of formula and hospital machinery was a little overwhelming at times. There were four beds in the first room. Most of the time, each was with a child. And most times, upon my arrival, they were all crying.

After soothing them, I had about thirty minutes to do some studying. We lived thirty minutes out of town, so even though practice wasn't till seven o'clock, I had to leave by at least six thirty. That drive killed me. We didn't even have the gas to make it, but somehow I always figured it out. I started coaching at the cheerleading gym I went to, and that helped a lot. But nonetheless, times were hard. We didn't have money for food; our phones were always off and on. You just never knew when you would have to do without, and that was extremely stressful. My job helped some, but it wasn't enough. Nothing was ever enough.

Faye had a spending problem. Money was like a drug to her. When she got her paycheck, I wouldn't see her for one or two days. She would leave, and well, I don't really know where she would go. When a check came in the mail, she would make herself up: makeup, hair, clothes, the whole thing. She knew all the expected arrival dates and would often meet the postman at the mailbox and leave. When she left, it's like she was excited and giddy. She would race out of the driveway in the van and head into town.

But when the money ran out, she returned; the high dissipated, and anger reappeared until the next check came. In all my years at that house, I could never figure out what she spent the money on. Faye made very good money working as a medical foster caregiver, but she never had anything to show for it. Not groceries, not clothes, not gas, nothing. Though we should have had money, we never did. So my job, as little as it brought in, was at least reliable for me. Faye would always ask for my paycheck, but I would cash it first, stash a few bucks, then give her the rest. I tried to ensure that she never really knew the full amount. Sometimes she would call the cheerleading gym and ask. Fortunately, I'd come up with a good excuse for the missing funds. I hated lying, but it was for the greater good. If we wanted to eat, I had to keep it that way.

But working wasn't on my schedule that night. I had an hour and a half of practice, and then it was back home to prepare for my test. History was never my favorite course, but my perfectionist nature was still present, even with things I didn't like. When I got to my room, I opened my text and gathered my notes.

"*Natalie*! Get your ass in here!" I was interrupted, as usual, by Faye's frantic screams. For whatever reason, no matter how close or far I was from her, she always felt the need to scream my name at the top of her lungs when she wanted something. I walked into the living room. Faye was sprawled out on the couch watching *Entertainment Tonight*. Her laziness appalled me, but I was used to it.

"Yes, ma'am?" I answered.

"What are you doing?" she asked with her eyes turning away from the TV.

"History homework," I said.

"You and your stupid books. I don't know why you care about that s— so much. Go make yourself useful. Wash the dishes in the sink," she ordered. Gosh, she was a piece of work. What kind of mother gripes about their children doing their homework? Well, Faye did. But then again, she wasn't really a mother.

"Yes, ma'am." I went over to the dishes and began washing them. Mostly, it was just syringes. There were some bottles, too, but those had to be sterilized. I got a pot and started to heat up some water to stick the bottles in it.

So much for my thirty minutes of studying, I thought. I'd be lucky if I wasn't late to practice.

While letting the bottles cool, I began putting up the other various dishes and medical equipment. I could hear Faye walking in behind me. "You are already done?" she asked.

"Yes, ma'am." My usual response in my usual tone. I kept my words to her at a minimum. It was best to answer in a routine way and not let my tongue get the better of me. But sometimes, I failed.

"Well, you shouldn't be done. You must have done a s—ty job, like you always do. Wash them again," she ordered.

"What? You want me to wash them again? I did them how I always do. I sterilized the bottles and syringes. You want me to do that again?" My blood pressure was rising. If there was one thing I hated, it was wasted time. And Faye, she wasted my time.

"Are you talking back?" Before I knew it, she popped me in the mouth with the back of her hand. I hated when she did that. No matter how many times it had happened, I never got used to the sting.

"See if that helps your mouth out. Wash them again. Oh, and while you're cleaning the dishes, we'll clean your mouth!"

She grabbed the Dawn liquid soap in one hand and the hair of my head in the other, tipping my head back, and pouring the soap in. I started choking as it took me a minute to respond. Finally, I was able to stop swallowing.

"There, keep that in your mouth. We need to make sure it's sterilized," she said in her evil voice. As she walked out of the kitchen, I just looked at her. Rephrase that—I glared at her. I'd never said it out loud, but I hated her. I absolutely hated that woman. I kept the soap in my mouth, knowing full well if I didn't, there would be severe repercussions.

I started to rewash and sterilize the dishes. I tried to calm myself down, but I was just getting more worked up. She was such an idiot. The soap was burning my mouth. My eyes were starting to water. It was becoming intolerable. I wanted so bad to spit it out, but I couldn't. I knew I couldn't.

Once I finished the dishes, I went back into the living room in front of Faye to await my orders.

"You still have the soap in your mouth? You better."

I nodded my head, not being able to respond. The tears fell unbidden down my face.

"Good. I'm sure your mouth is good and clean now. You may swallow," she said with a smirk.

What? Swallow? My eyes panicked. Oh gosh, how on earth was I going to be able to do this?

"Natalie. Swallow. *Now!*" Faye yelled.

I congregated all the strength in my body, forcing the liquid poison down my throat, suppressing my gag reflex as best as I could. Oh, how it burned.

"Open your mouth. I want to make sure it's nice and cleaned out."

Croaking and coughing, I finally managed to open my mouth.

"Good. Now get out of my sight. I hate seeing your ugly face," Faye said, waving her hand dismissively.

As I started walking to my room, I realized it was 6:45 p.m. I was late, and I needed to leave for practice. I ran to my room, grabbed my backpack, and started for the door.

"Where are you going?" Faye interrupted.

"I am going to cheerleading. It starts at seven, and I'm going to be late," I said coolly and cautiously, careful not to upset her. There was no way I could have handled more soap.

"Oh, you're not going to cheerleading tonight. You should have thought about that when you did the dishes s—ty and opened that smart little mouth of yours. That's your punishment, no cheerleading." She smirked.

My blood was boiling. Cheerleading was important to me. It was my sport, and I was pretty darn good at it. If I did anything, I did it to the best of my abilities. I was one of the top girls on my team, bound to get a scholarship to college, and Faye *was not* going to interfere with that. Over my dead body.

"I'm sorry, but I washed the dishes. Twice. And I swallowed liquid soap. I do believe that is punishment. Now, I'm going to cheerleading practice. We have a pep rally to prepare for," I said coolly, but with just enough fire in my tone to catch her by surprise.

She started to rise. "You're not going to tell me what you're f—in' doing. You little b—, who do you think you are? I'm the boss. I call the shots. You're not going to cheerleading, and if you keep pushing me, I'll call the coach and make sure you're not in that pep rally. I'll make sure you're not a damn cheerleader. Now get to your room! And make sure I don't see you until tomorrow morning!"

I don't really know what got into me, but my words, they just started flowing. "You are a b— straight from hell, and I hate you with every ounce of my entire being," I said calmly, but in a tone that even made me uneasy.

She just stood there, surprised that I actually expressed my feelings. I walked back to my room. And I heard her coming after me. That's the good thing about a trailer house and her being overweight; it wasn't a surprise when she came barging into my room. The rattling floors gave me good, fair warning.

As soon as I shut my door, it flung open. And just as I turned my face, it turned back with the blow from her hand. One thing about Faye, the lady had an arm on her. She always had. It knocked me off balance, but the second hit took me down. I hit my head on the edge of my dresser, and I was trying desperately to reorient myself.

It was the same pattern though. Faye had a routine to her beatings. Get her down with the hands, and then use the legs. This time was no different. She was kicking my ribs with all her might.

But I knew her routine, and the good thing was I was able to work around it. On her next kick, I rolled, and it just about made her fall down when the force of her leg didn't stop on my body. But at that point, she was pissed. She got on her knees and went after me with her hands again. But if she was pissed, I was infuriated.

Why am I letting her hit me? I thought. *Why?* Before I knew it, I spun around. I grabbed the arm that was about to smack me in the head. I held her at the wrist and slammed her arm back as far as her joint would allow and with as much force as my little body could harness. Holding her back, we just sat there in silence for a moment, until my words interrupted. "If you hit me again, I'll hit back," I said in a voice that had nothing but sheer warning in it.

Shock streaked across her face. She couldn't believe what I was doing, and frankly, neither could I. But I held my expression, making sure she would not doubt my seriousness. I knew she could tell by my grip that I wasn't kidding. One thing about cheerleading is that it gets you into shape. All those days of conditioning were now showing in my strength. I was small, but my muscles were as big as they had ever been.

It was a realization to us both that I was stronger than I used to be. If I hit, it was going to hurt. I'd make sure of that. She started to back away. As I let her arm go, I said, "I'm going to cheerleading practice."

"Go then," she said as she turned to the door and walked out. I couldn't help the triumphant smile that spread across my face. I could fight back, and that was exactly what I was going to do. I was sick and tired of her games. I was done being her punching bag. And I was finished with her thinking she could control my life.

On the drive to practice, I was all smiles and giggles. It was a moment of victory for me. When I arrived, I was late, but luckily the team was on break. I ran and joined them.

"Natalie, your back is bright red. And you have a handprint on your face!" one of the girls said to me. I forgot to look at the mirror before I went in. A few of my other teammates came over to check it out. You could tell that I had been crying. Though they weren't tears of pain, they didn't notice.

"I'm fine. No worries, you guys. Let's do some stunting," I said in my perkiest tone. "Come on!" I said with a smile. They were skeptical, but it worked. We went on with practice, and no one brought up the bruises that were forming on my back and arms.

As practice ended, my tumbling coach called me over.

"Natalie, come here please." He ordered.

"Why were you late? Why are there red marks on your back and face?" He asked in a way that that wasn't really a question but an order.

"It won't happen again," I said solemnly.

"Natalie. Tell me what's going on." Coach Blake was like that. Persistent. But then again, so was I.

"Nothing, Coach. Just was running behind today. Sorry. I promise, it won't happen again," I said, both of us knowing that it wouldn't go beyond this.

"Natalie. You can always tell me. If you need help, I can help you. If you…need protection, I can." His words were quiet but so serious. They almost brought tears to my eyes. He cared. I wanted to hug him, but I couldn't let on what was going. He was a great guy, but I knew there was nothing he could do about Faye and Jack. There was nothing to do. If he said anything, it would just result in me not being a cheerleader anymore.

"Thank you, Coach Blake. That means a lot. I'm okay. Promise.

No worries. God is love." That was his phrase. "God is love." That was our team's motto. Just a way of saying that if anything, God was in control.

"God is love," he agreed with a slight smile.

I walked away, still moved by his words. But truth be told, I had to put on my mask, and I wasn't going to have him trying to pull it off my face. And I was right. What happened tonight, the beatings, they wouldn't ever happen again. I knew it, and that night, so did Faye.

Pander Pimp

The evil that is in the world almost always comes of ignorance, and good intentions may do as much harm as malevolence if they lack understanding.

—Albert Camus, *The Plague*

....

Daddy Jack was now solely "Jack" in my eyes. And that's what I called him. The sexual abuse stopped around fourteen because I threatened to tell, but he never ceased being a creep. I was sure to never invite friends over. Never, ever would I put them in that position. I didn't know if he would do anything, but he was perverted nonetheless. He would try to walk in when he knew I was undressing or when I was taking a shower. Just to catch a glimpse, I guess. Disgusting, he was. He'd masturbate often when he was home. Just right there in the living room, with no regard for anyone else. However, he only did that when Faye was gone. Even she didn't allow that.

He was working as a prison guard now. Kind of ironic, I guess. That a man like him, one that belongs in prison, was guarding one. But after he wrecked his truck and killed an innocent man, he had to get another job. His driver's license was revoked, and he had criminal charges pending, along with a civil suit from the young man's family. He was under the influence, or suspected of being so, when the accident occurred. Now, he was home constantly. I felt so bad that the accident occurred for the young man's family, and now we had to suffer by more of his presence.

We had moved into town because the trailer house was too expensive, and we got evicted. Faye conned some man into renting us a townhouse. It was really nice, and there was no way we would afford it, so I knew it was just temporary. Money was scarce. Jack took a pay cut, and Faye had to because of state budget cuts. I was working at the cheerleading gym, but nothing was enough. I headed up the stairs to the room I was allotted. But I noticed Jack was following me.

"Don't even think about it." I turned before I shut my door, looking him dead straight in the face. He knew better than to ask what I was talking about.

Instead, he responded. "You have a…a date tonight." His voice had an odd tone.

"What?" I asked rudely. I didn't care about showing him any sort of respect. What was he talking about? A date?

"A date. His name is Ross. You're going…out with him tonight. Make sure you wear a dress or something," he simply said.

"What the hell are you talking about? I'm not going on a date with anyone." I was confused. What on earth was he even saying?

"Oh yes, you are. We made a deal. Ross and I. You'll go on that date, and you'll do as he wants." He was raising his voice.

A sick feeling came over me. *Do what he wants?* I thought. *Oh gosh. Did that mean what I think it means?*

"Do as he wants? What are you talking about?" I dared to ask.

"Natalie, we are all working here. And it's time for you to do your part. You have a date. He'll pay you afterwards. It won't be that bad. I'll let you keep some of the money, too," he explained.

The hysteria within me grew as I started yelling in outrage. "Are you kidding me? Have you lost your damn mind? You're pimping me out? Seriously?" Wrath filled my heart while tears filled my eyes. "You have the audacity to pimp me out to some man you work with?"

"Oh, it's not a big deal. I said I'd give you some of the money. It's not like it'll be for nothing," He explained calmly. "He'll be here around eight, so be sure and be ready."

"No! No! I'm not going anywhere, with anyone! Go to hell!" I screamed as I slammed the door and locked it. I was appalled, shocked, and infuriated. How could anyone do that? I mean, I wasn't his daughter or anything, but how could he think this was okay? That I'd willingly agree? That I'd go?

I was freaking out. I knew I had to get out of here. Jack was knocking at my door. "Natalie, I mean it. You better be ready by eight!" He shouted.

Gosh, what to do? I quickly called my friend Jennifer.

"Hey, girly, what's up?" she answered.

"Jennifer." My voice was serious. "I, uh, I need a ride. Can you come get me?"

"Yeah, sure, Natalie. What's wrong?" I knew she heard the panic in my voice.

"Oh, I just…I need to get out of the house. I'll tell you later." I needed some time to think of what to tell her. I wouldn't dare explain this.

"Okay. I'm on my way," she assured me.

"Great. Hey, just pick me up at the end of my street. Okay?" I asked.

"Uh, all right. Natalie, are you sure you're okay? What's going on?" she ventured again.

"I'll tell you later. See you in a minute." I hung up the phone. Jennifer didn't live far away, and I needed to get the heck out of the house. That was one benefit of living in town; there was a quick escape when needed. I knew there was no going out the front door, so I snuck out of my window. My room was on the second floor, so I had to jump, however, it wasn't unbearably high. I met Jennifer at the end of the street and climbed in her truck.

"What's wrong, Natalie?" she asked.

I just started to cry. There was no way I could tell her what happened. "I just need to stay with you tonight, okay?" I asked.

"Okay, okay." And nothing more was said.

San Antonio

There is only one success—to be able to spend your life in your own way.

—Christopher Morley

A biological equilibrium is a complex thing. There are many chemical levels that have to be balanced, however not completely. You see, if your biological equilibrium is perfectly balanced, you are dead. There has to be a certain level of disruption to keep the momentum, so to speak. However, if the disruption is not within the parameters of a certain range, like your pH being too high, too low, or any chemical for that matter, horrible results take place.

It's a complex system, an equilibrium. Our bodies need to be challenged in some sense; a little bit of a fight to force the continuation of life. But again, one must mind the parameters; there is always a breaking point.

I was sixteen years old, but that number did not describe me accurately. In reality, I had been through much and knew many things about life and the world we live in. By that point in my life, I had been through just about everything. I had been rejected, abandoned, beaten. I had my innocence stolen, along with my idea of self-worth. I knew that people were not reliable. I knew that they would leave when you needed them most. I understood that life was irrevocably hard, and that if you wanted something, it was up to you to get it because no one else would. Yes, I felt that I had been through just about everything. But I suppose that was the lesson I had not yet learned: the bad gets worse.

Friday afternoon at three o'clock, the bell had just rung to let us out of class. There was a vibrancy in the spring air as we all were ecstatic that it was spring break—a week with no classes or responsibilities. Yes, most of us were thrilled, and I have to admit I was excited, as well. I was taking three advanced placement classes, and I needed a week to recuperate from the intensity those classes held. A nice relaxing week to do a little catch-up work and perhaps read a nice novel that had absolutely no educational value. Yes, I, too, was looking forward to the break.

I was driving home, careful not to make any detours. Faye measured the mileage daily, making sure I wasn't going anywhere I wasn't supposed to and using up the gas. If there was one mile unaccounted for, I was in trouble. One time I had taken one of my friends home, and she freaked out. I was to go to school, cheerleading practice, and straight home. So on that Friday, I was headed home, where I knew I would probably be until school started again.

I walked in the door, and Faye was waiting with a look. The look. My mind panicked. *What had I done to make her mad?* I couldn't think of anything. I had done all my chores for the week, had taken care of what was needed. I had finished everything she had told me to do. There was nothing that I could think of that would cause her to be upset. That was until I noticed she was holding an envelope. I recognized it was from my school. *What could it be?* I thought, when I suddenly remembered.

It was my school schedule for next year, and instantly, I knew why she was mad. You see, I was planning on becoming a pediatric surgeon. I had been researching over the past few months about the process. And I had to admit, it was a long one. First, you had to obtain a bachelor's degree. Though it was not required to have a particular degree, you had to complete prerequisites in calculus, statistics, physics, organic chemistry, regular chemistry, biology, and English. After that, an applicant must take the MCAT, a test that is one of the determining factors on your application.

In addition, the medical school boards looked for experience in the medical field; volunteer work and shadowing physicians was among the list. They wanted excellence. The process of becoming a physician is harder than that of any other profession. It is rigorous and expensive, but I was set to complete it. I figured I had a little bit of an advantage. I had taken care of children my whole life, medically sick children. I had administered medication, fed through MIC-KEY buttons, and changed catheters. I had assisted during seizures. I had resuscitated several times. And I had lost children. I knew what medicine was. I also knew that it didn't always work.

In our house, it was not unusual to wake up and find a baby not breathing. It was not unusual to leave for school and there be an empty bed when you returned. Yes, I had experience. Much more than a girl at the age of sixteen should ever have, but I was thankful for it. I was going to be a physician. I was preparing myself to take an oath to forever help people. To forever help children that had been hurt. I could relate to that as well. So for my senior year, I decided to dive in. It was a long process, so it was necessary that I get started. I registered for college algebra, trigonometry, biology I, and biology II, all advanced dual-credit classes. I decided to take an advanced health course along with a college government and humanities class. It was a huge load, and I knew it would take all of my time to maintain straight A's. Taking that into consideration, I decided that I would not be a cheerleader. High school was fun, but it was time to grow up and graduate. I needed to start preparing to be a surgeon. I was going to replace my pom-poms with a scalpel. And that had Faye furious.

Why, you may wonder? Well, Faye loved attention. She loved people to look at her, applaud her, and I, in many cases and despite what she told me, was a nice little attraction for her. I was a cheerleader, and with that, she was a cheerleader's mom, gaining all the attention from my achievements. I suppose that's another reason why she let me be involved. She reaped the benefits by gaining the compliments of others on how she was such a good parent. I mean, look at me, her daughter doing so well. I also think she liked me to be a cheerleader so that she could live vicariously through me. Don't get me wrong; I loved the sport, but not as much as she loved the title of it. And now, it was about to disappear. And being a cheerleader your senior year at my high school held so much glory. No doubt, she was infuriated.

You know, I think most parents would be thrilled for their child to come home at sixteen years old and say, "Hey, Mom, Dad, I'm going to be a doctor. In fact, I'm going to be a pediatric surgeon and dedicate the rest of my life to saving children." But Faye was not like most parents, not in any case. She scowled at me for about five minutes before saying anything. In that time, I prepared myself. *Go ahead,* I thought. *I have one year and two months left to live here, so go ahead and try me.*

I had become a little rebellious, as I suppose most teenagers do, but I was becoming confident with age. When I turned eighteen years old, I was going to leave and never come back. No matter what it took, I was going to get away from Faye and Jack. I was starting my path now. I knew that if I took these classes and did well, a college would be willing to offer me a scholarship, independent of being a cheerleader. I loved sports, but being a cheerleader was a pastime. Being a doctor, I knew, was my calling. I was hoping to go to New York. It seemed like such an amazing city—so many people and so many opportunities. But honestly, I didn't care where I went, just as long as I was far away from Jack and Faye Winters. I was determined. Faye had stopped me from many things, but this was not going to be one of them. Not anymore.

"You wanna tell me what the hell this is?" she finally said.

"Oh, I believe that is my school schedule for next year," I said in a pleasant tone. I had been working on the "kill with kindness" technique. "I'm taking a lot of advanced classes."

"I don't give a damn about advanced classes. Why in the hell is cheerleading not on here?" Faye ordered.

"I'm not going to try out for cheerleader this year. I need to focus on my career. I'm going to be a surgeon, and it takes a lot of work."

I was shocked by her reaction. She didn't start yelling or screaming, hitting or whipping. No, what she did hurt much worse than that. She burst into laughter.

"You? A doctor? Well, that's the funniest bulls— I've ever heard," she said in between wails of laughter. "How the hell are you gonna get to college? I'm sure as hell not helping you. When you turn eighteen, I'm throwing you out on your ass. I'm sick of you in my house. You know, I've been sick ever since the first day." She went on chuckling. "Oh, you're gonna be a doctor, huh? Can you fix the sick? *Huh?* Hahaha, oh no. No, you can't. You won't ever. You're far too stupid for that. This better be fixed by Monday. You'll be a cheerleader next year. Over my dead body you won't be."

As much as I wanted this conversation to end, I knew that I had to stand up for myself. I couldn't back down on this. "I'm not going to be doing cheerleading next year, regardless of what you want," I said collectively. She needed to understand this.

Well, then screaming began. She lost it. I had grown used to her little tantrums. But nonetheless, they were ridiculous. Again, I really couldn't help but chuckle. My view of Faye was changing. I used to be scared to death of her. But now, I was just amused. She was an idiot. I knew that now. The lady couldn't even read, and she was going to tell me that I couldn't go to college. How does she know? She wouldn't even know what an application looks like, much less what one requires. Yes, it was humorous.

She looked up and saw the smile across my face. I immediately went into what I had learned as my fight-or-flight mode. My hypothalamus was jumping into action. A few years ago, I would have definitely geared toward flight, but not anymore.

I was a small girl, but I was strong. Put a little of the rage I had behind the back of my fist, I knew I could do a little damage. The last time Faye had taken a swing at me, I gave her a warning. This time, I wouldn't. She came toward me, all fired up.

"I dare you," I said coolly.

"What?" she said.

"Touch me. I dare you." I hardly recognized my own voice. "I'll hit you back. So strike me, I dare you."

For the first time in my life, I saw a twitch of fear in Faye's eyes. I had never been that confident, ever. But sometimes you get fed up. You get sick and tired to the point where you speak without the consultation of your mind. Your subconscious takes over because after all, it's more tired of dealing with all the crap than you are.

I was confident and prepared for whatever happened. I stood there like a viper, patient but ready. Faye took a step back and brought her hands to her side. She was uncomfortable and uncertain. However, she wasn't backing down just yet. She needed a moment to gather herself and figure out option two. I could almost visualize the wheels turning in her head. I picked up my backpack and went to my room. I'd won this battle, but it was time to prepare for the next one.

In my room, I started to outline a study regimen for the next week. I always tried to be at least two weeks ahead of the class. It was a good feeling to always know the answers to the questions the teachers asked in class. I decided that I would take this weekend off and read a novel of some sort. Monday, I would start prepping for my US History AP exam. We had been working on a project, so I was behind on my reading. That was my first priority. As I was planning, I could hear Faye talking on the phone to someone. I didn't know who or really care, as long as she wasn't talking to me. She seemed upset, which was the norm. I went back to my studying until the murmur of her voice morphed into footsteps outside my door. It slammed open.

"Get the hell out!" she screamed.

"What?" I asked. Had she lost her mind?

"If you're not going to do what I say, you can get the f— out of my house!" she yelled.

I sat there in silence. Did she just tell me to get out? I replayed her words in my head.

"I said, get the f— out!" Faye screamed.

"Right now?" I asked excitedly. *She wants me to leave?* I was ecstatic. *Yes!* I thought. *Yes! Okay, no problem.*

"Get your s—," she said.

"Yes, ma'am," I said with glee. I rushed around, grabbing my things. I got my cheerleading bag and stuffed everything in sight into it. I was too happy to care what actually made it in; I just wanted to go before she changed her mind. She was still in my room, yelling and lecturing. To be honest, I had no idea what she was saying. My mind was flooded with feelings of joy. Like a prisoner who was told he got let out on parole, I was shocked, but not enough to forget to be smart. I knew to hurry and get out.

I grabbed my cell phone and called a friend to pick me up a few blocks away. I also knew I didn't want her to know where I was going. I started out the door. She was still talking, but it was as if she was speaking another language. I couldn't comprehend anything other than the fact that I was leaving that house, with permission! I took off down the street. My friend and her mother saw me and rushed me to get in. They knew how Faye was, at least to an extent. I jumped in the truck and headed toward their house. I was so happy that I didn't even notice the tears running down my face. Freedom, liberation, is an indescribable feeling. My friend Morgan just looked at me, worried. She knew a little about Faye's way of doing things.

"Did she hit you this time?" she asked.

"No. Not this time." I smiled.

"Why are you crying?" I could tell she was confused.

"These are tears of joy, Morgan. Tears of freedom."

She looked at her mom and looked back at me. We both knew she didn't understand completely, but she was there anyways. Tonight, I was going to her house. I was going to be safe. This was going to be a great spring break.

We arrived at her house soon enough, and I went to her bedroom and started to unpack my bag. You know, I think you learn a lot about yourself when you have to pack in a rush. I learned that I thought my history book was more important than a toothbrush, and geometry homework was more important than underwear. Her mom told me that we would go to the store and grab a few things. She was such a kind and loving lady. Their family was very welcoming, and in the most appropriate way. No one asked as to why I was there, where I came from, or how long I was going to stay; they just welcomed me into their home.

I decided that I would call my friend Bethany. She was a nurse in our home at the time. She always looked out for me. I know that she knew that Faye was crazy, though I had never told her the extent of what happened or was happening to me. I had known her since I was nine years old, and from the first day I met her, I always hoped that I could one day have a mother like her. She was so nice, caring, and understanding. I could trust her.

"Hello?" she answered.

"Hey, Bethany, it's Natalie! I just wanted to tell you that I left Faye's house. She told me to get out, and I left."

"What? What happened?" She begged me to talk, and she listened as I told her the story of what happened.

"Well, Natalie, I'm glad you made it out but be careful. You know how Faye can be," she knowingly warned.

"Yes, I know exactly. Thanks, Bethany! Talk to you later."

As I hung up the phone, I thought about what she said, and slowly, a fog of fear crept upon my skin. This is way too easy. It had all gone way too smoothly for Faye's taste. She had something up her sleeve, though I had no idea what it could be. My thoughts were interrupted by laughter from the living room. I peered out from the hallway, and to this very day, I will name it as one of the most beautiful scenes I have ever witnessed. My friend, her mom, dad, brother, and sister were sitting all around each other, talking. There was such love. It was a scene that for me was out of a fiction book, but I was now shown that the story was real. They were real, and I felt so blessed to be welcomed into the picture.

The afternoon passed on, and my worries settled. Right now, it was going to be okay. I would think about repercussions tomorrow. I just wanted to enjoy the moment of being welcomed. I noticed that ever since I walked into the door, I had a smile on my face. I was unbelievably happy. At least, before the phone rang.

Morgan's mom brought it to me. "Natalie, it's Bethany," she said solemnly.

Curious, I answered, "Hey, Bethany! What's up?"

"Natalie, does Faye know where you are?" she demanded.

"What, no! No, why?"

"Natalie, Adrianna and Cole are coming for you. I called Faye to see what was up, and she is planning, Natalie. She is planning."

"Wait, what do you mean Adrianna is coming? Why?" I was concerned.

"I don't know, Natalie. I have no idea. Just be careful," she said.

"Okay, I will." I hung up.

What would Adrianna have to do with me leaving? She, her husband, and kids lived in San Antonio. Why would they be coming? Why would she care? It wasn't her concern. As far as I could think, she would be happy for me to be out of her life. And that feeling was mutual. I searched for reasoning but could find nothing. I calmed myself. There was nothing to be worried about. I was here and safe. Faye had no idea where I was, and I knew my friend and her family agreed to keep it that way. So coming for me? That just made no sense, no sense at all. I soothed myself with that. They didn't know where I was. I was safe. I was fine.

The family sat down to dinner. We were complacent. And somehow, I felt complete. Until I heard the knock at the door. I can't really explain how I knew. I can't explain how I knew exactly who it was. I just did. This was all too easy, too perfect. It was time for a disruption. My life was full of them. Every time I can ever remember being happy, it was taken away. And this time was going to take the same form. Morgan's dad went to answer the door.

"Hello. I'm Adrianna Conner, and this is my husband, Cole." Her voice had me frozen stiff. I had been classically trained that her voice linked with pain. It was like Thanksgiving—mental, physical, and emotional pain. I panicked. This was bad and was heading toward the worse. They were heading my way. I could hear their footsteps.

When I looked up, my eyes instantly set upon her face. She had the same green eyes as Faye had and the same capability of looking at someone in a way that stirs fear, no matter who you are. Her husband, Cole, was flanking her. He, too, was staring harshly. I couldn't bring myself to look away. My stomach felt as though it were inverting. They were here. It was not my imagination, even though I would have given anything for it to be.

Suddenly, a smile of malevolence streaked across Adrianna's face. "Hi, Dear! How is my darling little sister?" she asked in a kind but simultaneously evil voice. I didn't say anything. I just kept my eyes on her. At the mention of the word *sister*, I felt a hardness seep into my eyes.

"Why aren't you going to come give me a hug? I haven't seen you in a long time, and oh! How I've missed you."

Oh! How I despised her, almost as much as I despised Faye.

They say the apple doesn't fall far from the tree, and that was nothing but true in this case. She started toward me. My hands started to tremble; beads of sweat started to roll down my face. She leaned down to hug me. As she did, she whispered in my ear, "If you don't want this to get messy for your friends, I suggest you do what we say."

My breath escaped me. I scrambled for action but came up with nothing. Adrianna began complimenting my friend's home—sweet, perfectly sweet. Faye would have been so proud. I knew my friend's family was confused. This was a sticky situation.

"Natalie, may I talk to you for a moment? Privately?" Adrianna said so the others could hear.

Like I could refuse. She pulled me out of my chair, directing me to the other room. Her husband, Cole, followed.

"If you'll excuse us for a moment," Adrianna told my friend's mom. "I just want to talk with my sister for a minute."

As we stepped into the other room, her charm quickly faded.

"Okay, let me explain what's going to happen here," she said in a cool voice. "You are going to go get your s— and get your little, scrawny ass into that car out there. And you will do it in the next five minutes. If you cause any scene, I will make sure your friend pays the price. They have taken you into their home and are hiding a runaway. At least, that's what I'll tell the police, along with a few other things. You see, I don't have any problem with upsetting them. Because you, you upset me. From the time Mother took you into my home, you've upset me. And if you care anything for your friend, you'll do what I say before I start World War III."

She was inches away from my face. Like a tiger snarling at its prey, she threatened me. "On the count of three, I'll say go. You have exactly three minutes. Exactly. Don't test me. I promise it won't end well. Oh, and I suggest you do it with a smile." Again, her smile appeared. "One…two…three…go."

I instantly walked to Morgan's room to get my things. I knew better than to test Adrianna. She was an evil genius. I had no doubt that she would cause trouble, and I did not want that for my friend. I couldn't bear to stand the thought of upsetting them or getting them into trouble. This was my life, my problem, not theirs. So I went along with what Adrianna said, smiling along the way. As I got my things, Morgan came into the room.

"Natalie, what is going on? What are you doing? Are you seriously leaving with them?" she asked frantically.

Fake it, I thought. *It will be the best thing.* "It's okay, Morgan. They won't hurt me. It's good that they came. I'm going to leave with them."

"Natalie! Stop it! I know you are covering for them. Tell us to help you! Natalie!"

"Morgan, there is nothing for you to do. I have to go, I have no choice. Thank you for your help. It's been a great afternoon." I started to leave her bedroom. She knew that I was lying, but I think she also realized that there was nothing that she could do. There was nothing to do.

Before I knew it, I was in the backseat of the car. Adrianna and Cole were up front. I had no idea what was happening, and I had no desire to ask. *I'll take it as it comes*, I thought. *That's the only way I'll make it through.* As I peered out the window, I recognized the route we were taking. We were headed back to Faye's house. The same place I had escaped from a few hours earlier, I was now destined toward again.

As we pulled into the drive, I felt my spirit beginning to weaken. Hope, yeah, there was none. This was bad, I knew. Nothing about this situation was good. They ordered me into the house. When I entered, Faye was standing there with the same evil smirk that Adrianna had. They shoved me into my room, slamming the door. All I could do was what they told me. I was outnumbered. I stayed close to the door, trying to decipher what they were saying. It was hard to hear, but what I heard was unmistakable.

"Take her and do what you want," Faye said.

"That's fine, but you have to back us up every step of the way," Adrianna threatened. "I won't be responsible for whatever happens. And we need the extra car too."

"Okay, okay. Fine. I'll cover it," promised Faye.

They moved farther way, but I heard what I needed to. They were taking me. I wasn't sure where I was going, but I was sure that it wasn't a pleasant place. I started to plan. What was I going to do? How would I escape this?

I had no phone, but what I did have was my old computer that my teacher donated to me. And with that, I had Myspace. I was going to start messaging my friends. The people I knew I could trust. I wrote a letter of panic and desperation and sent it to all of the people I knew would help. I also sent one to my cheerleading coach. Luckily, a few adults in my life had no problem having a page on a predominately teenage website. Along with these adults was my history teacher, Ms. Herring. She would help me, I knew. I was just praying that on this Friday night, someone would feel the need to check his or her mail. My timing was good because as soon as I pressed send, my door flung open.

"What do you think you are doing?" Cole shouted as he marched over to my computer. Without thinking, I pressed the logout icon. I couldn't allow them to see that I was on my way to getting help. I couldn't let them know.

"What did you post? What did you say?" he demanded.

"Nothing, I didn't say anything," I said.

"Log back in. Now."

"No." The word was calm. Simply calm, but it had every ounce of authority I could muster. I was prepared for him to start shouting, screaming, and being dramatic. I wasn't prepared for the strike of a man's hand. Growing up, Faye had been the one who hit, not Jack. I had never known a man's strength, and I quickly was taught that it wasn't something to look forward to. He hit me hard, and it left me disoriented. When I gathered myself, he was ripping my computer from the wall.

As he walked out of my room with my computer in hand, he said, "Dare you to try anything else. I'll take pleasure in setting you straight."

So there I was. Out of options. No escape. I knew better than to try the window. And honestly, I didn't want another wallop from Cole. I sat up the rest of the night, hoping something would happen. Hoping that some miraculous rescue was on the way.

As dawn peeked its head above the horizon, I heard rustling outside my door.

"It's time to go," said Cole. "We have to take her while we still have a little darkness to work with."

At that, my door opened. I don't suppose they were shocked to see me awake. We all were aware that something was happening.

"Get some of your s—. Now. You have ten minutes to get what you want. Then we are leaving," Adrianna said.

"Where are we going?" I pleaded. I had to know. Where? What stuff would I need? I didn't suppose I would need a Sunday dress if I were going to end up in the woods dead.

"San Antonio," Cole stated. "Now get a move on it." He stepped closer. "Or do I need to set you straight?" A little smile appeared at the corner of his mouth.

I hurried to my feet and started grabbing things. It was the second time in twenty-four hours that I had to pack in a rush and for an unforeseen future. Before I knew it, I was being pushed out the door and shoved into a car.

As Cole got in beside me, he reached behind his back and pulled out a small gun. "Do you know what this is?" he asked in a condescending tone.

I froze. I had never seen a gun before. At least, not that up close.

"Answer me!" He interrupted my thoughts.

All I could do was nod, "yes."

"Good. Just so you know, if you f— with me, I'll use it on you. Don't try anything stupid. You best do exactly as I say. Understood?" he ordered.

Again, all I could do was nod. My mouth was unbelievably dry. My whole body was quivering with fear. I was utterly scared and drenched in sweat.

Soon, I was looking out the window at open road. Adrianna was driving the car that was donated, the one I usually drove. For what reason, I had no idea.

It seemed that had defined my entire state. I had no idea of anything. I refused to let my imagination wander. I needed to keep a hold of what reality I had. I needed to keep myself alert, but that was harder than expected. I was exhausted. I had been without sleep for much longer than I was used to. The road began to blur as my veracity was dwindling. As I knew we were getting farther away, I knew I was getting closer to danger. I didn't know what was happening, but one thing I was certain of: I was no longer in a fight mode as my hypothalamus had instructed the day before. I was definitely, willingly wishing for flight. But I also knew at this point, there was no escape.

I was heading into something I was not prepared for. The pH level of my soul was becoming toxic, and the chemicals of my very being were losing their structure. My balance, my equilibrium, was starting to push into those critical parameters, and there was absolutely nothing I could do about it. And in equilibrium, once something goes wrong, it goes really, really wrong.

Mind Over Matter

Desperate times call for desperate measures, and for me, this was the most desperate of times. I can't explain what it's like to be ripped from your surroundings as I cannot explain the fear I felt. I had felt scared before—scared of pain, emotional hurt, and many things in between. But this, this was a new level. I feared for my life. I had a fear for the unknown.

I must have dozed off because when I awoke, I didn't recognize anything out the window. There were trees, hills, and nothing but a winding road ahead. The landscape had morphed into something that I had only seen in textbooks and online pictures. For a moment, I lost track of what was really happening. It was beautiful. But that moment of bliss vanished at the sound of Cole's voice. "Have a nice nap?" he said kindly. His tone caught me off guard.

"Um…sure," I skeptically responded.

"That's good. I bet you were tired, huh?" he questioned.

"Um…sure," I repeated. What was going on? Was I dreaming? I suppose he saw the confusion on my face.

"I was just curious. I want to make sure you are okay," he stated, concerned.

I didn't respond. I couldn't respond. I had no idea how to respond. *What is happening?* I thought. A few hours ago he struck me across the face, had threatened me, and now he was asking how my nap was? If I was confused before, it compared nothing to what I was feeling now. Something was going on, and that something that was not right. His tone was too kind…

Looking out the window, I racked my brain for the reason or logic in this situation, but there was none. Why would Adrianna and Cole be taking me to their home? What was my purpose? I couldn't think of anything that wasn't crazy. But that's just the thing; they were absolutely, irreversibly crazy. In the distance, I could see a lot of lights and what appeared to be a huge city. And that's exactly what it was. Before I could decide which city it could be, I read the sign: San Antonio City Limits.

I figured it was to my advantage to keep gazing out the window. I had never really left the Texas Panhandle, and I had no clue about a city this big. I knew that I needed to start orienting myself. I shifted gears into survivor mode and tried to memorize the way to wherever we were going. If this was the way to get in, it was most likely the best way to get out, and that's what I was prepared for. No matter what was happening, I had a sick feeling in my gut. I knew, one way or another, I would have to get out. I'd have to escape.

We pulled up to their house. "Okay. Out," Cole said.

Wow, bipolar much? I thought. "What about my things?" I asked.

"Get in the house now. I'll worry about your things."

I started toward the door. It was a nice home. Cole was high up in the military and provided a good state of living for his family. The interior was well furnished, and by appearance, you would suspect a perfectly happy home.

"Up the stairs. That's where you'll be staying," Adrianna ordered.

I turned toward the staircase and started to make my way up. At this point, my fear faded into curiosity. I wasn't sure what they were doing, but at this point, I didn't think they brought me to their home to kill me. But what they were doing, I was unsure.

"In here." Adrianna pointed. "You're to stay in this room. Cole will bring your stuff up here. You are to stay in this room and not come out, unless you are bleeding, flying, or dying. We will call you down for meals, and at that time you can go to the bathroom. Understood?"

"Yes, ma'am," I responded. So I was a prisoner. Well, even prisoners got one phone call, so I asked, "May I use the phone? I would like to call one of my friends to let them know that I have moved."

Adrianna looked off in the distance, seemingly contemplating the request. Wondering the consequences of allowing me to do so, I suppose. "You have five minutes." She handed me a phone.

Smart but dumb, I thought. I was not going to be staying in this room for very long. I dialed a number on the phone; it was my best friend, Nicole's, cell. There was no answer. Next, I thought, *I'll call my coach. He'd promised to help me once. Maybe he would.* When he answered, I couldn't help the tears of happiness, shock, and thankfulness. It dawned on me that I was away from my family. I tried to explain to him in a hushed voice what was going on, but to be honest, I really didn't know. Nothing made sense, and there wasn't anything to do. He said he would call Faye and see what he could figure out. By the time I started to ask what I should do in the mean time, my five minutes were up.

"Done. Hand it over." Adrianna stood over me. I wanted to delete the number, but I didn't have time. I handed over the phone, and she headed out of the room.

I was stuck. There was nothing I could do about it. The room was small. The walls were painted a sage green, but for whatever reason, it had a musty smell. A small window overlooked the front yard. I could see the driveway and walking path to the front door. There was a twin size bed with beige sheets and a tan blanket. In one corner, there was a small white dresser on the adjacent wall. I had a small lamp and alarm clock placed on a table beside my bed, with my bags right beside it. In any other circumstance, I would have said the room was comfortable. But, in this situation, it was unnerving. And at ten o'clock in the evening, all I could do was wait for tomorrow.

I woke up the next morning to the light of the sun. For a moment, I had forgotten where I was and what was happening. For a moment, I was at peace, but unfortunately, yesterday came flooding back to me. I was disturbed by the sound of yelling coming from downstairs. I couldn't make out what they were saying, but neither

Adrianna nor Cole were happy. I just stayed in the room as they told me.

I couldn't help but cry. What was happening? I had been taken away from everything, and I sincerely didn't know what to do with myself. The day passed by. I went out for meals, though I didn't eat. I would go to the restroom, and then it was back in the room. There were no bars, no guards. There weren't security holdings or wire gates on the outside, but it was prison. I was in prison. And it wasn't iron bars that contained me. It was fear.

A few days passed, and I spent them crying. And when I wasn't crying, I was trying to figure out what to do. Monday arrived; however, it was spring break, so I knew there was no way for my school to be suspicious at this point. My friends, well, it wasn't abnormal for them not to hear from me for a few days. Most of them knew my homelife was a complex situation, though they didn't know of its depth. No one was looking for me. And even if they were, I wasn't going to be found.

I was emotionally exhausted, and physical exhaustion was soon to follow. I hadn't eaten, and I knew I was dehydrated. I frantically tried to figure out what to do, but I found nothing. All I could do was wait. Both Cole and Adrianna were at work and their kids were in their bedrooms, which were down the hall from the room I was in. I could hear the various media devices they had. They were distracted, and this waiting was killing me slowly. I had to do something.

I decided that I would venture out and look around the house. As I peered out my door, I could hear video games going on in Shawn's room and Disney movies in Ellie's. They would be preoccupied for a while. Time to venture.

During my trips to dinner, I paid very close attention to my surroundings, looking and eyeing the layout of the house.

Memorizing and planning for my escape. I crept slowly down the stairs. I went around the corner and found the computer. I went over and cautiously checked my MySpace. I had messages from a ton of people, but the response I looked for was from my history teacher. She asked many questions, but most importantly listed her phone number. I had to call her. The phone was on the same desk. *Take a chance*, I told myself. *What do you have to lose?*

But as soon as I picked up the phone, I heard the front door opening. I panicked. I had to get back to that room. I set the phone down, logged out of my account, and ran straight towards the staircase. I ran up them, taking three at a time. If I got caught... Well, I didn't know what would happen, but I couldn't help but remember that little gun of Cole's.

I reached my room and slowly shut the door. I couldn't let my anxiety cause me to make mistakes. I went over to the window, and Adrianna's car was in the drive. *Home for lunch*, I thought. *Holy crap, I didn't figure that at all.* It was close...too close. I needed to memorize their schedules. What time would Cole come home? I didn't know, but I knew that I needed to be more observant.

For the next two days, that's exactly what I did. I woke up early and listened to the sounds of the house. Adrianna left around 7:00 a.m., but Cole left around 5:30 a.m. He never came home for lunch, but Adrianna usually made it around 1:00 p.m. She left around 2:00 p.m. and was home at 6:00 p.m. Cole, though, he was home much sooner, around 4:00 p.m. The kids, they normally stayed in their rooms. However, Shawn often had visitors.

Shady people, to say the least. Luckily, my window provided me insight. Didn't take me long to figure out that he was dealing drugs—typical. Ellie, she was just Ellie. Consumed with movies and television, reality shows that she was way too young to be watching. But the family had a routine, and I had finally mastered it. I had two slots of time that I could venture out: 7:00 a.m. to noon and 2:30 p.m. to 3:30 p.m. I would always give myself room in case they were early or late. I figured forty-five minutes, just to be on the safe side. I couldn't be too cautious.

Friday morning had arrived. Today was the day. Time to make some phone calls. Throughout the week, I found an addressed envelope, and Google mapped it on the computer. I knew where I was, and more importantly, I memorized the route I needed to take to get back to Amarillo. I had to get out of here.

It was about nine in the morning. I went downstairs and grabbed the phone. I went to the front room that gave me a clear view of who was coming up the drive. I also memorized my history teacher's number. I dialed and waited while the phone rang.

"Hello?"

"Mrs. Herring!" I almost shouted.

"Natalie! Where are you?" she asked.

"I'm in San Antonio, Mrs. Herring. It's a long story, but Faye, my mom, kicked me out of her house. But her biological daughter came to Amarillo. They forced me to come with them. I don't know what they are going to do, Mrs. Herring, but I don't have a good feeling," I told her in a rush.

"You are really in San Antonio? Oh my gosh. Oh my gosh. Okay, well, I've notified Child Protective Services, but the investigation isn't getting anywhere. How are you able to talk to me?" she asked.

I ranted on about how I memorized their routines and that I was sneaking on the computer and the phone. It wasn't safe, we both knew. But it was the only way.

"Natalie, call the police. You have a phone, just call them," she instructed.

"No, Mrs. Herring. I can't. It's way too risky. He is in the military, and we are close to the military base. I can't be sure the real police will come or if it will be military police. And even if the police came, I'm not sure they would take me with them. And then… Well, who knows what they would do. These people are smart. Really smart," I reasoned with her.

"Well, so are we. I will figure something out, okay? But you, you call me. Every day at this time. All right? You stay in touch. Do you understand?" she warned.

"Yes, ma'am. I do. But it's the weekend. I can't be sure when they will be home or be gone. Help me find a way out, Mrs. Herring. This isn't good. And…I'm scared," I said.

"I know, Honey. I know. Now we better get off here. Just be careful, Natalie. Be careful. I'm going to call Officer Rodriguez, the school officer, and see what we can do here. We are going to get you out of there. I promise."

"I will. Thanks, Mrs. Herring. Thank you so much. Talk to you soon!" I hung up and deleted her number from the call history.

I snuck back up stairs. For the first time in a while, I had some hope. Mrs. Herring knew where I was, and she was going to help me. I was going to get out of here…somehow. Some way or another.

Friday night, I couldn't sleep. I was excited because help was near. I just had faith that it would come, and I was restless imagining how. As I lay there planning—well, dreaming—about how I was going to get out of here, I could hear footsteps outside my door, and quickly I went on the alert.

I heard my doorknob slowly turn. My door creaked open

slowly, and I could see his shadow. The scene was familiar. All too, too familiar. And just like before, fear has a way of freezing you to the point that even if you wanted to move, you couldn't. I lay there completely still.

He shut the door behind him and started toward my bed. But this time, I didn't pretend to be asleep. I was wide awake. Tears flooded my eyes. I knew what was about to happen. I knew as it had happened before.

As Cole walked over, he met my eyes. "Good evening, Natalie," he said in a hushed voice. He sat on my bed and put his hand on my leg. My mind lost itself to the terrible memories of my childhood days when it was Daddy Jack touching my legs. Part of me couldn't move, but the other part of me told me I had to. Not again. This couldn't happen again.

"Get away from me," I said in a rushed tone. He said nothing and only smirked as he raised his hand farther up my leg and tightened his grip.

"I said, get away from me," I repeated. The firmness in my voice shocked me. But I wasn't just going to lie there, not this time. He let go and stood up. He was looking down at me. Like I was his possession. Then a smile slowly appeared across his face. As he reached behind him, he pulled out his little gun. Fear soon replaced any ounce of courage I had. "Remember this?" he asked.

I couldn't answer as the horror had paralyzed my body once more.

"Answer me!" he ordered quietly.

All I could do was nod, "yes."

"Now, stand up."

Everything in me was freaking out. I couldn't tear my eyes

away from the little shiny piece of metal before me, capable of taking my life. I did as he said. I stood.

"Good. Now, take off your clothes, Natalie. Pants and panties first." He motioned at me with the gun. "Don't hesitate to think I'll put this to use," he warned.

I couldn't help but offer a silent prayer to God. *Please, help me. I'm begging you, please help me*, I prayed silently in my head.

"Natalie. Do it!" He was growing impatient.

I started to grab the waist of my pants and slowly slipped them down. They were draped at my ankles.

"Now underwear. Go," he commanded.

I was shaking. With fear, with panic, with everything far and in between the two. I repeated the previous motion, this time with my underwear, and they slid down, stopping at my ankles.

At that time, clothes weren't the only thing that was falling. So were my tears. The humiliation I felt in this very moment was soon to be followed by misery. Why did this have to happen? Where is God? Please, God. Please, not again. My thoughts were chaotic, frantic, and desperate. I couldn't bear this. I couldn't go through it again. It was all just too much. My eyes were squeezed tightly shut. I was all but wishing myself out of that room. *Please God, please!*

"Daddy!" My thoughts were suddenly interrupted by Ellie's call. It startled Cole as well. "Daddy!" she called again.

Cole was torn; I could tell by the look on his face. But he slowly put the gun back behind his back and stepped away. "Saved by the bell, so it seems, Miss Natalie. Maybe not tonight. But don't be stupid. You are mine now," he said then slowly walked toward the door and left the room.

I quickly redressed, putting my panties and pants back on,

and jumped back into bed. My tears flowed relentlessly. Now I understood. I knew part of the reason as to why I was here. I was a toy...a pet. But why would his wife, Adrianna, agree with this? Maybe she didn't know.

There were too many questions...and no answers. This was bad, and it was going to get much worse. I couldn't let this happen. Not again. I cried and cried. But before I drifted back to sleep, I thanked God. He saved me that night. I knew He did.

Part of me knew that He would have to save me again. But, I was comforted. I knew that He would.

The next few days were hazy. Mostly because I was weak and tired from the guard I had been holding up during the night. Sleep just wasn't possible now. Plus, the lack of food had me physically vulnerable. Something had to give. Cole had his eye on me and made sure I was aware of it. Adrianna made sure I knew how worthless I was. It was like I was kidnapped to a place that was exactly the same as the Winters home, except that I didn't have the comfort of cheerleading and friends to escape to. Sunday morning, we all went to church. How ironic. These two people seeking the Lord? I couldn't help but be a little confused by it.

During the service, I had to sit in between Adrianna and Cole. Adrianna left before the sermon was over and went to the car. I suppose the Word of God was a little much for her. But I wasn't happy to be alone with Cole. And it certainly didn't take long for him to make the most of the moment.

"You are mine. I mean that. All mine, Sweet Girl," he whispered in my ear. His voice sent chills down my spine. Then he leaned closer and draped an arm around me. Then, as he kissed me on the cheek, he whispered, "All mine."

I felt sick. I had to get out now. I couldn't wait to talk to Mrs. Herring. I had to get away from them as soon as I could. I'd pray for help. So I started to plan. I had to get a plan.

When we got home, I went back to my room, ruminating on how I could escape. My thoughts drifted to a Sixty-Minutes episode I watched once when they were talking about dangerous situations. A statement I remembered was "In a threatening situation, your mind is your greatest weapon."

They were right. I had a mind. A pretty good one, and I was going to use it. I had to find a way to ensure that I would be out of the house and in the public eye. A way that there was no possibility that I would be alone with either of them. A way that would force someone to listen to me. A way that was powerful…dramatic. I planned and I plotted. My mind was my greatest weapon.

Call Me Crazy

....

One person's craziness is another person's reality.

—Tim Burton

....

I f there was one thing that I had grown proficient in during the last few months, it was medicine. I was volunteering in the emergency room, and I learned a lot of how things worked, what symptoms led to what diagnoses, what procedures led to certain complications. I knew the processes, and this...this was my weapon.

If you'll remember, every child in our home was medically sick. Everyone was on medication for some reason or another. One reason was Faye liked the babies to be doped up so they wouldn't cry. Seizure medicine was a good remedy. So a lot of us had "seizures." Including me.

When I was looking through my bag, I found my medications. I completely forgot about them. I had Tegretol and Neurontin. I never took them, but Faye thought I did. I usually just washed them down the sink at home. I knew I didn't have seizures. I had never had a seizure, but Faye told the doctor I did. Why she wanted me doped up, I wasn't sure. I think she might have had a little bit of

Münchausen syndrome, faking childhood illnesses for attention. It all fit within her scope and psyche. But at this point, I had the medication. And oddly enough, it was exactly what I needed.

I had a plan, and it was an absolutely insane one. I had to figure out a way that would force me to be taken from the home, and a medical emergency was the perfect solution. I had to be smart about it though. I didn't want to die; I just had to make them think I did, at least for a little while.

I had capsules and tablets. I decided that I would take the tablets. They would give me more time to ensure the ambulance was coming. Another weapon in my arsenal was my ability to do math. I calculated the dose I would need to make my vitals unstable, but not enough to actually kill me. I was good with medication. I had worked with it my entire life, so I was confident.

My prescribed dosage was three 400 mg tablets a day—a total of 1,200 milligrams. This was the normal range, so I knew I would need to not only break that, but also to ingest enough to be a little on the dangerous side.

After I calculated three times, I figured that six 400 mg capsules would do the trick. I'd double the dose. With my weight drop, I was hesitant, but I didn't want to not take enough and be left drowsy. It was a huge risk. A huge gamble, but being here in this place was far more dangerous than a possible overdose.

I took out the six pills and a few extra. See, when a person tries to kill themselves with pills, it is easy to calculate how many they took by looking at the date in which the medication was given, the prescribed dosage, and the date it is now. It is a calculation based on assumption that the person took the medication regularly but is accurate in most cases. Cole was a nurse, and he would know this little trick. Luckily, so did I.

So I hid five more of the pills. Now, it would appear that I was headed right to death's door. This was a dark thought, I know. I didn't want to die, but I was willing to take the chance. I was on my last straw, and this was the only solution I could come up with. I had a water bottle left from lunch and just enough left to get the pills down. I would wait about twenty minutes for them to dissolve in my stomach. I knew it was best to take them on a dry stomach so it wouldn't be easy to get them back up. There would be no throwing them back up, something else I knew Cole would try.

As I held the pills in my hand, my anxiety was through the roof. This was...well, crazy. But desperate times, they call for desperate measures. I said a silent prayer before. *God. I love You. I don't want to die, but I need out. Protect me, please. If I do accidently kill myself, I'm sorry. It wasn't my intention. I love You. And if I do end up at heaven's gates, I ask that You have mercy on me. Forgive me for all of my sins. I love You, and I thank You.*

All or nothing, I thought. I grabbed the pills in my hand and swallowed them one by one. I couldn't help but cry because I knew there was a chance that my calculation was wrong. There was also a chance that they wouldn't get me help. There was a chance that I could die. The chance was there that I was actually killing myself.

But I was willing to take it. I was willing to risk death in order to live. I had been in a prison for over a week. Adrianna had yelled, threatened, and thrashed me, and I was about to be taken advantage of by Cole. I was fighting back, and this was how. There is a fine line between genius and insanity, and I was walking it.

The thirty minutes went by extremely slowly. I thought about life in general, how I didn't want mine to end. That suicide was a coward's choice. I had things to do. After all, I still had to earn my place up in the night sky as a star. My thoughts of the sky though, they were starting to get cloudy. I checked my pulse, and it was weak.

It was time to notify my caregivers that I needed medical attention.

I walked downstairs and into the living room.

"What the hell do you think you are doing?" Adrianna said as she was standing up. Up and ready to fight. So I tossed her the medicine bottle, smirking just a little. As she caught it and started to read, her eyes bolted up at me.

"Well, it seems I've taken a few of those pills. And it seems that you should probably call an ambulance. You're liable to have a body on your hands here in a few minutes," I said in a sly, drawn-out voice. The drugs were working.

"You little b—!" She came to me and slapped me hard across the face. The apple doesn't fall far from the tree, and she was her mother's daughter. She hit just like Faye did. Hard and fast, and it was no less disorienting. I stumbled into the wall; no doubt the intoxication from the medication affected my balance. She came at me flailing her arms, swinging. All I could do was crouch and duck. My body was weak and getting weaker.

All of a sudden, Cole pulled her off me. He grabbed my shirt and dragged me to the hall bathroom.

"You think you are so smart, don't you?" he asked as he stuck his hand down my throat. I gagged, but nothing came up. He did it again, but still nothing was emerging from my stomach.

"They aren't coming up. I took them on a dry stomach, you idiot," I said. Apparently, the medication was making me drowsy and just a bit bolder.

Glaring at me, he threw me against the floor. "You little b !
You little f—ing b—!" he screamed. Then he picked me up and pushed me up against the wall, pinning down my shoulders. I didn't feel very good and was starting to get nervous. They needed to call an ambulance, and they hadn't yet.

"You think you're so smart? What makes you think we care if you die? Who says we found you?" By the sound of his words, I panicked. I had figured that if they were going to kill me, they would have done it by now. What if I missed their bluff? Maybe they weren't going to kill me, but they wouldn't have a problem letting me die. But I didn't take enough to die, did I? No, I didn't. I didn't. I would wake up, then what? Then what?

He saw my panic. But what happened next, I wasn't prepared for. I couldn't breathe; I thought it was the medication before I realized his hands were around my neck. He was choking me. His grip was strong around my small neck, and my throat was closing in. My body was panicking beneath me. I tried to pull his hands away, but I was too weak. The meds I had taken were in effect; there was nothing I could do. My vision was going. My life was ending. It was over. It was too late. He was killing me.

Oh no... God, I'm sorry. That was my last conscious thought before I met the darkness.

I awoke on the floor, finding myself gasping for air. My lungs demanded air. I was coughing and panting.

"Call an ambulance," I heard Cole tell Adrianna in the background.

Everything was blurry. But I could hear sirens. Help was on the way. I was going to get out of here, and I wasn't going to die. Mind over matter... Mind over matter. That's what I told myself...

Soon the firefighters, police, and EMTs were there. Another situation I was familiar with. They took my vitals, and they were dropping.

"What's the estimate?" one of them asked.

"Um, by the dates, we expect she took about twelve pills. We have to get her to a hospital now. If that's how much she took, she doesn't have much time."

As they loaded me on the stretcher and shut the doors, I felt so relieved. I was really tired and knew that the medication was taking over as my body lost control. But I was…happy. I was getting the hell out of that house. Cole wouldn't be touching me. Adrianna wouldn't dare hit me. I was going back home. I was going home.

I guessed I dozed off because the next thing I know, I was in a hospital room. There was a nurse by my bedside. "Natalie? Can you hear me?" He was yelling.

"Yes, I can hear you. No need to yell," I responded drearily. Gosh, he was so loud. Everything was. My head was killing me. Everything was spinning like a merry-go-round gone wrong.

"How many pills did you take?" he asked. His tone was harsh. Of course it would be. Suicide patients don't get a lot of empathy, as the medical care now warranted was completely unnecessary.

"Um… I'm not really sure. What is your estimate?" I asked in a sarcastic tone.

"Do you think this is funny? You tried to kill yourself," he lectured.

"No, I took pills. I'm a girl who achieves and succeeds. I didn't try to kill myself." I slurred, all drunk-like. "Because I can assure you, if I wanted to die, I would be dead. Where is my doctor?" I questioned him.

He looked at me and was very confused. "He'll be right here.

In the meantime, drink this. It's charcoal to help get the pills out of your system."

"I don't need that. I didn't take that many. It's best to just let the meds clear out on their own," I advised.

"How many did you take then?" he questioned again.

"Where is my doctor? I'll discuss it with him," I stated fiercely. Jeez, I was really gutsy with these meds. Demanding.

A few moments later, a large man with a big white coat came into the room. I was as happy as a kid would be on Christmas seeing a large man with a red coat.

"Hello, Doctor. How are you?" I asked excitedly. He looked to be a bit surprised by my tone. I suppose it wasn't the typical suicidal patient to ask how someone else was doing, but I didn't want to be rude.

"I've been better. You want to tell me why you tried to kill yourself? What are you doing here?" he questioned me.

"Oh yes, sir, I can explain that. I didn't try to kill myself. I just needed it to appear that way." Gosh, I was slurring my words. It was so hard to concentrate. But I went on. I told him my story about how I had been taken from my home and how I was trying to get back. I told him about Cole's advances. And I made sure that he knew I wasn't emotionally unstable, just in need of help.

I pointed out the hand marks around my neck. The streak of red, which was bruising my face, that I noticed as I saw my reflection in the room. It was taking me forever to get my words out. I'd never been drunk, never intoxicated, but I imagined that this is what it was like. Frustratingly, I was trying to get my point across. I stated and defended my case. At least he was listening, though I'm not sure he understood the complexity.

"I don't even know what to say. You faked a suicide?" he asked skeptically.

"Yes, sir. I don't want to die, I promise. I just needed help. If I wanted to die, I would have gone with the Neurontin, the capsules. They dissolve faster. Also, I would have taken all of them. I wouldn't have calculated the dosage. It was the only way I could get out of that house. I need you to help me get back to Amarillo," I said. As I was talking to him, I watched his facial expression. One thing I didn't take into consideration was that faking a suicide was, well, kind of crazy. Faking crazy was crazy. Another thing I didn't take into consideration was the fact that the doctor might not understand. He might not help.

"Do you realize how insane you sound? How am I supposed to know that you are telling the truth?" he asked me, annoyed.

"You know, because I'm telling it to you. I'm here. Those people, Cole and Adrianna, they have no documentation on me. Go ask them a few questions about me. Birthday, history, my likes or dislikes. I can guarantee they won't know. Listen to me, I know how the game works. Please, contact social services. Please," I urged him. I was sure that he would believe me. I had a good case; we both knew it.

"I'll be right back," he said.

A few moments later, he came back into the room. I suppose he went to go talk to Adrianna and Cole.

He came back in the room and shut the door. "I don't know what the hell is going on here, but I know that I'm not getting involved. This is too much. I'm discharging you. Good luck." He started back toward the door, not looking me in the eyes.

"Doctor! Wait! Please, you have to help. You have to get involved. I'm right, we both know it! Please, help me. Please!" I begged of him, but I wasn't getting anywhere.

"I'm sorry. I'm… I'm so sorry, I just can't," he said hesitantly. What was wrong with him? Why wouldn't he do something? "I'm sorry, Natalie. I truly am."

"No! No! This is against hospital policy! We both know it! When a person tries to commit suicide you have to admit them! They have to be on a twenty-four hour observation and see a psychologist consult! You can't discharge me. You can't! Please!" I was explaining and pleading.

"I'm sorry. I just… I'm sorry," he muttered as he left the room.

I couldn't believe it. He just left. I knew he believed me, but why didn't he help? That's what he was supposed to do! Oh, what was I going to do know? It was all for nothing. All of this was for nothing. My door opened, and Adrianna and Cole walked in.

"Smart girl," Cole said. "I underestimated you, but I have friends in high places. This is the military hospital, Sweetheart. Couldn't calculate that, could you?" Fear overwhelmed me. There was a look in both of their eyes that was beyond the capacity evil could ever encompass. I had failed. My plan just didn't work out.

"Thanks to my sarge, you've been discharged. Don't worry, Sweetheart. I'm a nurse. I'll take good care of you," he stated in a depraved tone. "Let's go."

On the drive home, all I could do was weep. I gave it all I could. I used my mind, I pushed the limits, and I failed. My heart, well, to say it was broken, was an understatement. It was shattered, and I had no idea where the pieces had landed. I had no idea where to go from here. What to do? I had nothing left. My mind… my thoughts were shattered. And nothing I could do would matter.

Remember the Alamo

I found myself back in that room, back in the prison that a few hours ago I was sure I was leaving. My dramatic plan was well thought out, but it failed. Luckily, Cole didn't come to my room, and Adrianna left me alone. All I could do was cry. I cried to the point where even my tears were tired and ceased to come. My life, it was…well, I can't be sure what it was. But as far as I was concerned, it was over. There was nothing left for me to do. I had exhausted all of my resources.

On Monday morning, Shawn and Ellie headed back to school. I called Mrs. Herring and was able to get through to her, even though she was in class. I told her what happened, and all she could say was, "Oh my goodness… Oh my goodness." She said she was doing the best she could to get the school involved. They were starting to ask questions, but it would take time.

I decided to call a few of my friends. There was less of a chance of my getting caught with the kids gone, and to be honest, I really didn't care if I did get caught. What were they going to do? Kill me? Well, that was fine, because inside, I sincerely felt dead.

In talking with one of my friends, she said that she went to visit Faye. She urged me to call her.

"Natalie, you need to call her and suck it up. Tell her you miss her, tell her you love her, tell her whatever it takes to get you back," she begged.

It wasn't a bad idea. But the thought of giving her sentiments made me cringe. They'd be pure lies, but honestly, I was frantic, and at this point, I'd try anything. I hesitantly dialed the number I knew so well.

"Hello?" Faye answered.

"Mommy?" I didn't even recognize my own tone. It was foreign. I never referred to her as Mommy. I hardly referred to her as Mom. It was usually just "Yes, ma'am." But I continued. "I love you, can I please come back?"

"Natalie? How did you get the phone?" she asked. I refused to answer.

"Can I please come home? I miss you. Please let me come home. I'll do cheerleading next year. I'll do whatever you want. Please, just please let me come home," I pleaded with her. My words weren't real, but the emotion and my need to come home was. I hoped she could hear that.

"I'm sorry, Natalie. I just don't want you in my house. I really don't know why I ever took you from your daddy. That was a stupid decision on my part. But you can't come back. I don't want you," she said coldly.

"Oh please, please take me back. I promise I'll be good. I'll behave. I'll take care of the babies. I'll cook and clean. Please, please let me come back!" I begged and begged.

"No, Natalie. Good-bye." She hung up. Another plan. Another failure. I called one last friend, Olivia. Talking to them was the only thing that kept me going.

"Natalie!" she answered. "Where are you?"

"Hey, Olivia. Sorry." I explained the story, and she was outraged. Olivia always was one with quite a bit of temper.

"I'm coming to get you. They can't hold you. Where is Faye in all of this?" She was furious.

"She doesn't care, Olivia. That's why I'm here. There is nothing left to do."

"Oh yes, there is. I'm not just going to sit around. You just give me some time, okay, Nat? Just… Let me figure this out." She sounded determined.

"All right. I have to go. I'll talk to you later, Liv. Bye."

"Bye, girly. Hang in there."

I wanted to believe her. That she would figure out a way to help me, but I knew better than to present myself with that false hope. I couldn't bear another letdown.

All I could do was wait and hope. I knew that my school was digging, and they were getting somewhere. That night, I heard Adrianna talking on the phone to Faye. Of course, I would be in trouble for sneaking out of my room and using the phone without permission, but as far as they knew, I just called Faye. I deleted the history of the other calls. But their conversation was interesting. I could hear well if I was close to the vent, and fortunately, Adrianna had the speakerphone on.

"The school called, and they asked where she was. So I just went and unenrolled her," Faye explained. "But they asked where to send her records. According to law, she only has a few days to get back into school. You are going to have to enroll her if we don't want trouble."

"You want me to put her in school? How am I supposed to explain that?" Adrianna exclaimed.

"I don't know, but I don't want her. You took her, that was the deal. So deal with it!"

School, I thought. I could get help there. I could explain. That was the light at the end of this deep, dark tunnel.

The next morning, I arrived at the high school. It was huge, and there were people everywhere. They took me to the office, and I had no idea how, but Adrianna had the documentation. I guessed that Faye faxed it. I went to a counselor to figure out a schedule. The first minute alone, I tried to talk to her about what was going on.

"Miss, I need you to call my school. I'm not supposed to be here! I have been—"

"Yes, yes, darling. I've heard all about your crazy little stories. I also know that you tried to kill yourself. That's never the answer to the problem. We have to deal with our problems. Here"—she slid over a card with a suicide hotline—"you call this number if you get those crazy ideas in your head. Okay? Your sister loves you, and they are giving you a nice home and have brought you to a great school. So stop with the nonsense," she explained all chipper-like.

Seriously? A freaking suicide hotline? You have got to be kidding me. They were always one step ahead, no matter what. I started classes that day, and it was miserable. People were rude. I didn't know where I was going or how to get anywhere. They stuck me in the strangest classes. Apparently, that's all they had open. I had no advanced courses, and every class was…behind. They were learning stuff that I had learned months ago.

And to top it all off, Shawn went to the same school. He was, well, an ass. I saw him in the hallway pointing at me with a bunch of people laughing around him. Later on, I saw one of the kids with him. He looked at me and made a motion like he had a noose and was hanging himself.

Great, I was the crazy new girl. Could it get any worse? No, I dare not ask.

The days went by, and I was numb. I can't tell you about what happened because in all honesty, I wasn't there. I was…depressed. The only thing I was sure of was that there was no way out.

One night, while praying frantically, I called on God. I needed God's help. I really, really needed it. I begged of Him to give me a way. To give me help.

I prayed and prayed, more desperate than I had ever been. "Please, God. I know you are there. Please, get me out of here. I can't do this." I prayed on and on, but before I said amen, a solution came to me. A wallet. I had my wallet.

I went over to my bag and found it. Inside, I found what I was hoping to see. My PayPal credit card. No one knew I had it, but I had been putting money on it for sometime. I knew I had a little over a hundred dollars. That would buy a bus ticket wouldn't it? It had to.

The next day, I called the number on the back of the card. I had one hundred and ninety-eight dollars. I went to the library and looked up the price of a bus ticket: San Antonio to Amarillo. The charge was one hundred and sixty-two bucks. I had enough by the grace of God Himself.

At lunch, I asked this random girl to borrow her phone. Fortunately, she let me. I called Olivia.

"Natalie. Hey, I have good news. We are—"

"I'm getting out of here, Liv! I'm getting a bus ticket and leaving tomorrow!" I interrupted her.

"What? You do? You're leaving?" she exclaimed.

"Yes, I don't have time to explain, but I'm on my way out. Okay, I'll call you at some point! I have to go. Say a prayer for me!" I frantically said.

"Okay, okay. I'll talk to you later. Be careful, Natalie. Okay?"

"Yes, I will, Liv. No worries." I hung up the phone.

Tomorrow was Friday, and that was the next trip out. While at school, I located the bus station. It was a ways from the school, but not too bad. I planned to leave after first period. The bus left at 10:00 a.m. I had enough time.

Thursday night, I began to pack some of my things in a bag. I had to ensure that it was not conspicuous though. I didn't want Cole or Adrianna to become suspicious as to why I had so much. I picked the necessities but left it at a bare minimum. As I zipped up the bag, my door flung open.

"What are you doing?" Adrianna questioned.

"Nothing. I'm just...packing gym clothes," I answered hesitantly.

"Well, you certainly have been compliant these past few days. It makes me wonder. What are you up to?" she demanded.

"Nothing. I'm just getting ready for class," I lied out of need.

"Okay. Well, go to bed," she ordered while slamming the door.

"Ugh," I sighed. Close call. But soon, it would be over. Tomorrow was the day. I was heading home.

Tomorrow morning was here before I knew it. I got up and got ready, trying to hide my excitement. I got to school. Everything was on schedule. After first period, I went around the back of the school and started my route.

One thing that God blessed me with was an extremely good memory. It wasn't exactly photographic, but pretty close. After studying something for a minute, I usually had it down. Maps were a quick learn for me, a skill that was paying off.

Around 9:55 a.m., I got to the bus station. I was winded because I ran for most of the way. When I arrived, I was so glad I took that little sprint. There was a huge line at the ticket booth. I was anxious, because there really wasn't much time. *Gosh, hurry up!* I thought.

Soon enough, I made it to the front. I gave the lady my credit card and driver's license. She studied it for a moment before she asked, "Where is your guardian, Sweetie?"

What? Guardian? "Um, I don't have a guardian, miss. It's just me, but here is my license and money and everything," I explained.

Oh gosh, a guardian? I need a guardian to do this?

"Well, Hun, you are only sixteen. We can't let you on the bus unless you have your parents' permission," she explained.

"Oh, miss, please! Is there any way? Any way at all? I'm a good girl, I promise. Please let me on. Please!" I begged her.

"No, I'm so sorry. We just can't do that," she apologized. I suspect she heard the desperation in my voice, but there was nothing for either of us to do. "The rules are the rules."

I stared at her, disbelieving for a few moments. This just couldn't be. "Oh, please ma'am. Please let me go. You just have to."

"I'm sorry, Honey. I can't do that," she said sympathetically.

That was it. There was nothing more to be done. As I turned, the failure that hit me was overwhelming. I was never going to get out of here. There was no escape.

On the walk home, I took my time. I wasn't going back to school. I didn't care to. I meandered as I knew once I arrived, Cole and Adrianna would be furious. Part of me wanted to hide out, but I knew better. This was the big city, and there was probably just as much danger here as there was at home.

But on the journey back, I went through an array of emotions. First, I was sad, just crying relentlessly. Then I was numb. I had no feeling. Soon the numbness morphed into acceptance; the five stages of grief on steroids. But soon to follow was anger. Severe, potent anger. And when I finally arrived at the house, the anger changed into ferociousness.

It was noontime. I walked up and noticed my car. And, well, it dawned on me that I didn't need parental permission to drive it. I had money for gas. I knew it would be a fight to get it, but fortunately, I was mad enough for just that: a knock-down, drag-out fight.

Before I entered the house, I made up my mind. I was leaving. Both Cole and Adrianna were home. No doubt because the school called, alerting them of my truancy. I walked in, and I slammed the glass door behind me, and it nearly shattered, but it achieved what I wanted it to. I got both Cole's and Adrianna's attention as they quickly appeared in the foyer.

"I hate to break it to you, but I am leaving. That out there is my car." I walked over to the bar and picked up the keys. "These are my keys, and I'm getting the hell out of this house whether you like it or not. You are a bunch of sorry people, and you have no right to contain me. I've allowed it thus far, but that ends now," I stated in, well, a downright scary tone. I'd never spoken that way. Not to anyone.

Cole walked up to me. "You sound pretty confident, don't you?" he mocked. I saw his hand moving toward me.

"Hit me, you son of a b—. I dare you. But I'll hit back. And I know I'll lose, but one thing is for sure, we'll have a hell of a fight," I warned. The anger in my voice was sharp and strong. I had never acted this way. But weirdly enough I believed my words. I felt confident. I felt…powerful. Invincible. I was getting out of there.

The phone interrupted the tension. Cole just stared at me. Adrianna answered, and I recognized the voice on the other line. Again, my friend's mom's voice sounded through. Adrianna called Cole into the room. I have no idea what was said, but when Cole and Adrianna came back into the room, he said, "Get your s— and get the f— out of my house."

"Gladly," I said. I turned and started to walk out of the house.

"You don't even know your way. Your are going to get lost."

Adrianna sounded like a fifteen-year-old girl trying to scare me.

"I know the way. Don't worry your pretty little head," I said, and I got in the driver's seat and locked the doors. I threw that car into drive and took off like a NASCAR driver. I had to get out of there before they could stop me.

I had the route memorized, and I knew exactly what I was doing and where I was going. Before I knew it, I passed the city limits of San Antonio, Texas.

Tears of joy flooded my face and my heart. It was over; it was all over. I would never return to this city. I would never have to. On that drive, my thoughts drifted ironically to the Alamo. We lost so much…so many people. Though we were courageous and strong, we lost. But the perseverance of the soldiers lasted forever, and ultimately, Texas gained its freedom.

The story of the Alamo had a ring fairly close to mine. For the first time in a long time, I found myself smiling. Freedom. Liberty. Well, they just have a way of invoking a happy feeling, especially when they were gone for so long.

Under Arrest

Sometimes you're flush and sometimes you're bust,
and when you're up, it's never as good as it seems,
and when you're down, you never think you'll be up
again, but life goes on.

—Blow

During the drive home, I thought of my life and began to realize that so much was out of my hands. Things happen to you, and you can't control it. The only thing you can control is your attitude and how you handle it. I knew that I handled my trip to San Antonio all wrong. I should have never gone. I should have found a way to stand up for myself before it went that far. Fear can be a hard thing to overcome, but it must be. If not, it will overcome you.

I also thought a lot about the people who helped me during my time. My teacher, Mrs. Herring, was a saint in my eyes, as well as, my friend, Olivia, and her mom. I pulled over to call them, and they were actually going to come meet me halfway, right out of Big Springs, Texas. Olivia's mom was a wonderful woman. People were reaching out to help in a time of dire need, and that meant the world to me.

I also knew that there were going to be a lot of questions when I returned, questions that I wouldn't know how to answer. It was a story that I didn't want to recall. The loneliness, the heartbreak, the fear... I didn't want to remember any of it. And how in the world was I supposed to tell my friends about faking a suicide? They just wouldn't understand. And how could they? It was all just...crazy.

And that's another thing I thought about—suicide. Before, it was something I didn't really understand. Society puts a negative connotation to it that it is just for crazy people. And though I didn't have a desire to die, I was willing to take the chance just to be able to get help. I realized that's all suicide is—a desperate attempt to seek help. I don't think most who attempt it truly want their life to be over. They are just at a point like I was, with nothing left.

And the more I thought about it, I realized that people, they commit suicide every day, just in different ways. Some go to the bar every night and slowly drink their lives away. Some gamble until their life is all but empty. Some take drugs, stringing out the misery. Some isolate themselves. Some are slaves to guilt and heartache, and it too takes their life as they allow it.

Suicide is not about death. It's about trying to cope with the life you're living. I was not ashamed of my actions. It was desperate, but I was neither insane nor unstable. I was trying to deal with the present, though I knew most would not see it that way. But at this point, I really didn't have anything to prove to anyone. I was alive. I was breathing. And I could even take on a smile, something which I thought a few days prior would never happen again.

I was also very thankful that Cole never got his hands where he wanted them. I can't explain how relieved I was. I don't know if I could endure that from another man. But the whole situation bothered me. *Why would Adrianna support that? Was it just another way to hurt me?* The whole situation just didn't make sense. But then again, these were not sensible people.

My thoughts were suddenly interrupted by flashing lights in my rearview mirror. I instantly looked down at my speedometer. I knew I wasn't speeding because I had the cruise control set. I was just about thirty minutes away from Big Springs.

I grew nervous. I had never been pulled over before. I eased to the side of the road, and I noticed that my hands had begun to shake. I rolled down my window and waited as the deputy approached my car.

"License and registration," he said.

I pulled the insurance card from the passenger' glove box and prayed that it wasn't expired. Faye had a habit of "forgetting" to pay the insurance company. I reached for my wallet to get my license. My hand was severely shaking at this point that I couldn't get my license out of the slot it was placed in.

"Calm down. You're not in trouble yet," he said in an impatient voice.

Yet? I thought. *I'm not in trouble* yet? I was finally able to get it out. As I handed it to him, he read my name. "Natalie Winters." He reached for the radio clipped to his shoulder. "I got her," he spoke into it. "Out of the car, ma'am," he then ordered me.

"Um, yes, sir. But what is wrong?" I questioned in a shaky voice. I was petrified.

"I said get out of the car. No talking. Come with me." He grabbed my hands and held them behind my back as he led me to the front of his car.

Oh no, was all I could think. I was getting arrested. For what? I didn't do anything! My mind frantically searched for reasoning.

"Put your hands on my hood and don't move. I'm going to search you," he warned me.

"Yes, sir." At that point, I was in hysterical tears. I was going to jail. He patted me down, almost invasively.

"Stay there. Don't even think about moving." His voice was harsh, and I could tell that he was a smoker by the raspy gruffness in his voice along with a harshness that drenched his words in bitterness. I was nervous. No, I was freaking out. His radio went off, and he went over by the driver's side of the sheriff's car.

He sat inside his car and was using the computer. I was trying to listen to his radio. What was going on? I wasn't speeding. He hadn't even told me what I was being arrested for. I heard the radio static, but it was hard to make out what was being said.

"What is the name that the car is under?" the sheriff asked.

"Uh, Faye Winters," the radio responded.

"Well, her last name is Winters. What is the last name of the people who reported it?"

"Conner." Even the static couldn't tune out the sound of that name from my ears.

"Well, they aren't on any of the paperwork on this vehicle, so they can't report it stolen," the sheriff spoke into the radio. "Thanks, Joe."

He got out and came toward me. I was shaking and crying still, but at that point, anger was a big part of the reasoning. They freaking reported my car to be stolen. Are you kidding me?

"Ms. Winters. You can take your hands off the hood. It's all right now," he said, his voice shifting from harshness to a kind, fatherly type. "I'm so sorry about the misunderstanding."

"It's…it's okay," I stammered. He walked me back to my car. I suppose he noticed all of the clothes and random stuff thrown in the backseat.

"Are you okay?" he asked me.

"Yes, sir. I'm all right. I just need to get home," I said.

"Where is home?" he questioned.

"Amarillo. Amarillo, Texas," I said.

"All right then, drive safe. I'm really sorry about this. You didn't do anything wrong. Are you sure you are all right? What is going on?" He felt bad, I could tell. I wasn't mad at him. The man was just doing his job; he expected me to be a juvenile when he pulled me over, and he was cautious.

"Yes, sir, I'm okay. I'm just headed home. It's all over now. Thank you." I didn't know what else to say. I was in an emotional upheaval. These past two weeks had my nerves shot.

"Okay then, have a nice day. Drive safely," he offered as he walked away.

"Thank you, sir," I responded as I slid inside and rolled up my window. I couldn't drive away yet. I had to catch my breath. I'm pretty sure I had been holding it in for a while. I couldn't believe Cole and Adrianna. They had some nerve. And for what reason?

Why were they doing all of this? But these weren't questions I could answer. I had no earthly idea.

I drove the rest of the way to Big Springs and met Gina, Olivia's mom. I was really happy to see a familiar face. She was such a nice woman. And she knew exactly what to say: absolutely nothing. The last thing I wanted to talk about was my experiences over the past two weeks. I'm sure she gathered it was rough though. I still had slight marks on my neck and bruises on my arms. My eyes were raw and swollen from all the crying. I had lost about ten pounds. I was pale and looked extremely tired and emotionally exhausted. To be honest, I looked like I had been through hell. And, well, truth be told, I'd wager that it was something close.

She told me that she had talked to Faye. I was welcomed back to her house. Can't say I was happy about that fact, but it was what it was. And as long as I was in Amarillo, I didn't care whether I stayed under a bridge. I just wanted to be home. Cheerleading tryouts started Monday. Though I didn't want to try out, I knew it would make things easier with Faye. It was best just to try out. Besides, I liked cheerleading. It would preoccupy my time. And I was Cheerleader Natalie anyhow, and I had to continue to wear that mask, at least for a few more months. I turned seventeen in May, then it was just one more year. Only one more. I could handle that. I had lived through almost twelve of them with Faye and Jack. I could push through one more. I was almost at the end of the race.

We reached Amarillo shortly after midnight. I went over to Gina's house and saw my friend Olivia. When she saw me, she ran and gave me a huge hug, and we just cried. She too knew not to ask. I suppose my appearance told the story. I was so happy to see her. I was so happy to be home.

After hugs and, thankfully, food, I headed back to Faye's house. She was waiting on the porch for me. When I got out of the car, I couldn't help but notice the worried look on her face. And when she saw me, I also noticed a hint of concern. "Natalie?" she asked, making sure it was me.

"Hi," I answered skeptically.

"You look… Oh my gosh, what happened?"

She really didn't know? I thought. *Interesting.* "It doesn't matter.

I'm here now. Thanks for letting me come back." I thanked her, even though I didn't want to. I needed to. She let me come back, and Gina said she played a part in letting Adrianna and Cole let me go. Apparently, both she and Gina called, demanding to let me go. Gina said Faye called, threatening that she'd call the police. And Faye told them that she wanted me back and to let me leave in her car. I didn't really know how to handle that. Maybe she did care about me. Just maybe.

Monday morning was a big day. School. I was going back to Randall High School, and I was as excited as anyone could be about anything. I went to the office that morning and reenrolled. Once again, I was a student at RHS. It took awhile to get the paperwork done, but we had it handled. After Faye left, Officer Rodriguez and the counselor brought me to a conference room.

I told them everything. All that happened. My counselor started crying. And Officer Rodriguez, well, he looked mad. He asked me if I wanted to press charges, but I said no. I never wanted to see Cole or Adrianna ever again. I didn't care what they did as long as I never again had to set my eyes upon them.

By the time we finished talking, it was second period—my history class with Mrs. Herring. I was a little late, so I knocked on the door.

"Come in," I heard Mrs. Herring's voice.

When I walked in, almost instantaneously, cheers filled the room. Apparently, word got around that I was "gone." Mrs. Herring ran to me and gave me a huge hug. We both started crying. When I looked back up, the whole class was on their feet, clapping.

"Whoo, Natalie! You're back!" one of the guys shouted.

"Yeah! Woo-hoo! What happened? Where did you go? We heard you had been kidnapped or something crazy!" another one of the kids asked.

"It's a long story, but none of it matters. I'm back now. And I'm here to stay," I stated, smiling, stunned by the word *kidnapped*.

"Yeah! Cheerleader Natalie is back!" someone shouted. Another round of applause was offered. I couldn't help but laugh. That title, Cheerleader Natalie.

Yes, Cheerleader Natalie was back. And I wasn't going anywhere ever again. We sat down and started to get back on topic: World War II. As I took notes, I was so happy. History class, at that moment, was my favorite. And well, the topic, I could relate. Maybe I wasn't burned in an oven, stuck in a trench, or trapped on an island, but I felt I could extend some understanding when it came to the prisoner of war. To fight relentlessly and get nowhere. Truth be told, I'd been in a bit of a war myself. And parts of me knew mine wasn't quite over yet.

Home, Sweet Home

. . . .

A house is not a home unless it contains food and fire
for the mind as well as the body.

—Benjamin Franklin

. . . .

I ended up trying out for cheerleading, and I made it. I was on the Senior Varsity Squad, and I was actually pretty excited. I kept the same academic schedule though. I wanted to be a doctor now more than ever. Since my last ER visit, I realized that I was pretty dissatisfied with how that doctor "didn't want to get involved." I vowed that I would be a physician who did get involved. I would help when no one else would, regardless of what it would cost me.

Next year was going to be tough though. I had a lot on my plate, but it could be done. Where there is a will, there is a way.

Things at home were…well, different for a while, at least. Faye and I had a long sincere talk. We even decided to take counseling classes to "work out our differences." It was a long shot, but I knew it was best to try. I was about to turn seventeen, and I still had a year under her roof.

So we went to counseling. And it worked…for about a week. Not because I wasn't trying, but because I couldn't explain the situation. Faye and Jack were foster parents in the state of Texas. Therefore, anything said could be used against them, and their licensure would be taken away. And unfortunately, everything that I had to say, everything that Faye and I needed to work out, mostly fell on her account in conditions of neglect and harm, emotional and physical abuse. How could we talk about that without, well, talking about it? We just couldn't. The whole point of therapy is to talk about what's wrong, and I couldn't say a thing, or I'd be in trouble and back to square one.

We ended up only going to two sessions, which ended up being a complete waste of time. We tried to work things out on our own, but it only lasted about two weeks. Creatures of habit, I suppose. But things were back to normal before too long. I was back to taking care of the children, getting screamed at, having to do things that had no reasoning behind them. But even so, I was thankful. I was still in Amarillo, and that counted for something.

The beginning of April held hope. I had one month till my seventeenth birthday. Then, I had one year. That was my hope. No one would rescue me, but I would rescue myself. Before too long, I was going to be out on my own. I would be an adult and would make my own decisions. I started the application process to college, and I applied to every school except the ones located in Texas. I was going to leave, and I mean leave. New York was where I decided I wanted to go. Cornell University was a dream, and it was worth a shot. I had good grades, and I knew I could write a decent essay. I had letters of recommendations, and I felt I had what it took. I kept my goals a secret though. No one knew except me, and I was going to keep it that way. No one needed to know, and by the time they did, I would be long gone. It was my plan to leave and never come back. I couldn't risk Faye or Jack finding out. The whole reasoning behind my plan was to disappear. I realized, though, that had some downsides. I had good friends and teachers here in Amarillo, and I knew that I'd miss them. But there was no bond that could keep me here in the region of the Winters' home. Besides, most of my friends were going off to college as well. And regardless, people come and go. That's just how it worked in life. People would be there for you, for a little bit, and then they would leave. So honestly, there was no point to hold onto any certain individual. I could deal with being alone. I'd dealt with it my entire life. Now, I would just be alone in New York, which honestly sounded rather exciting.

I planned, because I knew it would be expensive and hard to even get there, but I had faith. My desire to leave was greater than any financial cost ever could be. To be honest, I didn't know how I was going to do it, but I planned to escape Faye and Jack's house forever. I needed to get a job that Faye didn't know about. I'd have to find a way to buy my own car without her knowing. I would save as much money as I possibly could in secret.

I would find a way. And I had just one year and a month to figure it all out. I had to get out of what everyone saw as a "home, sweet home."

Negligent Homicide

A little neglect may breed great mischief.

—Benjamin Franklin

The time passed quickly. I had two weeks left of my junior year. Finals were just around the corner, and I really needed time to prepare. One of the babies in our home, Emily, was really sick. She had kept me up the past two nights. She had chronic lung disease. The poor baby just couldn't breath. It was so bad that she had to get a temporary feeding tube placed through her nose because she was unable to get enough oxygen while sucking a bottle. Her condition wasn't getting any better. She had breathing treatments five times a day. Luckily, the nurse took care of her during the day and prepared the nighttime treatments. That saved me some time.

Tuesday afternoon, our coach informed us that cheerleading practice was put on hold for the next two weeks. She was giving us a break for finals, which was really nice and just what I needed. Normally, when I got home, I would go straight to my room. But today, I was starving. Fortunately, Faye finally applied for food stamps, and we got accepted. I suppose the hunger got to her, too.

For the first time in a very long time, we had food in the house. I went over to the pantry to see what would soothe my cravings.

"What are you looking for?" asked Faye.

"Oh, I'm starving. I just was going to get something to eat," I explained.

"Well, I'll make you something. What do you want? I have some chicken," she said nicely.

"Okay, that sounds good." I said in a leery tone. This woman, she had the craziest moods. You just never knew what she would be okay with, but I took what I got.

The chicken was grilling. The swing was right by the table, and little Emily was in it. She was soothed by the swing. I knew how she felt. But as I was watching her, I noticed her feeding tube was coming out of her nose.

"Hey." I grabbed Faye's attention. "Emily's feeding tube is almost out. I'll call the nurse," I offered.

"What? Wait, let me see." She walked over there and stopped the swing. I was watching her because I was confused. On a normal occasion, she would just say, "Yeah, call her." It was the proper procedure. Why was she checking?

But my curiosity ended when I saw what she did. Faye just pushed the tube back down. Which was the worst thing one could do. When these tubes come out, they have to be placed back in by a professional and, in most cases, x-rayed to make sure they are in the right place. It's easy for a small tube to enter the trachea rather than the esophagus, filling the lungs with milk rather than the stomach.

"Faye!" I shouted. "You can't do that. You have to—"

"Shut up, Natalie. You're not a doctor. She'll be fine," Faye said. But I was panicking inside. This was bad. Emily was starting to cough. Not a good sign.

"Seriously, you don't know if it went down her esophagus or not. We have to call the nurse." As I started walking toward the baby, Faye stepped in front of me.

"*We* are not going to do anything. *You* are going to mind your own business and get up to your room. I'm the mother. I take care of the children here. Now go!" She steered me in the direction of my room.

As I opened my door, I had the worst feeling in my gut, but I didn't know what to do. I knew that Emily was in danger, but so was I. Part of me didn't care. Part of me wanted to run back downstairs and pull the tube out myself and call the nurse. But I knew that even if that were my plan, I probably wouldn't succeed if Faye was still down there.

For about an hour, I pondered about what I should do and then I decided that I was going down. *The doctor who gets involved*, I reminded myself.

As I made it downstairs, Faye saw me but didn't say anything. I went over to the swing, and Emily was still in it. But when I saw her, she didn't look well at all. Without thinking, I went and turned off her feeding pump. Faye came over as I was picking her up.

"Call the nurse now," I demanded. Faye didn't hesitate because even she could see that Emily's color was not good. Her respirations had dropped significantly, and her heart rate was rapid and irregular. I decided to just go ahead and take the feeding tube out myself.

About thirty minutes later, the nurse showed up and took the baby's vitals. But by the next morning, little Emily was in pediatric ICU on a ventilator. Her lungs had been filled with milk during the time that I hesitated, and that time left her condition in a critical state.

The next morning, the level of guilt I felt was indescribable. Emily was now in the hospital, and I knew exactly why. I witnessed firsthand what Faye did. Not that she intentionally wanted to hurt Emily, but it was negligence. Medical negligence, and now there was a chance that Emily could lose her life. And I too was responsible. I had played a part in all of this. I shouldn't have held out for any amount of time. I should have acted quicker. I should have risked my own life before I let Emily's be put into danger.

I started to cry during government class that morning. I couldn't help myself. The whole situation was overwhelming. And to think that because of my actions, a baby could die… Well, I remembered that feeling, far too well… What it was to think a child would die by my hands. My cry broke into a sob. A friend sitting next to me asked if I was okay.

"No, I'm not okay. But I'm going to make it right," I stated through the tears. She had no idea what I was talking about, and she didn't need to. I just needed to hear myself, to tell myself that I was going to make a difference. I was done sitting around, allowing Jack and Faye to continue to hurt children. I had to make a stand.

As I rose out of my chair, I felt nervous, but there was no turning back. Once I gave the opportunity to myself, my drive took over. I told my teacher that I needed to speak with the counselor immediately. She saw the residue of my tears and agreed without question.

I left the room and headed straight to the counselor's office. As I arrived, Mrs. Clements greeted me. She noticed the troubled look in my eyes and told me to come back to her office.

When I got in the room, I couldn't say anything. Every time I tried to explain, I just broke down into tears. I wept for about fifteen minutes straight. Mrs. Clements knew I had something to say, but she also knew that I had to be able to say it when I was ready. After I stopped crying, I looked up at her, pleading with my eyes to give me a little push. I needed encouragement.

"It's okay, Natalie. Go ahead. I'm here to listen," she said in a soothing voice, in a motherly tone, like she was talking to a sick child. Mrs. Clements was a kind woman, and I knew I could trust her. I knew I could tell her the things that happened in our house, and she wouldn't second-guess me. She wouldn't go and tell Faye what I told her. And since the San Antonio experience, no one would question my seriousness when I claimed she was irrational and impulsive. And so, that's what I did. I started with what happened to Emily and explained how she was now in critical care. Then, well, it all just started flowing. I told of the abuse in the home. I talked about our living conditions. I explained how I was the one who had been taking care of the children. I just talked. I didn't mention Jack's sexual abuse; I wasn't ready for that. I had to take it one day, one session at a time. Slow and steady. When I finished, tears were still streaming from my eyes, and my hands were shaking terribly. I looked into Mrs. Clements' eyes, and all I could see was shock, just sheer surprise.

"Natalie, how long has this been going on?" she asked.

"My whole life, Mrs. Clements. My whole, entire life," I said.

The rest of the day we spent time making an official CPS report. The process was long, and the worst part of it was that nothing would happen today. Because, well, government agencies aren't exactly time efficient. All I had left to do was wait and act completely normal when I got home. I couldn't tip Faye off to what had taken place just a few hours before. And that was hard. It was difficult to know that I had to just come home and act like nothing was wrong. But at the same time, that's what I had always done. I came home and continued with the routine. The mask on my face. I decided that I would just act like nothing had happened and nothing would be done because, well, there was a chance that would be the case.

Later that week, Faye was notified that CPS was involved. A case was opened on Thursday, closed on Friday. Like I predicted, there was a chance that nothing would happen because usually, nothing ever did. Jack and Faye Winters had been reported to CPS many times. And every time, the report would be dismissed; there wouldn't be enough evidence or was proved somehow invalid. There was always something that caused them to be able to scrape by.

Oftentimes, Faye thought it was a joke and would tease about it. When she saw the Child Protective Service investigators, she would say, "Oh, am I being investigated again?" along with a chuckle. "Who's trying to take me down this time?"

She used to threatened people, as well. She warned, "Go ahead and call CPS. I'll even give you a quarter to do it! Ha! A quarter for your call!" Because she knew she was right. The Winters home was one of the only "medical group homes" available in the Texas Panhandle. And well, there was nowhere else for the kids to be placed; CPS just wants the children somewhere, anywhere. It doesn't matter, just so that they are placed. The system is too bogged down to consider whether the kids are actually safe. Just as long as they are in a home, everything is deemed sufficient.

However, her luck was about to change. My report had been ignored as I knew it would. But it so happened that Faye and Jack Winters were reported three times that week. The other two people, I cannot accurately identify. But because they both made a step toward the wrongdoing that was going on, things were about to change.

Agents came down from Austin to investigate rather than workers from the local department. Apparently, something appeared to be "fishy" about this whole thing. And they were right. They found unfinished reports, investigations that were opened and closed in the blink of an eye. They found corruption and negligence in all parts, on all accounts.

So another investigation was underway and by the right people; something was going to be done this time. An investigator came to my school and assured me of it. There were six children in the home in addition to myself. The investigation had proven that all of the medically sick children were in danger and were to be removed. But there were two other kids that Faye had adopted over the years, and unfortunately, they hadn't gathered enough evidence to take them yet. Their investigation was still on going. However, as the CPS investigator continued to explain the situation, I realized that he had only mentioned six children.

"Sir, what about me? Are you going to take me?" I questioned.

"Well, Natalie, you have just turned seventeen. The State of Texas sees you as an adult, and so Child Protective Services cannot take you, even though we have evidence to do so," he explained.

"What? So what am I supposed to do? Where am I supposed to go?" I demanded of him.

"Natalie, calm down. It's going to be all right," he assured me.

"But what is going to happen? I mean, you are going to take the kids, and then you are just going to tell me it's all right? You seem to be missing the fact that Faye, she is *insane!* She will go crazy when you take the kids, I promise you that. And then you think she is just going to let me be there with no harm done?" I was shouting at this point. I was infuriated. I had waited my whole life to be rescued. I waited my whole life for people to listen to what I was saying, and now they were listening. I was believed, but I couldn't be helped?

"Natalie, listen. We are talking to the District Attorney. Both Faye and Jack are in a lot of legal trouble right now. You are going to be emancipated. That means you will be able to leave no matter what Faye says. This situation is not a good one, and the ongoing police investigations have continued to prove that. I spoke with George Atkins, the DA, yesterday, and we are determining what needs to be done," he explained. "When you are emancipated, you will be able to leave. You will be an adult."

"But I thought you just said that at seventeen I was considered an adult in the state of Texas?" I questioned him. This just wasn't making any sense.

"Almost. There are still stipulations and roads to cross. You need to be emancipated to prevent yourself from getting into any trouble."

"Trouble? What do you mean trouble?" I demanded.

"Well, if you left right now, Faye could put a runaway report on you, and you would be taken to juvenile hall. There are a number of things that could happen, and well, none of them would be good for you," he said.

"Well, thanks. Thank you so much for all of your help!" I said in a sarcastic tone. "So when will I know that it's okay for me to just get up and leave?" I asked.

"I'll call you and let you know. It's all a process, but Mr. Atkins is trying to expedite everything," he promised. "Just be careful in the meantime. I'm sorry you are in this position, and I wish there was more I could do."

"Me, too," I uttered under my breath. "Me, too."

Summer had begun, along with cheerleading practice. Four weeks had passed since I last talked to the CPS worker, and I had heard nothing. To say that I had doubt about what he said would be an understatement. To be honest, I didn't trust them. I never had trusted those officials, and I wasn't going to start now. Often, I didn't know how good of an idea it was to report Faye and Jack. I mean, after all, they were a foster home. Possibly they were all this way. What if I was sending the babies to a place that was worse? At least here, I knew that I could take care of them. The thoughts weighed on me. The whole situation did.

I had cheerleading practice starting at nine that morning, and it was 8:15 a.m. Time to get up and go. On my drive to the school, I heard my cell phone ringing. I figured it was Faye calling to see if I had made it yet. Her control issues drove me crazy, and as I reached for it, I was half-tempted not to answer. But then I realized it was a number I didn't recognize.

"Hello?" I answered.

"Hi, Natalie, this is Tom Wilson from Child Protective Services. I just wanted to call and give you the news," he explained. "And well, I needed to warn you. We are coming this morning to remove four of the six children from the home. The investigation is still pending on the other two. But, you, you may leave. I got word from George Atkins, Natalie. You have been verbally emancipated. There won't be enough time to go through the formal process. Now, this is very unofficial, but you may go. You can leave."

I tried to respond, but I couldn't. I mean, I was happy, nervous, and petrified all at the same time. I had been emancipated and told to leave. Something I wished for my whole life, but that's just the thing. It wasn't my life I was worried about.

"I'm sorry, sir, but I can't leave. Not until all of the children are safe. Plus, I still have to figure out where to go. This isn't as simple as you make it sound. And on that note, sir, I just want to warn you. I hope you have the police force to accommodate you during this pickup," I warned him.

"What do you mean?" he asked with a nervous laugh.

"Well, you can believe me or not, but Faye is going to lose it. I mean, she is going to go crazy. And if you don't have evidence for the other two children, you soon will," I said in a steady voice.

"Yes, ma'am. Well, we are going to arrive about nine thirty. I will give you a call and let you know what's happening," he said.

"Yeah, good luck," I stated with slight sarcasm, but with underlying seriousness. As I pulled up to the school, I felt bad for those agents. They seriously had no idea what they were embarking upon.

Cheerleading practice was a killer. It was extremely hot outside, and our coach was in a conditioning mood, but I was thankful for the distraction. The push-ups took my mind away from what was happening at home. They distracted me from the realization that my life was being turned upside down.

We stopped at noon for lunch. I went to my car and checked my phone. I had about five missed calls from various numbers. *Yep*, I thought to myself. *She went crazy.*

I called the Mr. Wilson back first. As the phone rang, I grew nervous. I knew that whatever the situation was, it probably wasn't a good one.

"Natalie?" he answered the phone.

"Yes, sir, it's me. I'm sorry I missed your call, I—"

"Natalie, listen to me," he interrupted. "Do *not* come home. Do you hear me? Don't come back." He warned me with a seriousness that sent chills down my spine.

"What happened?" I asked.

"You were right. Faye lost it. Luckily, Jack is at work. I don't know if we could have handled the both of them. I brought two cops with me, well, really just to humor you, but you were right. She went ballistic on us as we were taking the kids. Like she had a psychotic break. You cannot be around her. If you go back, I'm worried that you will be in danger. The cops had to hold her down, Natalie. They almost arrested her right there." He talked in a tone that was serious. But there were things he wasn't taking into consideration.

"Did you take the other two kids?" I asked him.

"No, Natalie. I didn't have the authority. The little boy in his statement he claims that Faye has never abused him in any way. And the girl, she won't talk at all. Because Faye adopted them, it is much more difficult, as I told you before."

"Look, Mr. Wilson," I said very sternly. "The little boy is not telling the truth because he is scared. Faye threatens us, and he is silenced by fear. The little girl, she is mentally challenged. Faye and Jack adopted them so they could get their disability checks. You know, for steady income. Trust me, you need to get them out of there, Mr. Wilson."

"Natalie, I am trying my best. But please, for once, think about yourself. Don't come home. Don't," he urged.

"Sir, I don't think you understand. There are still two other children in the home. And if it's dangerous for me, it will be dangerous for them. I have to go protect them. Until you can get them removed, my place is there," I said with a tone of despair. Lord only knows that I wanted to leave, but I knew I couldn't.

I went on. "And besides, even if I didn't go back, tell me, where should I go? What should I do?" I waited for a moment for his response. When he said nothing, I continued. "You see, you say nothing because you have no idea. I'm not saying I'm not capable of being an adult, but my leaving cannot just happen overnight. I have to have a plan as to what I need to do. I cannot jeopardize my future. And I certainly will not jeopardize the safety of the other children that are still in danger. You, sir, have underestimated me. I speak the truth. I told you today would be bad, and I will say that the days forward will only get worse. I suggest that you get the evidence prepared for the other children as quickly as possible."

He didn't say anything at first. I suppose he was shocked at my tone, but it was the truth. I knew what I had to do. I had to go back. I also think he realized there was no talking me out of it.

"Natalie, be careful. I will do what I can on my end. Just know that at anytime, you may leave," he repeated. "Just be careful."

As I hung up, I couldn't help but notice the anxiety in my stomach as I headed to my car. I had no idea what lay ahead, but I knew that it was going to be… scary. Part of me wanted to rush home, for the two kids, but the other part of me wanted to take my time. I wasn't looking forward to seeing the situation firsthand.

My speed reflected my hesitation. The engine would roar when I accelerated with my urge to arrive. Then dwindle when I ceased to press that gas pedal and eased the brake, wishing I could just turn around and never look back. But before I chose that route, I turned into our drive. I had no idea what was going on in the house. As I approached the door, there was an eerie silence.

When I walked in, the house was a disaster. There were tubes and equipment thrown all over the place. Things were crushed and shattered all over the floor. It looked as though a tornado had somehow demolished the inside.

I went to find the two kids. There were in the playroom. When they saw me, neither said anything; they just looked at me with worry in their eyes. They were young, but they knew we were not in a good situation.

"It's okay. I'm going to protect you," I promised them. And I meant it. I wasn't going to let anything happen to them. But I needed to know where Faye was. "Where is Mom?"

The five-year-old responded, "In her room."

"Okay, stay here till I come and get you," I told him. The other girl was about ten, but she was mentally challenged, and her mental age was probably around four. "Lamar, you make sure Taci stays here, okay?" I asked the little boy. I knew he understood what was going on.

I walked toward Faye's bathroom. I could hear the water running. I braced myself for anything because Lord only knew what I would find when I opened that bathroom door.

As the door creaked open, I saw Faye in the bathtub. She was just sitting there with the water running over the edges. But she was rocking back and forth like an autistic child, holding a razor in her hand. Even though I tried to prepare myself before walking in, the sight of her was shocking to me. She had lost her mind.

"Faye," I interrupted. "What are you doing?"

"They took my babies. They took my money," she said in a voice that was emotionless.

Part of me thought, *You have to be freaking kidding me. Your money?* But I didn't say anything about that. I just asked, "What are you doing?"

"Doesn't matter. Nothing matters now," she said.

"Faye, it does matter, okay? I'm still here, and so are the other two kids," I tried to console her.

"I don't want you. You don't bring any income in! And the other two, their checks are only $500 a month. It's not enough to support us," she said hopelessly.

I stood there. I always knew it was about the money to her, but hearing her reasoning, was appalling to me. And my sympathy was decreasing by the second. Watching her rock back and forth, it was something I'd never seen in her before: despair. I knew that all her misery had been caused by herself, but seeing her, somehow, I felt the need to help her.

"Faye, can I see the razor?" I asked cautiously. When she didn't respond, I knew what was going through her mind. Again, more sternly, I said, "Faye, give me the razor. Now."

She looked up at me. There was a hopelessness in her eyes. As much as I despised this woman, I didn't want her to die. It just wasn't in my nature not to care.

"Please, Faye. Give me the razor. You don't want to do this. Okay, give it to me."

My coercion was working. She handed over the razor and said, "Just go. Leave me alone. I'm not going to kill myself. Just go. I want to be alone."

I believed her and took her advice, along with the other razors in the bathroom. Just in case. I sat and watched the children in the playroom, thinking about what I needed to do. This was a hard decision, but I knew it was the only way. I needed to get a full-time job, and in doing that, other things had to go. Faye was right, $500 a month was not enough. And Jack was undependable. I couldn't let these kids do without. I didn't know how long it would take Mr.

Wilson to gather the extra evidence. Surely from the outcome today, he knew. But, I was responsible for them until then. I had to work and my coaching job wasn't enough. I had to be some kind of parent to them. And part of me knew that over the next few weeks, I was going to have to take care of Faye, too.

I grabbed the kids and put them in my car, along with a bag that held all of my cheerleading uniforms. If there was one thing I knew, it was time for me to grow up. It was time that I became an adult. These children needed me, and I was the only thing they had until they were removed. I always had been. I couldn't leave them. I couldn't leave, even though I wanted to. Even though I had permission, nobility came before self-gratification. I had to do what was best for them, not what was best for myself.

The drive back to the school was one I didn't forget. That morning, I told the CPS that becoming an adult didn't happen overnight, and I was right. For me, I didn't become one overnight. I became an adult within about a half an hour. I knew the kids were hungry, so I stopped at Sonic and bought them some corn dogs and drinks. I didn't have much money, but they needed a treat. I couldn't imagine what their little eyes saw this morning, and thinking about it made me cringe. I let them start eating as I drove to the cheerleading gym that held our afternoon practice. I couldn't help but cry, and I put the car in park. I turned to the children and told them we were going in for a moment and to just stand by the door.

"I'm just going to drop something off. I'll be right back, okay? I won't be gone five minutes. Just wait right here," I ordered as we stepped inside.

"Yes, ma'am," little Lamar responded. I grabbed the bag that held my uniforms. The bag that held the rest of my teenage years. I realized that a few months ago, I didn't care whether or not I was a cheerleader this year. But somehow, as the time passed, I realized how much it meant to me, to my sanity. And it was something to just not try out, but now I was quitting. And if there was anything I loathed, it was quitting. I just didn't believe in it. But, I knew that there were bigger things to be concerned with.

As I walked in the gym all of the girls knew something was wrong. I was not one to be late, and practice had been going on for almost an hour. And I know they spotted me carrying my uniforms.

I walked up to my coach. "I'm sorry I am late, and I'm also sorry that I can't explain why I'm handing you my uniforms. But I cannot be a part of the squad any longer. I have other obligations that have arisen. Please forgive me." As I handed her my bag, the gym was dead silent. Everyone was in awe. "Natalie is quitting?" said the expression on their faces.

"Yes," I wanted to answer, but I said nothing. I just turned and walked out. No one stopped to ask why, and I was thankful for that. To be honest, I just didn't have it in me to explain. And I just really needed to get out of there. I couldn't let anyone know that I was about to break. Plus, I had Taci and Lamar to take care of. I was the only constant they had. I was their mother. I was sixteen. I was an adult.

As the old saying goes, the bad, well, it usually get's worse. And that's exactly what happened. The summer was horrid. The two children were still in the home because, well, l don't know. I hadn't heard from Mr. Wilson. But if it was a case of "not enough evidence," they would soon be taken because the very ground was crumbling beneath our feet.

We had always been poor, but we were now at a new level of poverty. We had no money. I mean we had absolutely no money. The bank repossessed the van, and our electricity was shut off for most of the summer. Our house smelled terrible and was becoming infested with bugs—worms, roaches, you name it. I couldn't sleep because I didn't dare shut my eyes. There was no telling what would be in your bed when you awoke.

We still had food stamps, thank God. If it wasn't for that, we wouldn't have been able to eat at all. That summer, was the summer of hell. And honestly, it was as hot as hell fire. The one hundred degrees outside was cool compared to the inside of the house. Faye was no longer sad. Now she was angry, looking for someone to blame. And of course, I was a great target. She patronized me. I knew she knew I had something to do with what happened, but I wasn't stupid enough to admit it to her this time. I remembered all too well what happened the last time I made a report. Even though those wounds were years old, they were still very fresh. But a new level of evil had arisen in Faye. She used her weapons, and she used them well. She was threatening me constantly. I wasn't allowed to go anywhere alone. And I mean anywhere at all. Even trips to the library were timed and monitored. I was her captive. And she had nothing else to focus on other than me and what I was doing. Later in the summer, I finally talked her into letting me volunteer at the hospital for about four hours once a week. That was my recreation.

Jack was still working at the prison, but there were complications there, too. The night he got in a wreck and killed an innocent man was coming back to haunt him. He ended up going to jail for a few weeks. It was nice having him gone, but it was also more difficult. In the past few weeks, he had been bringing some money home. That was helpful, and at this point, I'd take all the help I could get. I had started working at Kohl's Department Store. I had to quit my job at the cheerleading gym; it was too emotional for me. I was working as much as they would let me, trying to bring in an income to support five people. But it wasn't enough. Nothing ever was. And even if it was enough, it wouldn't be for long.

Every two weeks, Faye forced me to give her my paycheck. I never saw a dime of the money I earned. Sometimes she would pay the bills, other times she would blow it. Every week, I just hoped she'd let me hold on to some of the money, just so that I could at least get the electricity and water paid for. But truth be told, I couldn't win for losing. We were constantly being bombarded with a new problem, and Faye and Jack were getting deeper and deeper in their legal problems. By mid-July, both Jack and Faye had investigations of negligent homicide currently ongoing against them.

But, the hardest thing to deal with was the hatred. Faye had risen to a new level of mean. She told me the most hurtful things, and during that time, every blow, whether verbal or physical, hit me hard. Everyday, I listened to at least one thirty minute lecture after my shift at the store. She would tell me that I was stupid and ugly. That I was a piece of trash. She would spend forever explaining how much she thought God screwed up by creating me. I tried not to listen, but during these times, I was required to look at her. If not, the back of her hand would refocus my attention.

The worst of these days was on my seventeenth birthday. It was like the day itself gave her a new found fury to fuel her comments. She proceeded to tell me that "it must have been hard for your mother today… Knowing that she gave birth to a worthless piece of s— like you." On and on and on she ranted, making me agree.

"You are stupid aren't you?" she'd ask.

"Yes, ma'am," I agreed.

"You are hideous, aren't you?"

"Yes ma'am."

"It would have been better for the world, if you wouldn't have been born, right?"

"Yes ma'am."

That conversation carried on for the day, and frankly, for the rest of the summer.

After a while though, I grew tired of her comments and threats. They were starting to affect me, even though I tried not to listen. The heat and the hate were rubbing off. I became angry. I had become an angry and hateful person over that summer. I knew I couldn't stay there much longer. It was becoming too much to handle. I cared for the children, so I stayed. But before too much longer, my presence wasn't going to make a difference. I was coming to a point where planning my escape became all I could think about. I wouldn't leave in the summer. I knew that I would need the help of the school to pull this off. I would need the protection of the school day.

I talked Faye into letting me volunteer more at the hospital. Some days she'd let me go so "she wouldn't have to see my awful face." But some days she wouldn't. Everything that summer was a gamble. You just never knew.

I loved volunteering. I loved seeing people overcome their problems and get better. Somehow, it gave me hope. When I did volunteer, Faye would call just to ensure I was there. But, after a while, she stopped. One day, I decided to chance not going. I went to see one of the nurses that used to care for the children, Bethany. I was incredibly thankful she opened the door. When she saw who it was, she just hugged me. "Natalie! What are you doing here?" she asked.

I told her all about what was happening at home. How bad everything had gotten. She knew a lot about Jack and Faye's behavior, though not all.

"Natalie, it's time for you to leave. You have to let Child

Protective Services take care of Lamar and Taci. You have to get out of there... if you don't soon, you might not ever," Bethany said.

"I know, but... What if they don't get the kids out, Bethany? What if they are hurt?"

"Natalie. You are seventeen. It's time for you to take care of yourself and not everyone else. You cannot hold this weight anymore. It is too much and not your responsibility. Leave it to God to take care of the kids. He will. But you have to take care of you. For once, Natalie, put yourself first."

I listened to Bethany. Her words resonated with me on a deep level. I cared for Taci and Lamar, but I, myself, was falling apart trying to care for them. And when they left, who's to say that I would have been able to leave after that? The summer had taken a toll on me. I hardly even recognized myself.

"I know I have to get out of there, Bethany. Will you help me? Please, I will need your help to do this," I begged of her.

"I know. We'll figure it out... Natalie, have you ever thought about contacting your biological family? On your mom's side?" she asked.

"Um, no. Why would I do that?" I wondered aloud.

"Well, I was just thinking that if they were good people, it would be a good thing for you to be with them. To be with your family. I have your mom's obituary, and it lists names that we can look up."

"My mom's obituary?" I asked.

"Yes. When she died, I saved it for you. I knew Faye would never let you see it," she explained.

"Oh." I felt a little overwhelmed. I'd never seen my mother but only imagined what she looked like. When she died, I didn't have the courage to look up her picture. I knew it would be too much for me to handle, in addition to the regret I felt about not calling her. But I suppose the image I had wasn't very accurate, as I had Faye's negative connotations about her embedded in my brain.

As Bethany came back into the room, she held a small folded slip of paper. As she handed it to me, I became very nervous. My thoughts drifted to the chance I missed just a few years back. In some sense, I felt like I was meeting her for the first time. As I unfolded the paper, I saw my mother for the very first time. She was…beautiful. She had long curly hair with a perfect smile. Her eyes held a color of hazelnut brown, as mine did, placed underneath perfectly arched eyebrows. Her nose was small and rounded—symmetrical. She looked happy. She looked perfect. And as I looked closer, I couldn't help but recognize some of the features we had in common. I looked like her.

My eyes filled with tears. My mother was beautiful, regardless of her actions. And in that moment, I grew to love her. I don't guess that follows logic, but it was the truth. When I saw her, I saw myself, and that was something I had never experienced. It was real.

Listed under her picture were funeral dates and times, but most importantly, a list of remaining relatives. I pondered and supposed I should give it a try. I saw Kellie's name, along with Robert's and Morgan's, though we all had different last names. My grandparents were listed, along with my great-grandpa and aunt. I was skeptical, but then I realized that I really didn't have any other options.

"Yeah, we could find them. Maybe they will help me," I agreed. It was a start.

For the rest of the summer, that was my project: to find my family. I would go to the hospital for about an hour then just head to Bethany's house to research.

It didn't take long before I found my aunt. Turns out that my cousin was actually a girl on my former cheerleading squad. I knew who she was. Bethany and I decided to call my aunt. And not too long after that, we met. Her grandparents had passed away. But my great-grandfather was still alive. She explained so much about my family. About my mother. There was so much information.

I couldn't help but ask, "Why didn't you all want me? Why didn't you contact me after my mom died? Kellie, when I talked to her, that was the last time I saw her. I never heard from her again," I explained.

"Natalie, we tried to contact you. My mom, she called Faye and talked to her about you meeting us. She called long before Kellie even talked to you. My mom and your dad's mom both called Faye. Faye told us that she told you and that you said that you didn't have any interest in us. And, well, we believed her. But my mom and dad, your grandparents on your mom's side, they kept an eye on you. I found a box after they died. They had pictures of you from your cheerleading games. Newspaper reports from the honor roll. They had your original birth certificate and other things that belonged to you when you were younger. There were pictures of you with your dad and Charlotte holding you. I can show them to you if you like, sometime. But, Natalie, they did love you. We all did, but we just assumed you were happy. That you were living a normal, happy life. I once called Faye because I knew my daughter, Rachel, would be cheering with you. When I told Faye, she became very upset and told me not to say anything, and Rachel couldn't either. I knew she was controlling, but I just figured she was unsure of us. I had no idea. None of us, we had no idea."

I couldn't respond. I was so shocked. My family... They loved me. And Faye had prevented us from being together. All of those nights, I believed no one cared for me. That no one loved me. Faye and Jack Winters stole from me—memories, laughter, and smiles. I cried at the thought, knowing that I missed out on so much. But also at the fact that I knew someone cared. My grandparents had been watching me. They had seen me cheer, seen my grades. They cared about me. They loved me.

Both Bethany and I explained that Faye was much worse than controlling and what was going on. I knew my aunt was skeptical, but after observing the lengths we had to take to be able to talk to her—the sneaking around, the careful planning—she began to understand. After a while, she agreed that I needed to get out of there. She told me that I could come live with her. I was so delighted and thankful. She didn't even really know me and was offering me a place to stay.

I was also able to meet my other siblings, Morgan and Robert. It was kind of strange. We were all really different from one another. I mean, we just grew up in different worlds. And though they were skeptical of me, they were nice enough. Everything was coming together, slowly but surely.

The final week of July arrived, and we had a plan. I was going to wait until school started before leaving. It was best that they knew what was going on so they could help. Jack had started working the night shift at the prison, and Faye got a nighttime job, as well. The hunger and heat finally got to them both, motivating them to actually work.

On Labor Day Weekend, it just so happened that they were

both scheduled to work that Monday night. It was perfect. I had the first week of school to perfect everything and notify my counselor of what was going on. I felt bad that I was leaving the two kids, but I was able to speak with Mr. Wilson. It wouldn't be long before they were taken out of there, too. As I told him what I was doing, I made him promise me that he would rescue those kids.

"Mr. Wilson, please. You have to get them out of there. I've stayed as long as I can bear, but I just can't do it anymore."

"I know, Natalie. You are so brave. The papers will be filed soon, and they will be removed. Faye and Jack's legal trouble has all but paved the way. I promise, I'll get them out." His words were sincere.

"Okay. Thank you, Mr. Wilson. For everything."

Early August had finally arrived. The Sunday night before school started, I was so anxious. I only had one week left, and even still, that seemed like an eternity. Part of me was so nervous about this plan. I was scared that it wouldn't work, something would go wrong, and I would end up in a worse situation. But I had to take the chance.

Both Faye, Jack, and I had been working, but regardless, Faye and Jack took control of the money. I'd try to get them to pay the bills, but Faye and Jack took care of their wants and needs before anyone else. There was money coming in, but honestly I had absolutely no idea where it was going.

Our electricity had been on and off throughout the summer. I just couldn't understand how that was not a priority for them. It seemed to me that would be the most vital of the bills, but not in their eyes apparently. The electricity had been out the whole weekend, during the dead heat of August. However, Faye went to the store

Friday afternoon before it was shut off. She bought a whole lot of groceries, including a load of meat. But by Friday evening, the power was off again, and we had no way to keep the food cool.

I asked Faye if we could take them somewhere, but she refused. Slowly, the smell of spoiled food filled the air. By Sunday evening, the entire house smelled like rotting meat, a smell that I will never forget. Our place was infested with bugs and mice. Being inside was nauseating. The whole place was dirty and disgusting. We were without running water, and there wasn't enough soap in the world to cleanse the inside. The air was stuffy and hot. And though the physical atmosphere was toxic, the emotional tension was fatal.

One more week, I told myself. *One more week.*

That Sunday evening, I was working on homework. My goal was still set on becoming a physician, and I was trying to do some reading for my AP biology course. But it was just so hard to concentrate. I was nervous about everything. The plan. The future. *Everything.* But while my worries were numerous, I realized sitting there, reading by candlelight, soaked in sweat, with the smell of putrid food in the air, fighting bugs and rats, that I had to take the chance. No matter what happened, I had to leave. Whatever the future held, I doubted it could be any worse than this, than here. This was rock bottom. In all actuality it was far past that. This was a pit, surely like the ones scattered amongst the grounds of hell.

Labor Day

This giant fleet of American warships—a modern armada—churns across the ocean day and night for a journey of four thousand miles. It moves with the inevitability of a railroad schedule. It stops for nothing, it deviates for nothing. The United States, having been surprised at Pearl Harbor and then raked in battle after battle by the onrushing forces of imperial Japan, has finally stabilized and gathered its strength. Now the American giant is fully awake and cold-eyed. It is stalking an ocean, rounding the curve of the earth, to crush its tormentor.

—James Bradley, *Flags of Our Fathers*

The first day of my senior year was a big day. My schedule was insane. First period, I had advanced health occupations, then AP biology, AP government, then college algebra. After lunch, I was in a dual-credit humanities class, then I had English and Spanish 3. It was a large load to carry. And by the end of the day, with all that was happening, I didn't know if I would be able to hold it together.

During lunch, I went to talk to Mrs. Clements and Officer Rodriguez. I told them my plan. I was going to leave early Labor Day morning while both Jack and Faye were at work. My uncle and brother were going to come over that evening to help me get my things, and then I was out of there. But there was a slight problem, as Officer Rodriguez explained, "Natalie, this is well thought out, but you are missing one thing. There are two kids in the home. If you leave them, Faye could charge you with abandonment, and from what we've learned about her, that is something she would do."

"Abandonment?" I questioned.

"Yes, Natalie. Leaving minors alone, when they were under your supervision," he explained.

"Abandonment. Leaving a vulnerable child, in an unknown, dangerous situation. Leaving them alone, and walking away for yourself..." I started to cry. I knew what it was. I had been through it.

"Natalie," Ms. Clements soothed me. "It's alright, don't cry. We'll figure a way around it, okay? Don't cry. Don't lose hope."

I listened to her words, but that's not what concerned me. Here I was planning my escape and was leaving two children... I was acting in a way that my father did. And the very thought of having those kids feel the way I did was gut wrenching. I broke into sobs.

"Natalie. Calm down. It's going to be alright, shhhh." Officer Rodriguez was trying to console me, but I knew that he had no idea why I was crying.

"Abandonment. That's what I should be charged with. Because that's what I'm doing. I'm just leaving these kids. I... I can't do it. Maybe I shouldn't go. They need me... They..."

"Natalie, stop." Officer Rodriguez was very stern. "Listen to me. These children are not your responsibility. It is the State's responsibility to care for them. Not yours. You cannot carry this burden. Maybe legally it is abandonment, but in all actuality, it isn't, because they are not, should not, be in your care. You are a child, Natalie. You've been through more than I'll ever know. And I say that, because I look in your eyes, and I see the hurt. I see the pain. There is a sorrow that doesn't belong. Natalie, I know this is hard, and I know you have carried the burden of caring for these children your whole life, but it's time to let it go. You have to do what's best for you. You have to walk away. What Faye and Jack do, you cannot predict, and you are no longer in a position to protect. Natalie, you've thought about this. And I know you want it. There comes a time, when you just have to jump. You have to go forth, even if you have no idea where forward is. You love those kids, and they love you. But Natalie, for once, love yourself enough to walk away. If you don't now, you might not ever."

His words were profound. But they held resonation with me and I knew that he was right. And as much as I hated myself for leaving them, I knew that Officer Rodriguez was right. I knew that I had to chance it. The time had come where it was too much. What if I never escaped? The thought haunted me. I had to get away from the Winters' home. I just had to. My tears were steadily streaming down my face. I looked Officer Rodriguez in the eyes, and said, "What are my options?" I had to keep moving forward.

Officer Rodriguez thought for a moment. "Is there any way you can stay at the house until one of them comes home, Natalie? That would resolve the issue."

I thought. "Well, Jack usually gets home first. I... I could wait for him to arrive before leaving, but before Faye gets home."

"Okay, good. Good. If you leave with an adult there, it'll be fine. There will be no basis for the charge."

"Alright. But what about the emancipation? Mr. Wilson said that I could just go. Right?" I wanted to make sure everything was in the clear. I didn't want this situation to be harder than it already was.

"Well, I spoke with the DA's office. Your emancipation was verbal and, well, under the radar. All of the official documentation is absent. All of this is off the record because to do it formally, well, you would be eighteen before it was completed. So technically, Faye can file a runaway report on you. Nothing can be done, just as long as you come to school, but if she does, it will take a while to clear. George Atkins will have to jump through some hoops for you."

As he spoke, I began to get cold feet. My biggest priority was to leave, but I also had to make sure I wasn't going to get in any kind of trouble. I couldn't have anything on my record that would cause me to lose scholarship opportunities or prevent me from getting into medical school.

Officer Rodriguez saw the worry on my face. "Natalie, we will help you. It's going to be okay. Just make sure you are careful. Here is my number. If it goes bad, call me. Okay?"

"You're sure?" I looked to him and Mrs. Clements for reassurance.

"Yes, Natalie. We are here for you. It's time," Mrs. Clements soothed.

"It is going to work out, Natalie. One way or another. Just have faith," Officer Rodriguez reassured me. "Just keep a hold of my card. And seriously, call me if you need *anything*. Anything at all."

"Yes, sir," I responded. "I will. Thank you." I left the office feeling a little discouraged, but not enough to back out... At least not yet...

The week flew by. I hardly saw Faye or Jack because I was too busy with homework. I already had tests and quizzes to prepare for. As I said, school was a heavy load this year.

But before I knew it, Sunday evening had arrived. I was nervous and doing my best to present myself as calm, normal. But I was afraid some nerves were showing through. I started to gather some of my stuff together. I needed to get things where they could easily be transported out. But Faye noticed.

"What are you doing?" she said from my door.

"I'm just cleaning my room. Going through things I don't need," I said nonchalantly.

"Oh, okay. Good to see you doing something useful rather than having your head stuck in a stupid book," she lectured.

"Yep!" I said as she walked out. What an idiot she was. I mean, seriously? Like reading really is a hindrance to one's usefulness? Moron.

By seven o'clock that evening, both Jack and Faye were gone. Jack would be back about 5:30 a.m. Faye would be back around 6:00 a.m. I had a thirty-minute slot. I would leave when Jack arrived. He was too slow to catch on to what was really going on. I went to my room and packed everything I could. I planned on taking everything. I didn't have much, but what little there was, was all that I had. It was best just to take it all and never look back. I was sure not to take what wasn't in my room though. That was another thing Faye could pull on me, theft charges. And I knew she would do whatever she could get away with.

Around midnight, there was a knock on the door. My uncle and brother had arrived. I couldn't help but be in awe that they showed up. I had only met them a few weeks ago, and here they were to my rescue. Just like a family would be. Nevertheless, the idea of a family, it was all still foreign. They took all of my stuff and loaded it into the truck.

"Is that all?" my brother asked.

"Yes, that's everything," I said. "All that's left is me."

"Okay. Well, I'll be back around four thirty. I'm going to park down the street. If you aren't out of the house by six o'clock, I'm coming to get you. All right?" my uncle said. He was very nice. Caring. I think that he more than any of my family members grasped how crazy Faye was.

"Okay, okay. Sounds good. There shouldn't be a problem. Just as long as Jack gets here before Faye, all will be well," I ensured.

"All right. Good luck," my brother said.

"If you have any trouble, call us," my uncle ordered.

"I will. Thank you so much. I know I don't know you, but I am so thankful that you are my family," I said tearfully. Neither of them responded. They just nodded. Over the past weeks, they had learned about the life I had lived. My siblings grew up with my grandparents. Though Charlotte was in and out of their lives, their childhood was relatively normal. They grew up loved and taken care of. I knew they felt sorry for me. I also knew that they saw the fear in my eyes when I spoke of Jack and Faye. So they were helping. And I was thankful.

I waited around for the rest of the evening. My nerves were on end. My mind lingered and drew conclusions and summaries for tomorrow morning, most of them bad. *Stop it*, I told myself. *Think positively. In a few hours, it will be over.*

As the night rolled by, I wandered to where the two children were sleeping. They looked so peaceful, so innocent. I began to be immersed in guilt. I felt so horrible about it, but I knew that this was my chance. It was my opportunity, and they would be removed soon.

I walked over to Lamar and gently woke him. I needed to tell him something. "Lamar! Lamar!" I whispered quietly while slightly shaking him. He awoke, but it took him a minute to emerge out of his sleep.

"Hey," I whispered. "I have something to tell you."

"What, Natalie?" he asked in a confused and sleepy voice.

"Lamar, I want you to know that I love you very much. I love you with my whole heart. I will always love you, and I'm so sorry that I have to leave you. I'm so sorry for walking away, and one day I hope you will forgive me." Pain, fear, and hurt were stuck in my throat. The feeling of what it was like to be left, to be abandoned, was flooding back to me. "And soon, you will be leaving, too. You'll get a new family and be so happy. You are going to be wonderful. You are smart and talented and perfect. Okay? Remember that, Lamar. Please remember."

"But, Natalie, where you going?" he asked with a yawn.

"I'm going…home. But I love you, Lamar. Don't ever forget that. Tell Taci tomorrow that I love her, too, okay?" He was confused, but I prayed he heard the words that I spoke. I can't help but think that if my father would have said something along those lines, it would have helped me. "Now, go back to sleep, Sweetheart. Good night," I soothed as the tears rolled down my cheeks.

Faye always told me I was worthless. And honestly, I agreed with her on this night. As the hours passed, I would talk myself in and out of what I was doing. *Stop, Natalie.* I instructed myself. *You can't stop a moving train.* I just hoped Mr. Wilson would get them out before the end of the week. I felt horrible about all of this, but I had to do it. And now, there was no turning back.

Five o'clock was here before I knew it. I had half an hour before Jack showed up. It went by soon enough, but Jack was nowhere to be seen. Before I knew it, it was 5:45 a.m. Then 5:50a.m. Then… 5:55 a.m. I was beginning to panic. I had five minutes until Faye pulled up the drive. She would be on time. She always was. Where was he?

Then out of nowhere, I saw him pull up. I was about to faint from anxiety waiting by the front door. He walked in.

"Hey, Jack. I'm going for a run! See ya!" The run was accurate. In no way was I lying. I was running. Running away from there and never coming back.

He just nodded his head. "This early?" he asked.

"Yep, see ya!" I walked out the door, and out of the corner of my eye, I saw Faye's van pulling up the drive. Fear surged through my body. And I ran, and when I say ran, I mean I ran for my life. In that moment, I'm pretty sure I could have beaten an Olympian with my speed. I pushed myself hard, trying to muster all the speed that I was capable of. The thought of Faye finding out; the thought of what she would do; the thoughts of what she'd done; the many times I'd been struck down; all of the times that she screamed at me, telling me I was stupid, that I was ugly, that I was a mistake; the nights of torment from Daddy Jack; the hurt; the pain; the tears. Everything surged through my mind. Running. Fast. I didn't care to look back. I was *running*. When I reached my uncle's truck, I jumped in and screamed, "Go! Go! Go!"

He peeled out. I knew it wouldn't take long now. She saw me, I knew she did. I had the cell phone in my hand. I didn't plan on answering, but I was expecting calls. Part of me was unsure of what her reaction would be. Luckily, voice mail would give me a good indicator.

Fifteen minutes later, my phone was ringing. In about five minutes after that, I had eight missed calls and seven messages. Then six minutes after that, my phone service was cut off. I listened to the messages. The first one was just sheer screaming. The second consisted of screaming, too, but I could actually hear Faye make out my name a few times.

The third one was Adrianna. "You little b—. I can't believe you did this. I hope you know you are going to go to jail now, and after that, you're going to rot in hell, you little f—er," she warned.

The next message was Faye again. On the fourth message, Faye's words were actually decipherable. Knowing she would be belligerent, I wrote her a letter and left it on the counter. If she would stop acting like a lunatic and look around, she would see it. The letter explained and discussed all my reasoning. Where, in loose terms, I was going and why I felt it was time for me to leave. But then neither Faye nor Jack was ever the calm type. And never were they ever rational. The next few messages clearly outlined that.

"Where are you?" she yelled in a heated voice. I could imagine the fury in her eyes through her voice. "You better tell me because I am the guardian. You can't do anything without me. Without my permission." The next message was a little more forgiving about my leaving.

The next message…

"You know what, stay gone. It's better when you're not here. I don't know why I ever took you into my house anyways. The biggest mistake of my life! And I hope you know you had it good! Have a nice life living on the streets!"

And the next…

"I found your letter. What family are you talking about? No

one wants you. No one ever did, that's why I took you in. Out of the kindness of my heart, and this is how you repay me?" She was yelling into the phone. "I just can't believe this. By the way, I'm cutting off your phone service. If you don't live under my roof and go by my rules, I won't provide for you."

At that one, I just laughed. Provide for me? Well, she rarely did that anyways. And Faye, she just was a vindictive sort but was never really clever about it. She shut off my phone, not realizing what she was doing. If your daughter or son ran away in the middle of the night, you would be worried, right? Yes! Scared to death. And if you knew they took their cell phone, and that was the only way you could get a hold of them, why would you cut the line off? She was only proving that she didn't care. Faye wasn't a loving mother who was scared or worried. She was a lady pissed off that something of hers, her property, was not there in her possession and under her control.

My aunt and uncle listened to the messages and were shocked.

"She already turned off the phone?" my aunt asked.

"Yep. I knew it wouldn't take long," I replied. It really didn't make a difference to me. "They are usually off anyway. We could never pay the bill. It's just by happenstance that they were on this time."

"But she won't be able to get a hold of you," my uncle reasoned.

"Exactly. That's why I'm okay with it. I don't need to talk with her," I said. They both were just looking at me.

"Are you okay?" my aunt asked.

"Sure. I'm fine," I reassured them. I knew what they were thinking. This girl just heard six messages. None of them were of compassion or worry. They were all of malice and hate. The woman who claimed to be a mother to me was acting like a warden who had lost a prisoner. I could tell that they were shocked by Faye, but also by my reaction. I wasn't crying at her words, nor was I phased by her threats. I knew my rights, and I also knew that Jack and Faye were emotionally charged people who never thought anything through. Besides, what could they do now anyways? I left, and I wasn't going back.

That Monday morning, Labor Day, was a joyous one. I started going through my things and getting them unpacked. My aunt had given me a room and was helping me. She didn't talk much, but that was okay. I appreciated the silence to think. All of this was a little hard for me to believe. About six hours earlier, I was running for my life. Now here I was unpacking, preparing for a new one. It was strange and very surreal. I hadn't heard anything from Faye since those messages. That was also strange but delightful. I knew that I would have to reorient my thinking. I wouldn't be scared of her or Jack anymore. They weren't a part of my life any longer. I had new people. I had my family. Though I wouldn't dare ask them for anything, I knew that they were at least there for me.

I couldn't help but keep asking my aunt if it was okay if I stayed there. "It will only be for a little while," I assured her. "I plan to graduate early so I can get out on my own soon."

"Natalie, you're welcome to stay here. All of Charlotte's children have. We won't kick you out," she said with a chuckle. "And you don't have to graduate early if you don't want to. This is your senior year. Those only come once, and you should make the most of it."

"Thank you. You're so kind. I...I... Well, thank you." I couldn't really find the words to say. How could I have missed out on these people my whole life? Why didn't I end up here when my daddy left me at that building? But those questions couldn't be answered, at least not today. I had things to do and homework. I wasn't going to let my grades suffer just because my whole life was changing. I had a biology test on Friday, and I intended to make top score.

The day went and passed. That night, I lay in bed smiling, truly smiling, for the first time. Well, since memory serves me. It worked. My plan worked, and tonight I slept in a place where I knew I was safe. For the first time, I felt that I was at home. I dozed off with a smile, and the next morning, I awoke with one. I was happy, and I felt so incredibly blessed.

I showed up at school the next morning. Of course, none of my friends knew what had taken place that weekend, and they wouldn't. I didn't discuss my personal life with anyone, and that was for the best. I talked to my classmates, answered questions in class, and walked through my same old routine. But one difference was that my smile was so real. And when the three o'clock bell rang, the smile wouldn't fade away because I had to go home. Because now my home was a place that was safe.

During the day, it was a bit hard to concentrate. My uncle told me that I could paint my room. I was so excited. I had never been able to do that. I was daydreaming about colors and designs and about all aspects in my life. Painting is nice. You can just cover up the old, and no one ever knew what was there before. I knew that I would be painting my personal walls that I had built. I wasn't in a position to take them down, but I was ready to at least change the color. Something bright. Something hopeful.

My thoughts were interrupted. My teacher came to my desk. "Natalie, you are wanted at the office."

"Oh, okay. Thank you," I said. As I got up and headed toward the door, I could see Officer Rodriguez just outside. "Hi, Officer Rodriguez! I left! I did it! My plan worked!" I told him in an excited whisper.

"I know, Natalie," he said, but he wasn't excited. He seemed worried.

"What's wrong, Officer Rodriguez? What's happened?" I asked, even though deep in my heart, I begged his answer to be different than what I knew it would be.

"Faye has filed police reports on you. Good thing is that most of them are superficial and won't be taken into account. She was trying to say that you stole from her, but the officers that came to the house sidestepped that one. But, Natalie, she has filed a runaway report. That won't be as easy to get around," he warned.

"What do we do? I mean, Mr. Atkins said I could leave, so she can't do anything," I reasoned.

"Well, remember, your emancipation is not documented. It was just verbal, a gamble on Mr. Atkins' part. I don't suppose he thought Faye would put up a fuss. But the good thing is, you came to school today. So in the state of Texas, you technically aren't running away. You just left home. I'm going to call the DA's office and see if I can get it dismissed without her knowing," he explained. "That's our best bet."

"What if it doesn't get dismissed?" I asked, panicked.

His initial silence answered my question. "We'll cross that bridge if it comes, okay?"

"Yes, sir," I said nervously. My happy feelings were slowly deteriorating. Officer Rodriguez must have seen the worry in my eyes.

"Natalie, it's going to be just fine. We are going to protect you. You won't go back to Faye's house. All right?"

"Yes, sir," was all I could say.

"Natalie?" he asked and waited until I looked up. "I'm proud of you. It was a very brave thing that you did to leave. Most people wouldn't have had that kind of courage, but you did. That's something to be proud of."

I smiled at that. Officer Rodriguez was such a wonderful person. He always knew when a girl needed a nudge of confidence. "Let's get you back to class," he said. "We can't let those good brains of yours go to waste." He winked.

"Thank you, Officer Rodriguez. Keep me updated," I said as I headed back to class. I told myself it was going to be okay, but I couldn't help the worry that was in my stomach. Faye was stupid, but she was persistent when she wanted something. But then again, so was I…

Officer Rodriguez handled the runaway report; it was dropped, thank the good Lord above. Though I had faith in Officer Rodriguez, I couldn't help but wonder what would happen if it didn't go away. I researched at the library on Wednesday at lunch and feared for my life when I found out that most runaways were immediately taken to Juvenile Hall. But it was over by Wednesday afternoon, however, just the police part of things. Faye, like I said, was persistent and was doing everything in her power to make my life a living hell. She called up to the school several times a day, offering threats. It was to the point that Officer Rodriguez initiated a protection plan for me; I wasn't allowed to go anywhere without someone with me and a teacher being notified.

When the phone calls didn't work, she started to come up to the school, driving around the parking lot. And when that failed, she decided she would just check me out. But luckily, it was caught before I came to the office. The lady was insane, and at this point, she was desperate. I was taking classes through the college, and she went up there and unenrolled me and tried to get the money back, even though it was paid for by scholarship. Luckily, the money was nonrefundable. But that didn't stop her from taking me out of them. Every few hours, my counselor would call me to her office to reregister.

"Natalie, we can't stop her from dropping you from the classes. But we just have to make sure we get the last move. Friday at noon is the last time to drop. If you are registered at 12:01 p.m., we are good, and we won't have to worry," she explained.

Though I was trying to keep a lid on all of this, Faye sure wasn't. By Thursday, a lot of my cheerleader friends knew something was up, because Faye had been harassing them, too. My friend, Nicole, had even received a threatening message. Her dad handled that, but Faye was getting out of control. It was one thing to harass me, but my friends? Then she started to call some of my teachers, pretending to be someone else. I don't think she realized what a fool she was making of herself. But I won't lie and say that I wasn't scared. Because I was. I knew in my heart that if she found me, it would be all over. Jack was stupid, but Faye, she was deadly.

I did consider the possibility that Faye was acting this way because she missed me. Maybe Jack and Faye were trying to get me back because they love and miss me, but I quickly dismissed those beliefs. I knew in my heart that just wasn't the case.

Faye just wanted her property, not her so-called daughter. In one encounter at the school, Officer Rodriguez brought Faye into his office to try and reason with her.

"You know, I don't really want Natalie. I never really did. But she took a picture, which is of her that I paid money for, and I want it back. If she gives it back, I'll leave her alone," she explained to Officer Rodriguez.

"You mean you want a picture of her. Why?" I suppose Officer Rodriguez was trying to understand.

"Yes. I paid money for it. It was in the mall for the school cheerleaders. I don't know why that lady insisted she was so pretty, but I paid for it. Only half, but it was my money, and she doesn't need it," Faye said.

"I see. I'll tell her to get the photo of her back to you. And then if you promise to stop harassing her and the school, I will drop all of these reports," he bargained.

"You know, I really don't see why Natalie wants to leave. I gave her everything. Absolutely everything. I hope she ends up on the streets," Faye went on.

"Yes, Mrs. Winters. I'm sure you did. Thank you. That will be all," Officer Rodriguez said.

After she was escorted off campus, Officer Rodriguez called me down to the office and recalled that story to me. It didn't surprise me. Faye always had some sort of ridiculous request. I quickly remembered what photo she was talking about. I had my pictures made for the cheerleading squad. I remember the photographer telling me I was so gorgeous. I kept blushing. No one ever called me that. I mean, my whole life, Faye insisted that I was hideous, and I believed her.

But for some reason, the photographer thought I was pretty, and she insisted on using my photograph for her display in the mall. It was a very large photo and was on display for about five months. I remembered she offered us the chance to buy it for I think two hundred dollars, if my memory serves me. Faye, much to my surprise, bought it. It was for my birthday and Christmas, both. That was the nicest thing she had ever done for me. Now, it only made sense that she would want it back.

Though I didn't understand why she would want a photo of me, but I was glad to give it back. It didn't matter to me. I didn't need a picture of myself. And anyways, if I could trade a picture to get her to leave me alone, that was perfectly fine.

But as Officer Rodriguez told me that story, I couldn't help but shake my head and chuckle a little. At least I was happy that Faye's true colors were showing.

Officer Rodriguez just looked at me puzzled and said, "Natalie, promise me that you will never go back to that place. Promise me. No matter how hard it gets. No matter how many struggles, promise me you will never go back?"

"Officer Rodriguez, I can assure you, you have my word. I'd live under a bridge before I would go back to that place. I'll sleep in a car before I ever step foot in that house again," I promised him. And it was the honest truth, I would never go back.

Methamphetamines

. . . .

*I am not bound to win, but I am bound to be true. I
am not bound to succeed, but I am bound to live up
to what light I have.*

—Abraham Lincoln

. . . .

When an individual is using meth, there are a variety of telltale symptoms: high heart rate, days without sleep, jitteriness, dark circles under the eyes. Along with many other repercussions, speed is exactly that. Your body moves fast, and you are able to stay up hours on end. Elevated mood, determination. A person using speed, to some extent, believes they are unstoppable, and ironically enough, they go so fast that to some extent, they aren't.

Those few weeks were extremely hard to get through. I was going to school from seven o'clock in the morning to seven at night, trying to finish up all of my classes to graduate early. Thankfully, my school kept me focused, or distracted rather, from reality.

My biological family was really nice, but it was bizarre. I was living with strangers. And it was all just a completely different lifestyle than I was used to. I knew I didn't fit in from the first time I met them. But then again, I never really fit in with anyone, so I didn't think much of it.

I was gone most of the time during the week, but I was home on the weekends completely. I didn't go anywhere. My main goal at that time was to stay out of the public eye, and everyone who knew of the situation agreed with that. However, on the weekends, I noticed suspicious behavior. My uncle was nocturnal for sure, but I noticed that he would stay up for days at a time and then pass out cold. It was so strange to me, and as a curious person, I couldn't help but look into it.

Over the next few weeks, I realized that he didn't have a job but worked for my great-grandpa. My great-grandpa lived in a neighboring town and was a very wealthy man. We went to visit one weekend, and I was introduced. He was very nice, but very skeptical of me. I suppose he had his reasons. Most of his grandchildren wanted his money, but I had no interest in that sort of thing. I was interested in a family, in having people that cared for me in my life. However, I suppose that was strange to them. He offered to buy me a car, but I refused. I would earn money on my own and work my way to getting what I needed. Not that I didn't appreciate what he offered, I just didn't want to be seen as the new family leech. It bothered me how my fellow family members talked to me about his money. He was ninety-two years old, and they were like vultures waiting for nature to take its course. Well, I was not that person, nor would I ever be.

I continued to observe the situation. My uncle's behavior was odd. But everyone just sort of ignored it. There was an obscurity that I couldn't place. One afternoon, I came home, and my uncle was revved up, waving a gun around, yelling erratically.

I wasn't scared per se, but even more curious. Finally, I came to some conclusions. Either he was schizophrenic or was taking drugs.

My guess was drugs, meth in particular. It explained everything. But I have never been one to make accusations, so I decided to ask him about it. Though he tried to deny it at first, it didn't take long for him to cave. We talked for a while, and he told me stories about himself and my mother. How they used drugs together, and then got sober together, and then got back into drugs. And it was all just a little too much for me. He had a daughter who I didn't think suspected anything. Though I knew his wife had to know.

They were my family, but I wasn't there to play rehab or change their way of life. I hated to know that it was going on, but I had my own life to handle. I decided that it was best that I leave. I despised drugs and what they did to people's lives. To ignore is to condone, and I would not tolerate living in a house where drug use was subliminally accepted. So, I moved out. I believe that when you see wrong and don't correct it, you're guilty by silence. I knew that because I had been dealing with the culpability for years in staying silent about the things in the Winters' home. I couldn't do that anymore. I had left that life, and I had no need or desire for another version of it. Though I didn't really have anywhere to go, I would just have to figure a way… I always did.

I ended up staying at a variety of friends' houses, sleeping on couches and the like, though I felt bad for it. I didn't like charity. It reminded me of Faye and how she would scuttle money from people. I was still in school, but I wheeled and dealed with some of the possessions I had and did a little work for some of my teachers, grading papers and stuff. Soon, I had enough to buy a car. I paid $250 for it. A skateboard was probably more reliable, but I couldn't help but be proud. I bought a car all on my own, and it was mine, an 1992

Oldsmobile Achieva. It was almost as old as I was. With maroon interior, it smelled like old man and cigars. The locks didn't work and the driver's door didn't open, so I just had to climb in through the passenger's side. Sometimes, the engine didn't work either, but it was my very first car, and I loved it. I was proud.

The nights I didn't have anywhere to go, I slept there, under the only roof I could afford. I know that people looked down on that sort of thing, but I didn't mind. I would try to find a well lit parking lot, for safety precautions. I had a flashlight to read my books when it turned dark outside. I just thought of it as camping. And it was nice. After I finished my homework, I just gazed at the night sky. The vastness, the opportunity my life was presented with.

I think a lot of people would see this as horrible, but for me it was perfect. Was I homeless? Well, yes. But not hopeless. My life was now mine. And honestly, that's all that mattered. Choice. Freedom.

I kept my volunteering up at the hospital some, and it gave me access to a place to stay, too. I memorized the access code to the doctors' on-call room and slept there when it was too cold outside. My Oldsmobile wasn't very insulated. Plus, I could shower, and then I'd head off to school. No one ever really noticed. And, if they did, I'd just say that I was a volunteer and too tired to go home—a logical answer that wasn't questioned. Oddly enough, I slept so well at the hospital. It comforted me somehow. I felt safe. Plus, when the night's insomnia struck, I could saunter down to the Emergency Room and learn. Perfect home, if you ask me.

I also kept in touch with Bethany. When she found out that I was sleeping in random places, she let me stay in her back room. She gave me food and helped me quite a lot. She was such a wonderful woman, so kindhearted. What she was doing truly meant the world to me.

I did menial work so I could pay for gas. I wasn't making much, but it was a start. Bethany helped me out with money as well so I could buy lunch and stuff. But I knew I had to stand on my own two feet. I wasn't going to let her take care of me. That wasn't her responsibility. Soon, I was able to get a job at a doctor's office. I was thrilled! I would not only get experience in the medical field, but a paycheck that was all mine!

My rate was minimum, but I made about $675 a month. And, I have to say, I felt wealthy. That was the most money that had ever been in my possession. I didn't have to worry about Faye taking it. Slowly, I was moving forward. I saved as much as I could afford to.

The semester flew by. I graduated high school December 17, 2008, and that very same afternoon, I enrolled in college. Though it wasn't Cornell or Columbia in New York, I was excited.

Amarillo College was the local community college. I knew many people who recommended that I attend there.

Though I knew I had to take care of my adult responsibilities, school was my first priority. Many people told me that I should be more worried about working rather than getting degrees, but I ignored them. I wasn't going to give up on my journey of becoming a physician. And I for sure wasn't going to let my circumstances prevent me from becoming educated. God would provide a way. And He certainly did. I didn't have one expense to go to school my first semester; through grants and scholarships, everything was paid for.

However, my living circumstances were a little more complicated. Bethany had three other children, and I knew it was difficult to have an extra head. Over the next few months, my college schedule was the only thing that was reliable. I was still working, but finding a place to stay was even more difficult. I was seventeen and technically still a minor. Though I was emancipated, most of the apartments were owned by corporations, and no matter what my circumstances were, they wouldn't let me rent. So I had to look in the more sketchy areas of town, for lack of a better term.

I finally found a place, privately owned, and the owner agreed to rent it to me. Now, one thing was for certain, it wasn't the Ritz. I was definitely in a really dangerous neighborhood, a place where you didn't go outside your house in the nighttime alone. My windows were bolted shut, and there was no entry that didn't have three dead bolts. It was a place in a neighborhood that a small young girl shouldn't be alone, but it was affordable And, I would just have to make it work.

My rent was $375 with a deposit of $200. My gas bill was about $50 a month, but you had to pay a $100 start-up fee. And for me, it was $150 because I had no credit history. Electricity ran about $100 a month with a start-up cost of $100. My place was small, but the heater and air conditioner were in no way efficient. There were extra costs and stipulation with everything. Then I had to worry a bit about food and how to put gas in my car. Insurance and phone bills. It didn't take me long to realize that my whopping $675 a month wasn't going to cut it. I got another job at a hotel as a clerk. I was working full-time and going to school full-time. I was absolutely exhausted.

If a glass wall is defined as an obstruction to move within an organization because of prejudice, if a glass ceiling is a limit to professional women's advancement, and if a glass escalator is the advancement of men over women in the workforce, then minimum wage is the glass cage. I was definitely in the "working poor" class. I worked so much and gained so little. It dawned on me that this was a vicious cycle. I never really understood how people would just stick with low-income jobs and forfeit their education. But now I understood. When I wasn't working at a job, I was working on my classes. And on top of that, it was just me. I didn't have children. I didn't have anyone else to care for, and I was struggling. I saw how easily it would be to give up school just to be able to work a few more hours in the week just for a few more bucks. However, I knew better. It would be hard for a while, but I had faith it would get easier. Certainly there were times where I didn't know where my next meal would come from or where I would sleep. But I had school. I had a job. And I had God. There were worse lives to live, I knew. But nonetheless, times were very hard.

I remember there were times I was so tired that a flight of stairs brought tears to my eyes; just thinking about having to climb them seemed to be an insurmountable task. I was seventeen years old with so much responsibility. Some days, the A on my biology test would make me feel like I was on top of the world. While the late nights studying and the bills piling up, I felt like the world was on top of me. I was becoming a woman, and I was trying to understand life. And there were times when I was just downright angry.

I would see kids, hear them talk in my classes, and complain about what I considered were the stupidest things. Like their parents making them pay their car payment or suggesting that they get a part-time job. They would gripe and complain that it was too hard. Honestly, it made me sick. There were so many kids who had it all and didn't even know it. And it made me angry, but most of all, it made me jealous. It wasn't that I wanted someone to pay my way; I just wanted to know that someone was there for me who was honest and true, not using drugs. I was in sole control of my life. I made all of the executive decisions, and while that might seem wonderful, it was hard. I mean, if I decided to quit school and start doing drugs, there wasn't anyone to prevent me from doing so. I wouldn't be grounded. I wouldn't be punished. And while I had no intentions of doing those things, it was hard just knowing that I could, and no one was there to stop me. I was walking a tightrope, with no net to catch me if I fell.

The simplest comments cut me to the bone. Once, I was talking to my calculus professor about my future plans in school and about working at the doctor's office. She said, "Wow. Your parents must be so proud of you." I tried to stop the tears, but I couldn't. I broke down right there in her office. I was doing my best to stay afloat. But I had so much pain and hurt in my heart. There were times when I felt utterly and completely alone. I didn't know if my parents were proud, and I never would. I knew God was there, and I knew He loved me. But I just couldn't help but question. My faith was wounded by all of the things that I had been through and endured.

I built walls for so long, but my feelings were beginning to break through. One can only keep things bottled up for so long. I began to vent about my struggles though my writing assignments and essays. And soon, my story was being heard. In one essay for a minority studies course, I wrote of my experiences, described the feelings of what it was like to be alone in the world where survival was for the financially fit. My professor found me after class and took me to her office to talk with me. I began to open up about my past, though it was hard. However, it was necessary. To grow, you have to break out of your shell. I was learning that. And, surprising to me, people at my college, they listened. When I shared my story, I noticed that it had an effect on people. And once people knew about me, once I knew they had faith in me, it gave me the courage to continue. I couldn't let them down.

Sometimes I felt as if I were a daisy piercing through a crack in the sidewalk—strange and peculiar, out of place and alone, though gaining attention and catching the eyes of people on their daily strolls. But most of all, I began to feel unique. Yes, unique, because most seeds that find themselves surrounded by cement and inadequate environment give up and accept failure. However, I worked to extend my roots past the rocks and stubble, I soaked up the sunlight that was given, and I soaked in the rains when they came, thankful for them, as I had the privilege of knowing the dryness. The bad times make the good ones all the better.

I learned that the majority of people faced with extreme challenges or disconcerting events forget that they are a seed; that even though they may find themselves placed in a difficult milieu, they still have the ability to cultivate. However, I knew I must remain determined to not let other's mistakes and choices determine my future. I would not accept the paths others had chosen, nor the one-way streets they lost themselves on. I have made myself believe that I am a seed, and I have all the potential in the world to grow into a beautiful flower, just as those that have been planted in the gardens. No matter the circumstance, we all have potential; the hard part, I found, is just realizing it.

Once I broke out of my shell, I excelled. The next fall semester, I was accepted into the honors program. I was inducted into Phi Theta Kappa and started to receive awards in academic excellence. Finances were still hard, but I was able to move out of the neighborhood and get a better-paying job at the hospital. At eighteen, I graduated with my first associate's degree. A semester later, I had another in psychology. By nineteen, I was a senior at West Texas University. I went fast, taking up to twenty-four hours a semester. I worked nights at the hospital so I could focus completely on my studies during the day. Soon, I was sharing my story with students, ones who were in similar situations. I had to give them hope and set an example. Anything is possible by the grace of God.

I was moving quickly, engrossed with school; accuracy and efficiency were not sacrificed. I absolutely loved the classroom and my studies. I was growing into a very strong person. The walls of distrust and fear were soon falling down. People believed in me, and I soon found that I could also believe in them.

People watched in disbelief; some were expecting me to fail, I know. But I persevered, no matter what obstacles came my way. And honestly, I grew to love my chaotic schedule. A mentor of mine jokingly told me once, "Every time I see you, you move up a grade or get another award!"

And honestly, that was the truth. I was blazing through my classes. Academia was my passion. It was my focus. Every semester, I undertook a bigger course load. My logic? Well, if I can make four A's, why not try for five? School, it was my addiction. With the rate that I was going, sleep was a luxury, and extra time was rare. My social life consisted of visitation while waiting to check out at the library. My professors were my friends. I know my classmates thought I was some kind of crazy; that's all right, been there… heard that…

I was also aware that I was losing weight, and I had dark circles under my eyes because I was up for days at a time. There were times when I'd crash, but times where I felt invincible. You know, unstoppable. In studying psychopharmacology, we went over the effects of methamphetamines. Oddly enough, I myself appeared to be suffering those symptoms.

Surgical Solutions

....

*Then the Lord God made a woman from the rib he
had taken out of the man, and he brought her to the
man. The man said, "This is now bone of my bones
and flesh of my flesh; she shall be called 'woman,' for
she was taken out of man." For this reason a man will
leave his father and mother and be united to his wife,
and they will become one flesh.*

—Genesis 2:22-24, nkj

....

I wish I could say that all of my achievements and hard work were helping me get out and away from my entire childhood trauma, but I'm afraid I still had a bit more suffering to endure.

I knew I had a problem. And I knew that it was getting worse as the pain grew. I also knew that the thought of visiting the gynecologist was terrifying, even though I was almost eighteen years old. I still remembered my visit from four years ago. The flashbacks. I just didn't want to remember the days, well, the nights of my childhood.

But, I knew there was a problem with my anatomy. I didn't know if I'd ever, by my own volition, become sexually active. Boys, well… I didn't have the time or desire to deal with them. I was constantly working. And all of the guys my age just didn't get it. They were so immature, and I couldn't afford any distractions. Dating was an exhausting thought and marriage seemed outrageous. I wasn't ready for marriage, thus I wasn't ready to have sex. However, I knew it was important, regardless, to be functioning anatomically. And I was concerned that I wasn't.

I set the appointment with the same doctor. Dr. Williams. He was a nice man, and, oddly, I trusted him. I knew he tried to help me, even though I prevented him from doing so. And I wanted to minimize all of the small talk.

My appointment was set on a Thursday morning, but I didn't sleep the whole night before. I was freaking out about the whole thing. When the morning arrived, I got sick. And thirty minutes before, I called and canceled. I just couldn't go through with it.

The following month I tried again. I made it into the lobby this time but left before I got up to the elevator.

On the third try, the nurse called and asked me what was wrong. I told her that I had a bad experience and I just needed time. She offered to prescribe Valium to help me relax, but I declined. I refused to use drugs as a coping mechanism.

On the fourth round, I made it into the exam room, praying the whole way. But before she started with the questions, I stopped her, knowing it would freak me out.

"I'm not a virgin. I'm not currently sexually active, and I don't intend to be. Don't ask me when I became active, please." I stated, looking away.

"Yes, thank you, Ms. Winters," she said as she handed me the gown. I knew the drill all too well.

Doctor Williams came in. He looked much the same, except his hair was greyer than before.

"Hello, Natalie… Winters." He looked at the chart, then up at me. Instantly, I knew he remembered.

"Hi, Dr. Williams."

There was a moment of silence. I think both of us were at a loss of words.

"What brings you in today?" he asked cautiously.

"I… I need an exam. I think there are some issues that need to be looked at."

"Alright. We'll take a look," he said, looking at me then at the nurse.

But before I lay down, I knew I needed to explain. "I left my underwear on. Please don't take them all the way off. And please be as quick as possible. I will cry, but still do your job, unless I say stop." My tone was very informative and firm.

"Okay, Natalie. We can do that. But I need you to relax, okay? I'll do my best to make it as fast and painless as possible."

"Yes, sir," I said as I laid back and closed my eyes.

The whole process didn't last but five minutes, but it seemed like five hours. I was right in knowing that I would cry. I still couldn't keep those dark, black memories at bay. It wasn't as painful as I thought. During what I thought would be the worst part, he stopped and told me to get dressed. He said he'd come back to talk to me.

I was greatly relieved when I had my clothes back on. Lost in thought, there was a knock.

"Come in." It was Dr. Williams.

"Hi, Natalie. I wanted to talk with you about the exam."

"Alright," I said hesitantly.

"Well, you were right about thinking there were some issues. I couldn't perform a whole exam on you, because it seems you have some extra vaginal tissue… It's almost completely closed your vaginal opening."

"Tissue?" It didn't make sense to me… How was there tissue?

"Yes. Some of it appears to be scar tissue," he said quietly.

Tears immediately struck my eyes. "I see," I responded solemnly.

He handed me a tissue. "I know this is hard, Natalie."

"What do we do about it? How do we fix it?" I asked earnestly.

"I'll have to do surgery. Not a big surgery, but you'll have to be put under anesthesia. I'll go in and remove this tissue from the opening and around the area."

"What… what if I don't?" I asked, tears falling now. Surgery? Down there?

"Natalie, it needs to be done. If you don't, you will have many complications. At this point, it would be exceedingly painful, if not impossible to have intercourse if you wanted to. And you could get endometriosis, cervical cancer. A number of issues could arise," he said urgently.

"I see." I couldn't think about all of this. Why was this happening?

"Natalie," Dr. Williams said soothingly, "I can schedule you for next week. It will be a quick recovery. We'll put you under what's called twilight anesthesia, and we can do it here in the office. I'll talk to the anesthesiologist. That will make it less expensive and... easier to you for to cope with."

Expensive? That's right... the cost. I didn't have insurance. How was I going to pay for this? How was I going to handle all of this?

"Dr. Williams, I understand I need this done, as hard as it will be. But financially, I can't afford a surgery."

"Don't worry about the money. We can set up a very flexible payment plan. Natalie, this is really urgent. I don't want this becoming worse for you than it already is. It could prevent you from having children."

Those words hit me hard. I wanted my own kids more than anything. And because of this, I might not have them. The thought shook me. *No.* I thought. I will not let anything from my past effect me or my kids. Though I didn't know who my little ones were, or how many their might be, I would do anything for them. Including this...

"Yes, sir. I guess... okay." I said.

I went ahead and did the paperwork for the procedure and set up a payment plan. I was going to have to pay one hundred dollars up front and then pay out the rest as long as I needed.

By the time I left the office, I was so angry. How many times was I going to have to pay for what "Daddy Jack" did?

For the next week, I practiced going to the doctor's office. Up the elevator and into the lobby. I didn't want to have a freak out on the day of the surgery. That would be humiliating and I didn't want to waste Dr. Williams' time.

The day came before I knew it. I wasn't ready. But, honestly, even if I had five more years I still wouldn't have been ready.

I made it to the lobby as I had practiced and was called back. The same old doctor-patient routine was followed.

I put on my gown but left my underwear on.

They brought me into the room where the operation would be. Dr. Williams came in.

"Well, Natalie. It will soon be over. Do you have any questions for me?" he asked.

"No. But I have instructions," I said, smiling meekly.

He returned my smile. "Okay. Let's hear them."

"I have my underwear on. Please keep them on until I am completely out. And please, please don't let me wake up with them off," I said, my voice shaky with emotion.

He just nodded his head, not looking me in the eye.

"And I have an apology, Dr. Williams."

He immediately looked up in surprise. "An apology?" he questioned.

"Yes. Four years ago I lied to you. About being abused. I'm sorry, I'm sorry for lying," I stammered, not able to prevent the tears from rolling down my cheek.

"Don't apologize, Natalie. You did nothing wrong. You were a child. You still are. I'm sorry I didn't do more for you." He looked down. I knew he was becoming emotional.

"No, Dr. Williams. It's okay. You're doing a lot now. I trust you. Thank you," I encouraged him.

He shook his head again. "I'll see you in a bit."

The anesthesiologist came in. He did the whole counting thing. I promised him I'd get to ten, too. He laughed. Then it was dark.

I woke up to a lot of pain. I was happy my panties were on, but I was oddly ready to have them off. This was violating in many ways. I just wanted to go home.

My friend drove me. I told her a little bit about what had been done, but not the whole extent. I didn't want anyone to know.

Later that afternoon, I thought about having a husband and family one day. I didn't know if I ever would. I was far from perfect. Surely, my ideas of Cinderella would fade when it came to a Prince Charming. But the one thing that never faded away was the want and desire to be happy, to be cared for. I wanted to be loved, and I wanted to love someone else. It seemed that every time I had ever tried to someone, the walked or past away. Over the years, that left me with a lot of love in my heart, just waiting to be given.

I still had a lot of growing to do though. I had a lot to accomplish. In my mind, I needed to be successful before I found a husband. I needed to make myself worthy of a good man; one who wouldn't hurt me. Maybe if I were a doctor… Maybe if I were a distinguished professor, there would be a man to want me, and one who would overlook my many flaws, including this one.

Maybe one day the Lord would bless me with a kind, understanding man. I had hope, as I knew that of all the strength in medicine and knowledge, it would be love that would heal me, and my scars. And from what I hear, love conquers all…

Angels and Halos

. . . .

Not flesh of my flesh, Nor bone of my bone, But still miraculously my own. Never forget for a single minute: you didn't grow under my heart, but in it.

—Fleur Conkling Heyliger

. . . .

Though during that time I was struggling to be on my own, my problems were nothing compared to the struggles of little Emily. She was a victim of Faye's negligence. And, well, mine, too. I felt responsible for her.

Not long after I was emancipated, I contacted her social worker. She was still in the hospital and wasn't doing well. She had a new foster family. I was able to meet them, and they were very kind people and were visiting her daily. But I couldn't help but feel accountable for her condition.

I visited her every day. Sometimes rather than sleeping in the on-call room, I slept in her room while holding her in my arms. She had been off the ventilator for a while, but her condition worsened, and she had to be placed back on life support. But we all still had hope she would make it through. I needed that hope at the time. I needed a reason for all of this. I needed to know that all of the hardship was worth it. I still had my studies to think about, so instead of reading the children's books to little Emily, I read my biology book. Maybe it wasn't interesting as puppies and birds, but she enjoyed my voice, and by the end of it, I think she found amoebas interesting, too.

I cared for her as if she were my own, and I was adamant about staying up to date on the literature of her conditions. I read the statistics, memorized her medications, and studied the outcomes. No one really knew who I was, and I planned on keeping it that way for a while. Faye and Jack Winters had become public, and many people were aware that they were not as they appeared. And after all, I still carried their last name. But there was much skepticism. Some people who knew what I did believed that I was a liar, and all of the people involved in the investigations were deceitful. People couldn't believe that the woman who so often spoke of these children, who spent all of her time taking care of them, wasn't doing so. They couldn't believe that the family who had taken in children, removing them from dangerous situations for years, had actually been abusing them. However, mainly, I think those people just couldn't believe that they had been fooled.

It's sort of like a fairy tale. People love to hear happy stories, happy endings. They grow confident in the idea that the world is good. And when discrepancies occur, they ignore them because it's uncomfortable and hard to handle. The people who claim that the fairy tale isn't real become villains. So I kept my identity quiet and just made sure to mind my own…most of the time.

One day I didn't have class, so I was able to be there when Emily's primary doctor made rounds. I stood in the back of the room while he asked questions to the interns. Truth be told, I knew the answers to his questions, and I probably knew just as much about Emily's case as the interns. I enjoyed seeing the interns and attendings. Those situations provided me a good example of what I was getting into.

"Is she suffering from alkalinity or acidity?" Dr. Brian asked. He was a tall, very handsome man. But if I had to choose one word to describe him, it would be *intense*. He was every bit intimidating.

When there was no answer to his question, I decided to help out. "Acidity," I stated quietly. He didn't say anything but just looked in my direction and continued. "What type?" he asked.

Again, there was no answer. So I responded, "Respiratory acidosis. Her CO_2 levels are extremely elevated, thus through alveolar hypoventilation, her bicarbonate levels are low, thus reduction in her blood pH. It's chronic." I didn't mean to ramble, but when I'm nervous I tend to do that.

By the time I finished, everyone in the room was looking at me while Dr. Brian just stared, appalled. I knew he had no idea who I was, and he was trying to figure it out. "Who are you?" he asked.

"I'm...I'm her sister," I responded. I never used my name. It wasn't something I was proud to admit.

"Uh-huh. Name?" he prodded.

"Natalie," I stated meekly. His eyes were fixed on me. He knew about Faye Winters and wasn't a fan of her. And with my name, he placed my face. "Faye Winters' daughter?" His voice was raised. Faye was banned from the hospital, and I assumed he thought I was her spy.

"No," I quickly answered. "I am not her daughter. I was emancipated. My parents are deceased, and I have nothing to do with the individuals of the Winters family," I said sternly with just a hint of anger. I hated being referred to as her daughter because I sure wasn't, and I was quick to make sure everyone in that room knew it.

"Come outside." Dr. Brian motioned me. I was panicking. He was going to kick me out. I just knew it. We stepped next door into an empty room. "What are you doing here?" he asked me in an odd, almost concerned tone.

"Emily is my sister, and she is my responsibility. I have taken care of her most of her life, and I don't plan on stopping now," I responded matter-of-factly.

"I see. And you say you don't talk to Faye?" he questioned once more.

"No, I do not. I do not speak to that woman, and I haven't for several months. I have no contact. I was emancipated, and I am on my own," I said. Dr. Brian just looked at me. For the life of me, I couldn't read his expression. I had no idea what he was thinking.

"How do you know the answers to my questions?" he asked.

"I read. I've studied her conditions. And I'm going to be a physician," I stated simply. "It's only right that I know what's going on."

"Very good," he said and then just walked away, leaving me confused. I supposed he didn't mind me staying, and I was very happy for that. I was also very happy that he was Emily's doctor.

Dr. Brian was the best of the best. Though I wouldn't dare let him know it, I looked up to him. He was extremely intelligent, and he knew what he was doing. If I could pick anyone in the world to care for Emily, it would be him. I grew up watching him save many children. I was sure he was going to save Emily just the same.

Weeks went by. Dr. Brian talked to me and kept me updated. I knew my consistency in being there made him curious. But he didn't ask about my personal life. When we talked, it was about Emily. I was thankful for that. He treated me like a person, not like a victim or a villain, and I appreciated that. I had confidence in him, and most importantly, I trusted him.

One evening, I was sitting with Emily's foster mom. She and her husband had decided to adopt her, and I was so happy. Little Emily was going to get a home, and when she made it out of the hospital, she would have a happy life. I was overjoyed for her. Her new mother and I were just chatting when Dr. Brian walked in. He explained that Emily's labs didn't look good, and she was taking a turn for the worst. That night, she coded, but we got her back. The next morning she coded again, but they were able to revive her once more.

When Dr. Brian arrived that morning for rounds, his face was expressionless, but I knew what he was going to say. I also knew that I had no interest in hearing it. "Emily's condition has gotten worse. Her lungs have filled with fluid. We could do a pneumothorax, but it will just be a short-term solution. I believe we have reached a point in her treatment where the next step should be to do nothing," he said solemnly.

"Absolutely not!" I shouted. "The next step will not be to do nothing! We will do the chest tube. It can buy her time, relieve pressure from her lungs, and allow more time for healing! More time for them to rejuvenate! Lung tissue has that capability, if given a chance. I mean, more tissue will grow that is unaffected. She is just a baby now. In a few months... in a few years, her lungs will have normal capability. We will *not* stop at nothing." No one in the room said a word. They all just looked at me. To speak against Dr. Brian was a very bold thing. I wasn't one to raise my voice, but I didn't care. Part of me knew he was right, but the other part just couldn't believe it.

"Natalie. I know this is hard. It's hard to understand, but I think you know it's the best thing to do." Tears were streaming down my face. I couldn't bear this.

"No! No! We have to save her. You can save her, Dr. Brian. You have to! You have to save her because she has a family to go home to. She has a mom and a dad, new sisters and brothers. She has a chance at happiness. You have to help her have that. I…I have to make sure she has that. I…" The tears of outrage turned into the tears of guilt. I knew in my heart that I could have prevented Emily from being in that bed. I remembered the day in the living room when I noticed her feeding tube was coming out. I shouldn't have said anything. I should have just gone and removed the tube myself and called the nurse rather than have waited around. Or when Faye pushed it back in, no matter what she would have done to me, I should have gone and pulled it out. I should have grabbed Emily and taken her to the hospital myself. It was my fault she lay in that bed. And I couldn't bear to know that it would be my fault if she died. I remembered that feeling. I remembered what it was like to hold a baby, knowing that what you did has led to them dying. I was responsible for her. I was responsible for her life and for her happiness.

If there was one thing about Dr. Brian, it was that he was perceptive. I was trying to hold back my tears and my emotions, but it was useless. He came over to me and pulled me to the hallway. For a moment, he said nothing. He just looked at me or looked through me. I have no idea how he understood, but he did. Suddenly, he said, "Natalie. It's not your fault. You couldn't have done anything different. You may not understand this now, but Emily had weak lungs in the first place. She was a sick little girl, and this early death was a possibility presented since she was born. And you have to believe me. This is not your fault." He used a soothing voice. He was sincere.

Again, my tears started to fall violently. "But, Dr. Brian, it is. I was responsible for all of those children. I kept my mouth shut for so long. I just tried to do my best, but it wasn't enough. They died. And when that happened to Emily, I knew I had to stand up. I had to do that. This all can't be for nothing, Dr. Brian. It just can't be for nothing."

"Natalie, how old are you?" he asked.

"Seventeen."

"Exactly. You are a child. Someone should have been caring for you. You cannot hold these burdens. Emily's life is not your responsibility, and her loss of life is not your fault. And it wasn't for nothing. You have saved many lives. Faye and Jack will no longer have children. Because of you, they will never again harm another child. Because of your choice to stand up, because of your sacrifice, lives have been saved."

I have to say, I never saw it that way. I focused on what was in the past rather than what I had prevented in the future. I knew he was right, and part of me knew that I should believe him, but I just couldn't let myself off the hook that easily.

"But if I would have done it sooner—"

"No," Dr. Brian interrupted. "You will not go there anymore. You did more than most people do. You did what many people would never have the courage to do. And you don't have to understand now, but one day, you will. When you are a doctor, you will understand… You will understand that none of whatever happened is your fault. Now, you don't understand it, but I'm telling you to believe it nonetheless."

I couldn't say anything else. I just shook my head and let my tears that I had kept held up fall freely. I had faith in Dr. Brian, and due to that, I had faith in his words. He was right. I didn't understand, but I would have to believe for my sanity's sake.

That night I held her, baby Emily, in my arms. I told her I loved her, and I told her I was sorry. I couldn't help but apologize for everything that happened. But I knew in a few hours, she would be taken off life support, and I knew better than to have hope that she would be able to survive on her own. She was going to be in heaven soon. Teasingly, I told her to put in a good word for me. At least I knew she would be in heaven. She would be in a happy place, far in the distant sky...

At 9:45 p.m., Thursday, September 18, 2008, Emily was taken off life support. I stood by Dr. Brian. It was so hard to just stand there. Part of me wanted to run to her bed and reintubate her. As her heart rate slowed, I wanted to yell, "Emily, fight. Fight! Live." But I restrained myself. The tears that streamed down my face were steady, though Emily's breaths were not. The end was drawing near, and the minutes that passed were what seemed like slow motion. It was hard to believe this was reality, but Dr. Brian's arm was suddenly around my shoulders, and it brought me back. At 9:53 p.m., she passed. I waited for Dr. Brian to call the time of death. I had to be sure the monitors were accurate. They were.

I left the room and just walked. I went down to the basement of the hospital and mourned. I didn't want anyone to see me. I didn't want anyone's comfort. And the last thing I wanted to hear was that "it was okay." Because for me, it wasn't. I was angry with God. I was angry with myself. I was angry with all of the horrible things that happened in the world. And I was angry that I couldn't do a thing about it.

I knew people were looking for me, but I didn't want to be

found. I stayed gone for about four hours. I dealt with things my own way. I always had. I cried, but I also reasoned. There was nothing I could change. Life happened, and all I could do was look forward. I accepted that I had failed Emily. But I promised that I never again would fail another child. A promise that I had once made and failed… A promise that I was making again and vowed that I'd die before I broke it.

I wept and wept. And in the meantime, I prayed. I knew that God had a reason for everything, but why couldn't He save this little girl? Why didn't He? I questioned and questioned, but there was no answer.

I kept going back and forth, back and forth. Emotionally, I was trying to reason, which is virtually impossible. I was without understanding. Even in maturity, my seventeen years held no explanation as to *why*…

Then like a blanket, a spirit of peace washed over me. I was consoled somehow, and I knew it was going to be okay as God's words appeared in my heart, "My Natalie. You will save many lives. Do not burden yourself with this one, for Emily served her purpose."

I can't explain how you know it is God talking to you. You just do. This was my first, true experience. The Spirit of the Lord touched me in a way that I had never experienced. I immediately ceased crying. I knew that it was all right. That everything was all okay. I knew that little Emily was saved, and I understood that God had His purpose. I couldn't… wouldn't question what it was anymore.

When I came back to the floor, everyone just looked at me. I didn't understand their stares, but I knew something in me had changed. For whatever reason, I had hope.

A few months later, a friend who was there told me that I had left a sad, angry little girl. But when I came back, I was a content, strong woman. Emily had been there for me, even more than I had been there for her. I had a life to lead, lives to save, and things to change. Crying didn't serve a purpose, and wishing to change the past is a waste of precious time. I was going to dedicate my life to what God had in store for me. I would go to school. I would work hard. I would achieve. I would grow and conquer obstacles, because in her short little life, that is exactly what Emily did.

The following day after Emily's death, her new adoptive mother called me. Though there was still sorrow in the air, everyone was doing better. I suppose the cycle of grief was prepared by the months we spend in the hospital.

"Natalie, how are you? Is school going well?" Adele asked.

"Yes ma'am. I'm hanging in there. My studies help with that. How are the funeral arrangements coming?" I questioned hesitantly.

"Well, Natalie, they are going well… But actually, that's why I'm calling you. I have a request."

"Oh yes! Anything!" I responded urgently.

"Well Natalie, I know that you have a beautiful singing voice. I listened to you sing Emily to sleep every night you were with her. She was soothed by it. Comforted. And well, I just… I think you should be the one to sing her last lullaby."

I'm sure my heart stopped. I hadn't performed in ages, but more than that, I didn't know if I could sing under the emotional strain I knew I would feel.

"Ms. Adele, I just don't know if I can… I'm sure I would…" She interrupted.

"Oh Natalie, I know it will be difficult, but you can do it. Emily would love it. And only loved ones will be there. Please, please agree."

Despite every nerve shouting "no," I responded. "Ms. Adele, I'll do it."

She already had the song picked out: "Held" by Natalie Grant. Though I preferred country, I remembered singing this song several times in the hospital. The melody was soft and slow, perfect for rocking angels asleep.

The funeral was everything gloomy and solemn. In addition to being sad, I was scared. I couldn't mess up. Not this. Not here. I had to sing this song flawlessly for Emily.

As I took the stage, every one was crying. Seeing the crowd's tears, made mine anxious to fall. When the music began, I was shaky. *Oh please God, help me.*

When the lyrics began, I could feel the strain in my voice and the people who were crying previously soon began to sob, making composure all the more difficult. I scanned the crowd for a focal point. That's when I saw Dr. Brian.

He was in the very back row, dressed in a black suit. He was straight-faced, but there were no tears. *That would work*, I thought. *I'll just watch him.*

And so I did. When my eyes weren't closed, they were fixed on Dr. Brian. He had composure and his face didn't once flinch. Personally, I don't know how he did it. I'm sure he was the only dry eye there, but I was so thankful. And I knew, little Emily would be smiling down on us.

Soon, the song was over, along with the funeral. Weeks go by, and some days are better than others. But, I remembered what God had spoke to me, and in Him, I trusted. But, I would never forget little Emily. She was a precious little angel sent for a purpose far greater than I could have ever envisioned. She touched so many lives. It never ceases to amaze me that out of tragedy, wonderful things happen. She will always be the brightest star in my sky.

A Meeting of Memories

. . . .

*Disenchantment, whether it is a minor
disappointment or a major shock, is the signal that
things are moving into transition in our lives.*

—William Throsby Bridges

. . . .

When I finally was in a place in my life where things were steady, I couldn't help but ask questions. There was so much about my childhood that I didn't understand. So many questions with no answers. I wondered about my dad, John, and my mom, Charlotte. I wondered about their deaths. Why they died. But most of all, I wondered about their lives. I wanted to know the people who were my parents. Despite their flaws, I loved them dearly. I started doing research, but I can't say that I was prepared for what I would find.

I figured the best way to learn the truth was to contact my dad's mom: my grandmother. After a quick lookup of her name followed by a quick Google search, I located her address. I needed to speak with her.

As I pulled up the street, I can't begin to explain the anxiety

I felt. I was petrified. I didn't know how she would respond. Many years had passed since I'd last seen her. And the memory of our last visit was so very painful: the day she told me my daddy was dead.

When I parked my car, I couldn't help but cry. The house was so familiar. After all of these years, it looked exactly the same. Slowly, I calmed myself. Braced myself. It was time to learn the truth. I just prayed that she would give it to me.

I walked up the sidewalk, having to pause a number of times. For the last time I had walked here was the last day I saw my daddy. The emotion was overwhelming. That day came flooding back to me. The memories. The look in his crystal-blue eyes. Before I knew it, I was on the ground halfway to the door, weeping. I struggled to stop, but I just couldn't. I sat there for about fifteen minutes before I finally managed to console my crying. I finally reached the door, collecting myself, wiping my eyes, I rang the doorbell.

I half-expected no one to answer. After all, no one had noticed me falling apart on the sidewalk outside. But as I turned to walk away, the door creaked open. I gazed up to meet the eyes of my grandmother. She looked so much the same. Older, but the same eyes, same hair, same smell.

"Hi, Grandma," was all I could mutter. She stood there for a moment, just staring at me. I was sure she wondered who I was.

When I started to say my name, she interrupted me. "Natalie? Is it really you?" she asked in shock.

"Yes, Grandma. It is me." Before I knew it, we were caught in an embrace. Oh, my grandmother. My tears started to fall relentlessly again. She remembered me. I just held onto her. Again, I hadn't hugged her since that day in the store on the art aisle. I knew that I needed to calm down, but parts of me couldn't let her go. That twelve-year-old girl…that four-year-old girl longed to just be in her arms forever.

But slowly, we eased apart.

"Come in, sweet girl. Come in." She motioned.

As I walked in the house, I was overcome by memories once more. Everything looked exactly the same. In fact, nothing, not a single thing, had changed. The furniture, the smell, the pictures hanging on the walls. It was a direct reflection of my past.

"Do you want to look around?" My grandmother must have read my thoughts and sensed my curiosity.

"Oh, may I? I know this is odd, but…this is my home," I said, my voice shaking.

"Of course, dear, of course. This way." She led me through to the kitchen.

It was a pale light blue and white. I saw the stove where my daddy used to heat my horribly messy suckers. Those Sugar Daddies… He would hold them above the stove to soften them up so I could eat them easier. I smiled at the thought.

I then saw the canisters holding flour, sugar, and baking powder.

"Daddy would let me dip my strawberries straight into the canister, and you would always scold him for it, saying 'Johnny, it ruins the whole batch when you let her do that,'" I said, my voice shaking.

"You remember that?" my grandmother asked. She was shocked.

"Yes. And I remember this counter, where he'd give me vanilla ice cream with sprinkles…before dinnertime. I really liked sugar… Still do."

"Yes, that's right," she choked. "Here, let's go back here."

She led me, though she didn't need to. I remembered living in this house, just like I had lived here all my life. When we stepped into my daddy's room, the crying really began. The smell, that's what got me first. The smell of my daddy…whiskey and cologne. My daddy.

I cleared my eyes the best I could before I saw his bed.

"We'd sit here for hours. He'd read to me. And sing to me. And tell me stories," I stated as I wandered over to it. The same comforter was there, same Western Indian design. The painful memory also struck me, reminding me of the last time I had been to this room. The day I hid under the bed.

As I gained a little more control over the tears in my eyes, I looked around the room and spotted his jewelry box. I sauntered over to open it. And there were his turquoise rings. The ones I loved to play with. I picked one up. I remembered that when I'd play with them, I could stick four fingers in the place of his one. Now, as I mocked the motion, I could fit two. It made me smile. I had grown up. If nothing else, I knew it by this.

I placed them down and went over to the closet. I opened the door and was greeted by the wave of his scent. I stood there for a moment. Absorbing it. Taking it all in. I put my hands on his shirts and quickly found the one I remembered most. "This was his favorite. Maybe not the same shirt, but it's the same color," I said, stroking it. The tears were falling free once more.

"Oh, Natalie!" My grandmother broke out in sobs. "How do you remember all of these things? That was so many years ago," she questioned.

"I remember almost everything from that time because those were the happiest days of my life. I held on to my daddy, his memories, as long as I could. These memories… They kept me alive. They gave my heart a reason to keep beating."

"Oh, Natalie. I'm so sorry. I'm so sorry." She was hugging me now, holding me close.

"It's okay, Grandma. Don't cry. I'm okay now. I'm okay." I tried to console her. "Come, let's go back in the living room and talk."

We walked back to the living room, and I was very happy. The other rooms held too many reminders. The living room held the least amount of memories for me. I needed to, well, calm down a bit. Everything was just really overwhelming.

My grandmother and I talked for hours. I told her that I had been emancipated, and now I was in college, working for the hospital, planning on becoming a doctor.

"Oh, Johnny would be so proud of you, Natalie," she urged. I couldn't help but smile. That is one thing I could hear from him, which would probably mean the most. That besides "I love you."

We talked and talked. About life, about beliefs. I couldn't help but bring up God, and I was thankful when she told me that she had given her life to the Lord many years ago. But more importantly, so did my daddy.

"He went to heaven when he died, Natalie," she told me. "I know he did. In the hospital, he was ready to go. He told me that he was ready to go and live with the Lord."

Again I was crying relentlessly. I was so thankful. For one day, I knew for sure I would see my precious daddy again.

She showed me more pictures, some of family members and cousins. I remembered playing with some of them when I was little. It was all just surreal. Then I saw more pictures of my dad. In some he looked so frail, others so strong. I assumed the strong Dad was when he was on the wagon, the frail was when he'd fallen off. She showed me pictures of him holding me.

"You two were inseparable." She held them, remembering as well.

"Then why? Why were we separated?" I asked. I couldn't help it. I had wondered that my whole life.

She just looked at me with a mix of regret and sorrow in her eyes. "Natalie, it's a complicated story. And, well, I'm not sure it's mine to tell. I'm not sure John would want you to know."

"Well, John is not here. And I think I have a right to know. Please," I urged more sternly than I meant.

"Okay, okay," she agreed as she sat down across from me. She began to talk, careful not to look me in the eyes.

"Natalie, both John and Charlotte, they loved you. And you must never doubt that. But they had their problems. Charlotte, well, she was a wonderful person when she wasn't taking drugs. But when she was on them, she did horrible things. Your dad too was a good person, but the heroin changed him. But despite that, Charlotte and John were good together. They loved each other. They married, and about a year later, Charlotte was pregnant with you. She made a lot of mistakes, your mom. She had been married four times before and had four different husbands and a child by each of them. But you were her only child in wedlock."

"Four? I thought I only had two sisters and a brother. What about the other?" I interrupted.

"Your mom's firstborn, he died shortly after birth. I got all of this from your grandmother on her side. Charlotte was a wonderful person, but after she lost her baby, the drugs and alcohol consumed her. She was never the same and used substances to hide the pain of that. She got into many abusive relationships. She was beaten to a pulp by some of her husbands. No matter what or where, she was always in trouble. Always hiding, running from someone. She would get away from one abusive husband, only to get involved with another. Your grandparents on her side got to the point where they had to step away. When Charlotte was on drugs, she was destructive and dangerous.

"When your dad and Charlotte first met, it was much the same as her other relationships. John, he made mistakes, too. Drugs make you crazy, and that's what the two of them were together when they were on them. Absolutely crazy. But after a while, they found that their love was true. It was strong, and they quit the drugs together. Sobered each other up, then they got married, and she got pregnant. But addiction, it's a strong thing, Natalie. At the first sign of struggles between your mom and dad, Charlotte went back to cocaine. And shortly after, your dad was so distraught over it all, he went back to heroin. But then you were born—a new life to awaken theirs. You were so tiny when you were born and so sick. You were about as big as a Coke can, and the doctors kept telling us that you weren't going to live. But John and Charlotte, they didn't believe. They stayed with you. Day and night. Soon, they took shifts, watching over you. I was there. I just prayed and prayed. You were so little, but I knew that God had His angels on you. And for whatever reason, I knew you were going to be okay.

"Soon, they let you go home with Charlotte and John. Charlotte was working, and so was John. They were stable and were doing everything to take care of you the best they could. But still, you were so sick. And, well, as two drug addicts, they couldn't really handle themselves, much less you. They fought and fought and ended up back on the drugs. One night they got in a violent fistfight, and Charlotte…well…"

Her voice was weakening. I knew that it was so hard for her, but I needed her to continue. I needed to know what happened

"It's okay, Grandma," I soothed. "You can tell me. It's okay. I'm okay."

She looked weary but continued. "Well, she…she almost killed you, Natalie. She almost did. Then your daddy, he almost killed her for it. He walked in on her, trying to smother you… and he lost it. The police were called. And you were taken to your other grandmother's house while CPS investigated. But you were so sick, and she couldn't care for you. And at the time, neither could I. So we both decided to put you in temporary foster care. John was going to sober up again and get you back. Charlotte's rights were suspended. I was going to help him. It was just temporary placement until we could all just… get back on our feet.

"They placed you in the home of Jack and Faye Winters. A medical home they called it, where you would get all the care and help you needed. You had to go to so much therapy 'cause your legs, they were just so stiff. And you were so irritable. You wouldn't eat, drink, or anything. You hated to be touched as a baby. But your daddy, he was working hard. Harder than I'd ever seen him work. Unfortunately, Charlotte wasn't. And he told her that if she wasn't clean, she wasn't going to be around his daughter. He loved you, Natalie. He truly did. And Charlotte, she just couldn't do it. She tried, but it wasn't enough. John made her give up her rights. He wasn't going to let her or anyone else ever hurt you. He wasn't going to let anymore harm come your way. He felt so guilty, Natalie. But honestly, I think that's what sobered him up. Guilt.

"We started having visits with you, seeing you every week. But something about Jack and Faye Winters just wasn't right. You were different somehow. When we'd leave, you would cry and cry, begging us not to go. This got worse when we started having weekend visits. I remember one time I went to pick you up. You weren't as excited that it was I, instead of your father, but you were happy. It was strange because it was almost like you were relieved somehow. Then once we got into the truck, you said,

'Grandma, let's me, you, and Daddy run away. Let's get our stuff and run away, and no one will ever hurt us. Let's just run away.'"

I couldn't remember this, but I knew it was something I would have said. She continued, "I asked you why you wanted to run away, and you said, 'Those people are mean. They are nasty.' When you said those words, I had a sick feeling in my gut. But I didn't know what to do. We were under tight restrictions, and Faye had a good name with you. Your conditions were improving. Your walking was getting stronger, as was your speech. We couldn't prove anything, and the state was not on our side. I tried asking you what you meant by saying 'they are nasty,' but you wouldn't say much. Plus, your speech still wasn't all that good. Nothing more than 'I don't like them. I hate them.' I never told your father about it. I knew that if I did, he would do something stupid. Besides, all we could do was assume, and that serves no purpose. We're Irish, you know, and your daddy, his temper showed it. If I told him, there was no way we'd get you back because he was sure to kill them."

I couldn't question her logic. It was true. They were on the weaker side of the equation, and we had no room for new variables. Whatever was happening in the Winters home was just temporary, or so they thought. I wouldn't be there for long. Soon, I'd be back with my daddy, and everything would be just fine.

"But soon enough, your daddy got custody of you, and we took you home. Everything was just perfect. We were all perfect. You were getting so good at walking and talking. You were a little rambunctious one, that's for sure," she said, smiling. "But then Faye kept calling, asking questions, wondering how you were, wanting to see you. It was very strange. I didn't like it, but John thought it would be good for you to see them some. I mean, he saw that you lived with them, and they took care of you, so I think he felt he owed it to them for some reason, despite what I said. But Faye, she was a conniving woman. You give that lady and inch, she'd take you for a thousand miles."

"What do you mean?" I asked.

"Well, she started dropping by here unannounced. Bringing you gifts and clothes, making us feel…well, inferior. She started calling more and talking to John. I don't know what all she was telling him, but not long after, he started drinking again."

"Yes, I remember that. We'd go to the bar together. I…enjoyed it," I said meekly.

She smiled, shaking her head. "Yes, you did. You loved it, though I kept telling John that that alcohol would lead him back down a bad path. But you know kids. They don't listen to their mothers. But, well, I knew something was wrong. I asked him about it, but he wouldn't tell me. One Friday, Faye came over and asked to speak with your daddy. They left. They were gone for a while, and when they came back, Johnny was *so* upset. He went straight to the back room, picked you up, and woke you out of your sleep. He was crying, saying, 'I'm so sorry, Natalie. I'm so sorry. Daddy loves you. He always will.' He rocked and rocked you, wouldn't put you down. Later, I asked him what was wrong.

"He said, 'Mom, I'm just not a good dad. I can't provide for her. I have no money. I'm broke, and I'm a drunk.' His words pained me, and I knew better than to think they were his own. I asked who told him that, and though he never told me directly, I knew it was Faye Winters' doing. I tried to talk him out of that bad thinking, but he just wouldn't listen. He kept on. 'I'm not the best dad she deserves, Mom. She deserves more. Faye and Jack, they can give her much more.'

"I talked and talked to him. I tried to talk him out of it. I even told him what you told me. That got him all riled up. And fortunately, he let go of those silly thoughts of his. Or should I say Faye's. But unfortunately, it wasn't for long. One night, when he took you to the bar, Faye and Jack showed up. They threatened him. Blackmailed him, really. They were going to turn him in to get you back. They wanted you so much. John was so upset. He had lost his job, and we… Well, we were struggling. He came home that night and told me what happened. He then told me that he and Faye made a… They made a deal."

"A deal?" I couldn't help but ask. "What does that even mean?"

"I'm sorry, Natalie. Maybe I shouldn't be telling you this." She started to get up.

"No, please, Grandma. I want to know. Please, tell me. I deserve to know," I urged desperately.

She hesitated but then continued. "Natalie, Faye was going to turn your dad in. I don't know why she was so obsessed with you, but she was. I can't say I ever thought she loved you. She just… wanted you for some reason. It was like a competition, but John, he never got that impression. She told him that she would turn him in for taking you to a bar, or he could just hand you over, and he wouldn't get in any trouble. They… John, he didn't want any trouble. He was already dealing with legal fees and all sorts of things, so he—they—made an arrangement."

Her eyes weary and regretful, she continued. "The deal was that Faye wouldn't turn your daddy in if he just handed you over to them and let them be your parents. But in addition, Faye agreed to pay for his and Charlotte's divorce. Just to help eliminate Charlotte completely, I guess. She hadn't seen you in a long while, but Faye, she was very threatened by her. And then Faye… offered… She… she offered your dad some money. To get him on his feet and all."

"Money? She offered him money? For me?" I couldn't help the

outrage in my voice.

"Natalie, I'm sorry. I shouldn't be telling you this. No one was supposed to know." She got up and walked away, but I went after her.

"No! You tell me. I have a right to know this story. My dad is not here to tell me, and I want to know. He made a deal with Jack and Faye Winters. Me in return for a divorce and how much? Tell me, how much was I worth? Tell me!" I was yelling.

"Two hundred dollars," my grandma muttered as she turned.

Once again, for the thousandth time in this short time frame, tears were rolling down my cheeks. The realization of my dad selling me to that woman was mind-numbing.

We stood in silence for a long moment before I calmed myself enough to ask, "What was the building? The place he took me to. It smelled horrible." I recalled that incident, wrinkling my nose at the thought.

"It was an old run-down building downtown. Vacated, except for homeless people and drug addicts. They agreed to meet there. It was inconspicuous. No one could know what was happening."

"Yeah, I don't blame him. I mean, it was against the freaking law. He just handed me over? He didn't fight for me? What a coward," I said solemnly. I was ten different kinds of angry. And I couldn't help it. I was infuriated by all of this.

"Don't talk about your father that way, Natalie! He loved you," she scolded me.

"Loved me? He sold me. For a divorce and two hundred bucks! Why couldn't he see how evil she was? Who just hands over their child? And he never came to see me! He never made sure I was alright! Y'all never checked to see if I was taken care of! Regardless of his reasoning! I think coward suits!" I snapped back.

"He was anything but a coward. He took care of you. He loved you! Even when…you weren't even—" She stopped suddenly, holding herself from finishing the sentence. But I knew what she was going to say. I knew, but I needed to hear it.

"Weren't even what? Please, continue," I said, my voice laced with malice. When she didn't answer, I yelled, "Say it! Finish your sentence!"

"We weren't even sure he was your dad. Charlotte slept around. She was very promiscuous. And John, he didn't even care. There was a good chance you weren't even his! I told him to get a DNA test, but he refused. He took care of you when he probably didn't have to. He probably didn't even have any obligations to you anyways. He wasn't a coward! Anything but! And if that's what you call a man who takes a child who isn't his, there is something seriously wrong with your definitions!" she said with pure hatred, granting revenge for my words against her son.

I was shell-shocked. My daddy…the man I loved… Oh, I couldn't bear the thought of it. I turned, grabbed my purse, and walked out of that house. I went straight to my car, locked the door, and wailed like I never had before, not even in the darkest times in my life. For this was the darkest I had ever known.

I cried and cried. I was so upset with her, with my dad, but mostly with myself. I shouldn't have acted that way. I felt bad. I just wanted to know what happened. And now, I knew that I truly didn't.

I sat there in my car, thinking about all that my grandmother told me. My dad was, well, conned into giving me up to Faye and Jack Winters. But worse, he did it for something as meaningless as money. But I still considered the altruism he had. Perhaps if he thought he was doing me a service by sending me away with the Winters. Perhaps that was his way of taking care of me. And then there was the consideration that he might not even be my real father. I began to feel guilty for my outrage… I had no right to talk that way… My emotions just got the better of me.

But as I sat there sobbing, I realized that no matter what happened, there was no changing it. The past was just that—gone. John was my daddy. And regardless of blood, he would always be my daddy.

As I looked up while putting my car in gear, a red glare caught my eyes. As I turned, I spotted it. There it was: my airplane swing. The one that my daddy swung me in for hours and hours. The one where I didn't even have to look back to know he was there. The continuous momentum proved that he was. My daddy was there. My daddy, John Welch.

Trials and Tribulations

Wise are they who have learned these truths: Trouble is temporary. Time is tonic. Tribulation is a test tube.

—William Arthur Ward

I never found out if John Welch was truly my biological father. And honestly, I didn't care to. He was my daddy, and despite his mistakes, I loved him very much. My mother, too. It is a commandment to obey and honor your parents, and even though there was many a time that I was angry with them, I did my best to honor them by being the best person I could be. But forgiveness, it doesn't come easy. I still had so much anger and hurt in my heart. And some days, it got the best of me, especially when I learned more of the truth.

I contacted Mr. Wilson about Lamar and Taci. I needed to make sure they were okay. Unfortunately, he moved away, and the new caseworker, well, she wasn't so helpful. Because of rules and regulations, she could not disclose their location. Though I didn't like that answer, I was thankful that they were now following rules and regulations. Because, as I learned, for so long, they hadn't.

I spoke with the investigator handling Faye and Jack's case status. He too was very reluctant to give me information. But he allowed me to meet him and ask him questions.

As I pulled up to the station, it was just really intimidating. There were policemen everywhere with guns, badges, and radios. The environment was chaotic. And if I didn't know before that I never wanted to be a police officer, I definitely knew then. You could almost feel the stress in the air. I walked up to the counter and spoke with the receptionist. She was a very pretty blonde with perfect teeth. She was a little cold at first, at least until I mentioned my name.

"Hello, may I help you?" she asked matter-of-factly.

"Uh, yes. I'm here to see a...um, Mr. Myers," I said quietly.

"Okay. Do you have an appointment?" she asked hesitantly.

"Um, yes." My anxiety was creeping in.

"Okay. Your name?" she asked skeptically. I'm sure she thought I was a moron.

"Natalie Winters," I stated.

"Oh, okay, honey. Just give me a second to call him. Okay?" she said with a dashing smile, her tone changing instantaneously.

I waited for a few minutes until a large man approached the front desk. By his stance, I knew that he must be of extreme importance. He all but reeked of authority.

"Natalie, hello. I'm Detective Myers. Right this way to my office," he stated in an extremely deep voice. I quickly remembered what it was like to be arrested. Fortunately, that deputy wasn't as intimidating. If he had been the one to pull me over, I surely would have passed out. But I quickly dismissed the thoughts. I didn't want to reflect back on that time in my life.

As I walked in, I gazed around the office. It was decorated with plaques and numerous awards of achievement. There were degrees and diplomas. I hoped one day that I would have an office just the same.

Mr. Myers interrupted my thoughts. "Here, take a seat, Natalie. Can I get you anything to drink?" he asked.

My throat was dry from the nerves, but I said, "No, thank you." I didn't want to cause trouble.

"Okay. Well, I wanted to talk with you a little bit. I know that you've had a hard time with Jack and Faye Winters, and I just have a few questions for you."

"Yes, sir," I responded reluctantly. I hated talking about this.

"Okay, well, we are still investigating Emily's death. Can you tell me what you saw?"

Ugh, not this again, I thought. Why did I have to revisit this? "Sure, of course," I agreed. It was the least I could do for Emily, even as uncomfortable as it was for me.

I told him the story of that day. The feeding tube. My waiting. I half-expected him to arrest me when I told him that part. I knew that I probably deserved at least some jail time for how I neglected Emily that day. But he just took notes and listened patiently. He was very good at just letting me talk. After I finished, I had to get some tissues. Somewhere along the way, my traitor tears started flowing.

"It's all right, Natalie. I'm sorry. I know this is hard," he soothed. "Thank you for sharing. We are trying to make this right. I have some more questions for you, if that's okay."

"Yes, that's fine," I sniffled.

"Well, we've all done a lot of digging in the past reports made against Faye and Jack. I noticed one from you at an early age. Can you tell me a little about that?"

I was shocked by his question. That report, yeah, I remembered all too well. It was the only one I had ever made against Faye and Jack, and people, well, they betrayed me. My sadness was quickly supplemented by my irritation.

"Sure," I said. "I made that report as a child. It was my first and only cry for help, before the report on Emily's behalf was made. There was a girl in my class, Allison, who I talked to. She was my only friend at the time. We talked every day, and she asked me about my homelife, and for the first time, I shared the truth to someone. She then educated me on how those things that were happening were wrong and that I needed to tell our teacher. I was very reluctant, but I did. For the next few weeks, I was called out of class, examined, and the like. The caseworker told me that they were looking for a new home for me. But, well, that didn't happened. The case was dismissed, and Faye was somehow notified that I was the one who reported her. And I was punished." My voice grew quiet as I remembered the beating that followed.

"Punished?" Mr. Myers asked, prodding.

"Yes." I nodded.

"I know this is hard, but could you tell me a little about what punishment was?" he asked in a sympathetic but serious tone.

I paused for a long moment before I could answer. "My punishment, sir, was beatings. Severe beatings. Not by Jack, but by Faye. By her hands, by her legs, sometimes with a belt. Sometimes with a paddle or another objects. Whatever was near by. One time, it was with a flyswatter. Over and over again, across the face. Because I was a pest, or so she said. Other times, punishment was no food or water. And others, it was just extremely harsh words." My voice was quiet. I really didn't care to be talking about this.

"What about Jack?" he asked. "Did he ever hit you?"

"No. He never…hit me," I answered slowly. Gosh, I really didn't want to go there. I'd never told anyone about what Jack did, and I just couldn't. Could I?

"He never punished you?" Mr. Myers questioned again, reading my hesitant reaction, no doubt.

"He punished me…but not in the ways Faye did." My voice was wavering.

"How did he punish you, Natalie?" He was gentle, but I knew he wanted answers.

"He…Jack, he…He—" Oh gosh! I couldn't do this! *I can't talk about this.* I panicked. "Sir, I'm sorry. I just… I can't talk about this. I'm sorry." I started to sob. These memories were just too painful.

"It's okay, Natalie. It's all right. Here." He handed me more tissue. "I'm sorry. I'm so sorry." I knew that he knew the rest of my sentence though I couldn't say it.

We sat there for a moment in silence. He was letting me collect myself. I was appreciative of that.

"So you were never taken from the home? Is that correct?" He was changing gears. Thank goodness.

"No, I never was," I assured him.

"It is so strange. The documents that we found, there was a discharge report on you leaving the Winters home. It says that you went home with your father, John Welch. But you were never put back in CPS custody. I can't gather why you were back," he wondered aloud.

"Yes, well, my father and Faye…made a deal. I talked to my grandmother a few months ago. It was…under the table. Money and a divorce in exchange for me," I stated. The words still hurt. I knew they always would.

When I looked up at the chief, he had such anger in his eyes, but I knew it wasn't directed at me. Again, there was silence for a moment before he asked, "You never made any other reports other than the one from your childhood. Why?"

He was going back here? "I didn't make any reports because I was betrayed the first time around. No one listened to me. Faye and Jack they had a lot of people on their side. Plenty of the nurses and therapists went into the home. They had to see things, but Faye would offer them more hours—working hours, that is, if they kept their mouth shut. And it was a payoff for them. Those nurses would get so much overtime, and because Faye always had really sick children, it was a super steady income for them. The doctors, Dr. Schlock was the primary care for all of her babies. I can't say that he knew about any of the abuse, per se, but he gained a lot of income from her house. Faye was extremely good at hiding things. And as far as I can tell, Dr. Schlock just went along. People didn't question. Even though, they probably knew they should have."

He just sat there in silence, staring at me, shocked by my words, no less.

"It was a business, Mr. Myers. A corrupted business. Medicaid funded the way. Nurses got jobs. Caseworkers could pawn off some of their work. Therapists had it a lot easier. It was all tit for tat. Get what you can. And so, no one said anything. Dare you interrupt the status quo."

"Natalie, I'm so sorry. This is…outlandish."

"Yes, sir. It was," I agreed.

"Yes, but, well, I'm probably not supposed to tell you this. But I think you should know," he stated quietly. "You should know that there were many reports made against Jack and Faye. Tons of reports by various people. And when I say tons of reports, I mean hundreds.

But they were all just dismissed. Swept under the rug for whatever reason. Some, she got a slap on the hand, like a probationary period, but some, they were opened one day, closed the next with some sort of false misrepresentation bulls—."

He stopped and looked at me, asking excuse for his language, then continued. "But people, they tried. Natalie, there were people who tried to get you and the babies out."

Once again, I was crying. Somehow, his words were so relieving to me. All of those years I believed that no one cared, but clearly, that wasn't the case. I found so much comfort in knowing that there were people who questioned, even if they never got answers.

"There were reports from your teachers, from some of the nurses in the home, people from church. They tried, even though it seems it was in vain."

"Thank you, Mr. Myers." That was all I could manage.

"Natalie, still though, there is a lot of injustice here. I'm not sure that we are going to be able to convict Faye and Jack. These reports are outdated and not done properly. The evidence we have is circumstantial. The District Attorney is trying to push forward. But, unfortunately, there are some people…who are aligning themselves with Faye and Jack. Powerful people."

"What powerful people?" I demanded. Who was still sticking up for them?

"Natalie, I can't tell you that. But our case is quickly deteriorating."

"What can I do to help?" I asked before I even realized it. Did I even want to help? To be involved? I was trying so hard to get over this part of my life, but it just kept creeping up on me.

"Well, right now I'm not sure. I'll speak to the DA, but I need to know if…if you'd be willing to testify." He was serious now. His eyes were all but blazing with intensity.

"Like…in front of a courtroom?" I asked.

"Yes," he answered.

"I would…talk about what happened?" I questioned.

"Yes," he repeated.

"What about?" I asked, my voice laced with fear.

"Everything, Natalie. You would talk about everything." His answer all but gave me goose bumps. Everything? All of it? That was crazy. I couldn't, could I?

"Mr. Myers, but I…what if…" I stammered. My words were drenched in fear.

"Natalie, it's okay. Look, it's not going to be happening now. I don't know if it will happen. We just have to wait and see. Okay? You might not have to. It just depends. I just need to know if you are willing."

I paused for a long moment, thinking. Part of me wanted to run out that door and never come back. Leave here and just never return. But the other part of me wanted the fight. Not for myself, but for the children, for all of those years of pain and suffering inflicted on so many. And there was my answer. If I could do anything to make it up to those babies, it would be this.

"Yes, Mr. Myers. I'll testify," I stated softly, but with confidence.

"You're sure, Natalie?" he questioned.

"Yes, I'm sure."

"All right. Well, I'll be in touch with you. Like I said, the case is shaky. We might not. I just don't know." He was so conflicted with all of this.

"I'm here when you need me, Mr. Myers." I knew a short answer was the best route.

"Thank you, Natalie. You are a brave young woman."

"No, sir, I'm not. I'm just trying to do the right thing," I told him. I wasn't brave, even though people told me that often when they heard the story. People, they called me a hero at times, and I hated it. I was not worthy of such a title, and I would set anyone straight who thought that.

Mr. Myers didn't respond to my answer. I suppose he knew not to pick a fight you can't win. And judging by my reaction, I'm sure he knew I wouldn't believe a word he said with regard to my character.

"Okay, well, that will be all for now. Thanks for coming in, Natalie," he told me.

"You're welcome, sir."

"Did you have any more questions?" he asked, concerned, probably gathering the reluctance in me not wanting to leave.

"Actually, yes. I know you can't give me a lot of the information. But the reports… Is there any way I could get…information? I'm, well, I'm curious about it all."

He thought for a moment, gazing out his window. He was perplexed, no doubt. "Police reports are public record. You can… request them. It takes a while, but…" He took out a pen and grabbed a small card, writing something on the back. "She'll be the one to help you," he said, handing me the card with the name on the back.

"Thank you, Mr. Myers. Thank you so much," I said.

"Natalie, just be careful. Sometimes digging leads to some… Well, you just never know what you are going to find." There was so much warning in his voice. I knew he was probably aware of what I would see and was trying to protect me.

"I know, Mr. Myers. I do. But honestly, I know probably more than those reports could ever tell me. You see, I was there. I lived through them."

He looked down, hiding the pain that had suddenly appeared on his face. "I know this doesn't mean a lot, but I am sorry for your childhood, Natalie. I truly am."

"Thank you, Mr. Myers. But you needn't be sorry. For nothing that happened in that home was your fault. And, well, I'm okay now. I'm in college, and I'm… I'm all right." He needed some assurance.

"Well, for what it's worth, I'm… I'm proud of you, Natalie. I've seen a lot of people in a lot of bad situations, and, well, most of them, they don't end up with successful stories. But I know, I believe, that you will."

His words were so kind. "Thank you, Mr. Myers. That means the world to me," I said with a slight smile.

"Well, if you need anything, just let me know. My name and number is on the back of that card there," he stated, all businesslike again while rising.

"Will do, Mr. Myers. Thanks so much! I'll keep in touch." I shook his hand and turned to leave. I made it to my car and just sat there for a moment. Gosh, this was all just crazy. I had learned so much in this one morning. People had tried to help me, and though they didn't succeed, just knowing that they tried helped me somehow. That knowledge gave me hope—something I had done without for a long time.

After I made the information requests, the reports started coming in. Mr. Myers was right. Even though I had an idea of what

I would find, it was it wasn't any less hard less hard to read in black-and-white.

There were a ton of investigations on Faye and Jack Winters. All, like Mr. Myers said though, quickly dismissed. People had made reports on my behalf often. My nurse practitioner, teachers, and others I knew.

But, independent of me, there was a far greater upset. Throughout the twelve years I lived with Jack and Faye, eleven children died in the home. Eleven. Little Emily made twelve. A child a year. Some probably were because of initial medical causes from previous abuse. But I knew that the neglect they suffered shortened their lives. Some of the deaths were investigated by the homicide unit, however, the autopsies could never determine whether the deaths of the children were from the prior abuse that put them into the home or the abuse that occurred after they arrived. They never had a solid case, and this allowed Faye and Jack Winters to escape by the skin of their teeth every time. In addition, once they got away with one death, the next was much easier. Every investigation that came and went was a positive reinforcement for them, giving them more confidence, and ultimately, making them more daring.

I read the reports, but harder than that, I learned that even though there were many people who tried to report what Faye and Jack were doing and were suspected of doing, there were also many people who spoke on their behalf. That was very difficult to digest. Some I knew did it out of ignorance, out of blindness, not realizing what was really going on. But some, some I knew had done it intentionally for no other reason than to keep their jobs and to hold on to their paychecks. I couldn't imagine how money was more important to some than the lives of children. I just couldn't grasp and understand. And honestly, I hoped I never would.

A few months later, Mr. Meyers contacted me. It seemed someone again came to the Winters' rescue and offered expert testimony to relinquish Faye of her charges against her negligence against Emily. I was outraged when I heard the news. By the testimony of that person and a few others, the case was dropped. I offered my testimony once more, but Mr. Myers said that it wouldn't stand against the others. The case was dropped, right along with justice.

I was heartbroken by the news. Why did these people always get away with the crimes they had committed? I was angry, and I did more digging. I wanted to know who did this. But like Mr. Myers said, be careful when you go digging because you never know what you would find.

And that was the truth. I was not prepared for what I found. Dr. Schlock had offered the expert testimony. He stated that Faye's negligence was completely independent of Emily's death. He insisted that in all of the years he had known Jack and Faye Winters, he had never suspected any kind of abuse, neglect, or maltreatment. Because he was such an outstanding doctor, his testimony put a rather large dent in the case.

But that wasn't all. Bethany had testified, too. She said that Faye and Jack were not capable of taking care of kids, but that they didn't deserve jail time. She said that Faye never meant any harm, that she worked as hard as she could, and that she didn't think she deserved prison time. But a few weeks later, Bethany recanted her statement and told the truth about some of what she saw in the home. Unfortunately, it was too little too late. Her conflicting statements made her an unreliable witness; thus, the accreditation of what she said was completely invalidated. It was all over. I was no match for a doctor. At least, not at this point in my life.

Mr. Myers, I knew, was so upset over the outcome, calling it the largest case of injustice he'd ever seen. But that's just the thing. Justice will always prevail, in one way or another. Faye and Jack lost quite a lot, even though they didn't go to prison. They lost all privileges for taking care of children. They each lost their jobs, lost their income, and lost a lot of support from the people who they had conned over the years. It wasn't prison, but it was punishment. And, well, something is better than nothing. I know that Dr. Schlock had faith in Faye and Jack. And honestly, he should have. They conned him, and I knew that his testimony was his sincere, professional opinion. Though I wanted to, I could not blame him for his ignorance. The whole thing amounts to the fairy tale. It is much easier to believe than to realize that things aren't true, to realize that you've been helping the villain all along. Plus, opening yourself up to various lawsuits. And that was another thing— if all of these people who had seen and known of the abuse came forward, they too would be accountable; losing their licenses and would probably be reported for Medicaid fraud. Honestly, the whole situation was a horrible, negative feedback loop.

Bethany, too, I knew was scared. She had risked so much in all of this. Faye and Jack had a way of intimidating people, and she was one of them. Other nurses had refused to get involved, and I believe that Bethany at least tried, and I was thankful for that. It takes a lot to point out the wrongs of others while admitting your own at the same time.

I couldn't blame them for being scared. Because, honestly, I was, too. Mr. Myers also told me that when I was ready, I could assert individual charges. My statute of limitations didn't run out until I turned twenty-eight on most things. I considered it, but at that time, I just wasn't ready for something like that. I knew that before anything was done, I had to take care of myself. I had to cure the anger and resentment within my heart. I had to let go of the past, the mistakes of others, and the mistakes of my own. I had to learn to forgive. For any action taken in the spirit of revenge is a foolish one.

Trigonometry

....

In the middle of difficulty lies opportunity.

—Albert Einstein

....

Triangles are interesting in that if you know just enough about a few lines, you can figure out the angles and dimensions of the shape itself. There is a recipe, and once you learn all of the tricks, the math is very simple. It's just a matter of finding out the information. And that's what I continued to do. Even though I had learned a lot from my grandmother and Mr. Myers, I still had so many questions—not about my life, but the lives of the people who I had been around.

I began to do research first with police and what medical records I could find. I then went to the courthouse and pulled up old cases and documents. After that, I sought out people and did interviews. I found loads of information on my mom, dad, Faye, Jack, Adrianna, Cole, Molly (Faye's other daughter), my grandparents on both sides, my siblings. Everyone. During this process, I started to notice a trend, a heartbreaking one.

I started with Jack Winters. I learned that during labor, Jack got stuck in his mother's birth canal. During that period, medicine was not as advanced. He was deprived of oxygen, and that was the most probable cause as to why Jack was slower than most. I also found that his family rejected him. He had four sisters, all of which had nothing to do with him. His father was in the military, always gone. His mother was a cold woman who, from the words of others, never showed love or affection. Perhaps that's why sex was important to him. Maybe to him physical closeness was the only love he understood.

Faye's history was much worse. She was badly beaten by her mother as a child and was almost killed on several accounts. Her father was a very important figure in her life; however, he was not an emotionally strong individual. It took him until Faye was thirteen before he took her and left his wife. Faye was a fragile soul, a girl who had been hurt and told horrible things all her childhood. I realized that she carried the anger with her from those days and, unfortunately, was never able to outgrow that little girl. As I looked into Faye's psychology, I finally put it together as to why she loved taking the children from their parents. I figured it was because for so long, she wanted to be taken from hers. I think that's one of the problems she had. She took kids in her home not because she necessarily wanted children, but she enjoyed the taking itself. I believe she coerced my father into believing he was not a good one so that she could take me. Maybe she did love me, in her own way. Part of me believes that Faye, in her own way, sincerely believed that she did no wrong in her actions. That she was helping those children. But nonetheless, Faye Winters was angry. She passed on the hate and the anger to her two children, Adrianna and Molly, whom she also physically abused. I suspect Jack harmed them, in much of the same way he harmed me, but I don't know for sure.

Adrianna had children and continued that cycle of abuse and

dysfunction. I later found out that Jack was not her biological father. In talking to one of her friends, I found that Adrianna discovered this and did her own digging. Her biological father was in prison. She joined the army to get away from home but got pregnant and had to be discharged. As you know, she married Cole. Later, after my false imprisonment in their home, I found out that Cole was in some legal trouble. He and Adrianna had a disagreement, and he tried to kill her. His method? Strangulation. I suppose the man had a preference.

However, Cole, too, had a hard childhood. He lost his father at an early age and was forced to grow up far too quickly. His family was poor, and he worked his whole life while, I think, seeking for a father's love and never quite finding it.

Molly also fell into the bounds of these horrific chains. She was borderline in intelligence and was given a diagnosis of mentally disabled. Faye had abandoned her at some point, and she ended up on drugs. One day I was driving downtown to the library, and I saw her on the street. I stopped to talk to her. I told her to get in my car, and I drove her to a homeless shelter. We talked, and I was stricken with grief when she told me what she was doing for work. Molly was a prostitute. She was selling herself for money and drugs. I asked her if Faye and Jack knew what she was doing. She told me that they knew, as it was Faye and Jack who told her to do it, because they wouldn't pay her way, and she had to make a living doing what she could. I tried to talk to her, telling her that there were other options. I let her out at a downtown women's shelter, hoping she had listened to my encouragement to find work and money elsewhere. I called the shelter and tried to explain and urged them to help her.

Over the next few months, I called every week to see how she was doing. But unfortunately, one week I was disappointed when I found out that Molly hadn't done away with her past job and was suffering from cocaine addiction. She continually broke the rules in the shelter, bringing in men and drugs, and thus, had to leave.

A few months later, I got another call. Molly had returned to the home and had conceived a child. They asked me if I could take the baby. As much as I wanted to, I had to decline. I was a child myself, in many respects. I didn't have the money, and honestly, I didn't have the willpower. There is a point where you have to draw the line as to how much help you can offer. I knew by taking that child, I would be inviting a lot of things in my life. Not to mention Faye and Jack Winters. I felt sorry for the child, but I felt that I couldn't offer any more help than I already had.

The baby was born with several disabilities and ended up being placed in the system. Molly was trying to go through rehab to gain custody, but she relapsed. Later, I heard that her diagnosis had manifested into paranoid schizophrenia and she was hospitalized.

My father, John Welch, too had a difficult childhood. My grandmother lived a reckless life in her younger years. She had four different children, and all were without their father, and they grew up in poverty. My father liked to have fun but was also trying to escape his pain by doing so. He started drinking and then smoking. Not long after that, marijuana was introduced, which led into heroin and cocaine. But I know that despite his addictions, my daddy loved me. I know that he tried his best.

When I looked more into his records, I spoke with his brothers. They too had severe issues with drinking and drugs. But for the most part, they were sober. One of the men, Joe, was really nice. He told me a lot about my daddy. Joe explained that he was funny, smart, and was always making people smile. While we were talking, Joe told me that I favored John. Honestly, it was the nicest compliment I'd ever been given. Of course I favored him; he was my daddy.

I asked Joe why he thinks my dad did what he did. He told me that John just wanted the best for me, but he didn't believe he was the one to provide it. During that time, he was struggling every way a person could, and it was just too much. But Joe also told me that after John took me to Faye and Jack, he never really recovered. After that, he drank himself into his grave. The guilt was too much, and he never forgave himself but just prayed that God would forgive him for abandoning his children. When he spoke in the plural, I couldn't help but be astounded. I was informed that I had an older brother, but I was also encouraged not to speak to him. He was located in a Florida maximum security prison for murder. Joe explained that it would not be safe for me to seek any information there, as he believed my brother to be a very dangerous man. For that reason, Joe wouldn't even give me his name. I decided it best to take his word of advice.

My mom, Charlotte, had what appeared to be a pretty normal childhood. Her mom was a stay-at-home mom while her dad was in the military. They were good parents, but her father was extremely strict. Charlotte made straight A's in school and was on the gymnastics team. She even competed and almost got on the US Olympic team. However, in her older years, she became rebellious, and started to make bad decisions. She ended up in the wrong crowd and was introduced to the wrong things. She became pregnant and lost her baby boy. Never being able to recover, she went to drugs for escape. Before too long, she was in and out of abusive relationships and jail. When she died, it was from overdose. But the Tennessee medical examiner, when I spoke to him, said that he ruled it an accidental suicide, telling me that there was so much of so many things in her system, he thought that she must have had conscious awareness of what she was doing. At the time of her death, she was seeing a man, a truck driver, but their relationship wasn't working.

He left her three weeks before she passed. My mother died alone in a hotel room.

Family members—most, if not all—on both sides of my family suffered from drug and alcohol abuse. All had many struggles as children and were swept in the deathly currents of poverty and corruption. Some made it out without drowning. Others did not.

I also did quite a lot of research on myself. I received the reports from my earlier years in the system. As it turns out I was absolutely right about Faye not liking me. During monthly reports, she stated several times that she did not feel a connection with me, saying that it just "wasn't working." They claimed that I was hard to handle and not easily loved. On two occasions, she actually requested me to be moved from the home. Unfortunately, there was nowhere else for me to go. Their home was the only medical home in the area, and since my dad was working to get custody back, my caseworker said it was necessary that I stay in the area.

Oddly enough, I never truly got the answer as to why she and Jack brought me back. I don't suppose I'll ever really know. I just know that I was stuck there. The documents I found on my alleged adoption were sealed. And the ones that weren't sealed were blacked out and unreadable. There were many things that really made no sense at all, and part of me doesn't think that they ever will.

I also got access to the runaway report filed when I was emancipated. I couldn't help but be shocked. Faye and Jack called the police around nine thirty, three and a half hours after I had "run away." But when the police showed, they asked questions about me, like what I said when I left and how I had been acting lately, that sort of thing. As I read the report, I found it interesting how none of the officers' questions were accurately answered.

In the report, Jack said that I said I was going out for a job because I needed to get some money. Faye said that I had acted defiant and that I was a troublesome child, saying I was rebellious and reckless and that she thought I was on drugs. The officer then asked for my basic height, weight, hair, and eye color. What I was wearing. And, well, they didn't know. They told the officer that I was 5'2". I am only five feet. They said my hair color was blondish. Well, that's sort of right, if it had been three years earlier when I had highlights, but at the time, my hair was a hazelnut brown, my natural tone. My eyes are a light golden brown, almost hazel. Faye said they were dark brown and that I weighed about 125 pounds. That was the funniest. I was maybe 105 at the most. Maybe it's petty of me to pick at these things, but then again, I think not. From what I know about parents, they are aware of every freckle on their child, no less their height and weight. I knew they didn't care as normal parents would, but you would think after living in their house for about twelve years that they would at least know what I looked like.

One thing Jack did get right though. When asked about what I was wearing that morning, Jack said, "She is wearing her letterman jacket and red shorts that said *cheer* across the butt." I wasn't the least bit surprised he would know that. The man would be checking out my butt on the way out the door.

When I learned these things, I began to see everything in a different light. I began to understand somewhat of why these people behaved as they did. In some respects, I could relate to them. I saw them all as the children they once were. When I reflected on Faye's childhood, I saw her as a little girl—a lot like the little girl I once was. I saw the hurt that Jack must have felt, being abandoned and unloved. I reflected on the pain my daddy must have felt when he thought he failed his child because I too felt as though I failed many children. I saw Adrianna and Molly differently as I knew their childhoods were probably very similar to mine: hard.

And as I learned the things of their pasts, those things morphed into a key to the lock on the door of forgiveness in my heart. And with that, I was able to start to forgive. I don't excuse any of their behavior, and honestly, as an adult we all have our own choices, chances to change things. Though it is difficult, the possibility is there. But independent of that, these findings helped dissipate some of the rage in my heart.

I also learned by my research that one's choices are not solely your own as they affect many around you and those that come after you. It is a vicious cycle. And unfortunately, our way of thinking is often an impediment to breaking these cycles. I know for me it was extremely difficult. When I was homeless and on my own, when I was so hungry that I would have done almost anything for food, when I was so tired, so angry, so sad, so desperate, I understood how easy it was to slip through the cracks of the horrible world we live in.

And the worse part of it is, if I would have failed or ended up on drugs or selling myself on the street, society would not only expect it, but also most likely accept it. People say far too often, "Well, look what happened to them. Look what their parents did." I will say as a survivor, though those things are relevant, they cannot be used as means to an end. Abuse is terrible, and as much as I wish it was exonerated, it isn't. It affects you and, a lot of times, in ways you don't really notice.

Emotional abuse is no less harmful than a blow to the head. When people tell you things that are hurtful as a child, you believe them without question. I used to believe Faye and the things she said to me. When she would say I was ugly, I accepted it. When she told me that no one would ever want me, I thought it to be true. However, when I was older, I began to realize that perhaps Faye was mistaken. But honestly, there will always be a part of me, that little vulnerable child, that believes what she said. When I fail, when I make mistakes, my thoughts drift back to her words. Forever will they be etched in my brain. Though most days, I have the strength to ignore them.

Physical abuse is also something that I think most don't quite get. They limit it to being hit, kicked, punched, and restrained. But it's not just the physical pain. When you're hit over and over again, the physical pain starts to reach beyond the surface of your flesh. That sting goes deep, and it envelops your soul, taking over like a burning sensation. It becomes a continuously burning fire that you start to believe will never be put out. A bruise on your skin may last a few days, but a bruised soul may last forever. To this very day, if someone grabs me from behind, I freak out. When someone lifts their hand or moves too quickly, I flinch. My wounds physically are healed, but mentally I don't believe one can ever completely recover, but rather just learn to cope.

Sexual abuse, I feel, mostly affects one's mind. It alters your thinking before one can prevent it. It destroys your self-esteem to the point where you cannot grasp it until you are an adult. Most people who suffer from sexual abuse don't talk about it until they are about twenty to twenty-two years of age. Why? Well, at least for me, it took me that long to realize what happened wasn't my fault, and I wasn't responsible. It took me that long to realize that I wasn't dirty. I wasn't bad. That I wasn't a whore. I had to admit it to myself. I had to accept what happened and deal with it from within before I could let anyone know. I think a lot of women who are abused have the same type of reaction. Time. You just need a lot of time for healing. The first time I ever talked about my abuse was when I witnessed these very pages. That's what I needed. Because as I told the horrific stories, when I talked of the horrible fear, my blank pages didn't react. They didn't judge or comment. There was no gasping or tears. They just listened. I feel like that's what helps the most. You need someone to listen. Then you have to accept that you can't change the past. Then, you look to the future...

I look back on my childhood and its dimensions. How there were things that affected me and my position before it ever really occurred to me. People ask, after hearing a little about my story, what happened and why nothing was ever done. But not only that, they see my successes and dismiss the effect of the abuse and discount the work I have put into becoming a better person. People doubt. People ask why the abuse I suffered was not discovered. They ask why I am now normal. They question how I am who I am today.

For those questions, I cannot be sure of the exact answers, but here are my hypotheses: The main reason I believe that no one saw the abuse I suffered was because it was minimal compared to my surroundings. One must understand, the children in our home were sick. They were on ventilators; they had feeding tubes, missing arms or legs, body casts, malformed heads because parts of their skull had been removed. When walking into a room full of children like that, one hardly notices the little girl in the corner with a bruise on her face. One hardly sees the pain in the eyes of a little girl who is walking when focusing on a child who is fighting for their life.

In addition, I was the only child in the home with normal cognitive abilities. Those babies couldn't talk. Faye and Jack preferred medically fragile children, because of that very reason. They got a bigger paycheck, and they didn't have to worry about the kids talking about the abuse that was going on, because the children weren't able to. And their deaths, well, most of them were sick in the first place. It was very easy to cover up. And it was a very smart game to play.

In terms of being normal, well, I believe that to be false. I was never a normal child because I learned much about the world too early. My surroundings, my development was skewed on many different levels. I had to find different ways to make sense of the world I was living in. To be honest, I am very much an addict. My addiction may not be drugs, alcohol, or sex, but those things are replaced with school, achievement, and success. I am consumed with being a successful person, and it just so happens that my addiction is one of productive sorts. And for the record, I have no intentions to ever be what society refers to as normal. Though I tried my best to learn normal, I look at some of the things I did as a child to help myself cope with the world I was in. School was number one. Getting an A on a quiz was my encouragement. I also remember watching people as a child and learning from their actions. And there were little things that I believe severely impacted me.

One of my favorite TV shows to watch when I wasn't in trouble was *Walker, Texas Ranger*. I remember watching Chuck Norris come back every week for a fight. I remember thinking, *This guy never gives up. Even when he knows he's about to take a blow, he doesn't back down. And Walker, he always does the right thing.* I sincerely believe that Chuck Norris taught me to be tough. I'd watch him and all the fighting scenes and imagine myself fighting back one day. Standing up and taking down the people who hurt me. Not necessarily in a violent way, just figuratively. There was inspiration there. Endurance.

As a teen, I loved *Dr. Phil*. One reason is because when I watched the individuals on the show and learned of their problems, most of the time I could relate them to Faye and Jack. There were always similarities, and I would sit there and watch Dr. Phil tell them how much of a moron they were for behaving this way. I loved that show. It always made me smile. I figured if Dr. Phil was telling you that you were a moron, you probably were. And though he wasn't directly talking to Jack and Faye, I knew that he very well could be, and that was enough.

But, the most prominent reason I believe that I am okay is because the grace of God led me ever since I can remember. I don't recall ever being introduced to God, but I always knew His voice. For a long time, I thought of it like Jiminy Cricket from Mr. Walt Disney or what Oprah referred to as "your whispers." I also remember one week while attending Bible school, I prayed a prayer asking Jesus into my heart. I was only seven years old, and honestly I can't say that I knew what it meant, but I know that I meant it. That same week, I won a new Bible for memorizing the most Bible verses. I kept that Bible with me most of the time. It was so small I could just fit it in my pocket. Sometimes when I was in trouble, Faye would make me go to the closet. I'd have to stay in there for hours upon hours. But during that time, I would read the little Bible. It was very difficult, and most of the time I didn't understand, but I knew it was God's word, and it would help me. And He did. I didn't have my daddy, but I most certainly had a father.

Another part of my resilience was that I knew that Jack and Faye Winters were not my parents. I saw them as people. I believe my outcome would have been dramatically changed if my daddy was the one who sexually abused me or my real mom was the one who hit me and beat down my self-esteem. But I always knew that it wasn't them. Jack and Faye were just people to me. I never saw them as my parents. My ability to have logic and my intellect also helped me see past the things they said and the actions they portrayed.

However, at the end of the day, I do not have answers for all of the people who have questioned me. I have learned that pleasing people is a tiresome job that never ends, so it's better left undone. This is my story, and if there is one thing I have learned, it is that for every one person who believes you, there are five who won't. For every word of encouragement, there will be a sentence of disgrace. People are sometimes cruel creatures, but sometimes they are also beautiful. I know in my heart that there are worse stories. Many people suffer from horrid things, which they shouldn't have to. The world is sometimes a treacherous place. When there is a storm, it's so easy to be distracted by the thunder and lightning, but we must remember that even the most ferocious of winds still bring the rain… Those storms bring water, for nourishment and for growth. However, I believe that coming out of bad situations ultimately depends on how you look at them in the first place. As in trigonometry, it all depends on the angle.

Conditioning Forgiveness

· ·

To be a Christian means to forgive the inexcusable because God has forgiven the inexcusable in you.

—C. S. Lewis

· ·

As I began to forgive, I examined my heart and all of my wrongdoings. Sometime later, I wrote Faye and Jack a letter of apology. I lied to them on several accounts during my last months there. I knew that I needed to tell them what I did in order to escape, but nonetheless, they were lies. I also announced in that letter that they were forgiven, and I apologized for the way I left. I can't imagine what it must have felt like for them to just suddenly realize a person was gone from their lives, even if that person wasn't really wanted. But explaining it was the only way I knew. Doing this was a relief for me. I had to clean out all of the baggage that had been buried for so long inside my heart. I hoped that in my forgiveness of them, they could someday come to forgive themselves.

It was a battle for me to forgive and break the chains, but it was a necessary one. Forgiveness is necessary. Often, people question as to how I could do that, but it's not a step-by-step process. It is a daily process. And some days it comes easier than others. However, it's an important and essential journey. I knew that Faye and Jack and a lot of people have anger in their hearts. And what that does to a person is something I never wanted for myself. Hatred is poison to the soul, and even if it is hard to do, it's important to let go of that anger, as one's heart becomes hardened if you don't.

If there was one thing I learned in all of my research, it was that if you don't let go of the people who hurt you, you become those people. I continuously saw pictures of how people become what they hate, just because they didn't let go. And hate is very powerful. Before you know it, it will consume you. Antagonism and abhorrence are heavy things to carry around, so it's best just to drop them off, come to terms with what happened, and move on with the future. People will tell you to forgive and forget, but I don't agree with that. Most definitely forgive, but I think only a fool would try to forget. For the past is a part of what makes us who we are. The things I endured in my childhood were horrible, and they most definitely didn't make me who I am, but how I dealt with them did.

So I embarked on the journey of clemency. If not for Faye and Jack, for myself. However, nothing is worth anything if not tested, and that's exactly what happened.

One morning, I was at a local coffee shop when I ran into one of Faye's acquaintances. As much as I wanted to make a run for it when she saw me, I wasn't able to.

"Oh, Natalie! How are you?" she asked.

"I'm very well. And yourself?" I asked politely. Remembering her face, but not exactly placing her name…

"I'm good, but have you heard about your mom, Faye?"

Ugh, those words got under my skin quickly. I hated any reference to her as my mom, but I kept my cool. "No, I no longer speak with the Winters family," I informed her.

"Oh. Well, Natalie. Faye is dying. She has some sort of heart problem, and she broke her back a few weeks ago. She's been in the hospital for a while now." She stopped, gauging my reaction.

I tried to keep my expressions under control, careful not to give anything away. "Oh, well, I'm sorry to hear that."

"Natalie, I know that she would love to see you. I know...I know it was hard and all. The situation between you two, but she is dying..." She trailed off.

A situation? "Yes, well, what happened between the Winter family and myself was much more than a situation. And I think it best if I keep my distance."

"Natalie, I don't know what went on. I just know that Faye has been asking for you... She just... she really wants to see you. She has been adamant about it since she got sick."

This lady had some nerve trying to give me the guilt trip. But more so, I was astounded that the guilt trip was working. I responded before I knew what I was saying. "I'll think about visiting her."

"Oh, good. It's the right thing, Natalie. Maybe you two can put away your differences."

Not likely, my inner self coached. "Maybe. Thank you, I'll see you around," I stated aloud and walked away. I quickly hurried out of the building and got in my car, thanking the Lord above for an operating driver's door. I had saved up enough money to get a new vehicle. Though it had a salvaged title, it was an Infiniti G20 at a very good price and in excellent condition.

I drove away thinking about visiting Faye, and I continued

thinking about it through the rest of the week. I went back and forth, back and forth. Yes, visit her. No, absolutely not. You know in cartoons how there is the little devil and angel on either side of your shoulder? Yeah, that's exactly what was happening.

I had so much anger against both Jack and Faye, even though I was trying to forgive them. They caused me so much pain and so much heartbreak. And honestly, parts of me were still fearful of the both of them. No matter what I achieved, majored in, or overcame, there was a part of me that would always be that little girl, that scared little girl who was too many times the victim of Faye's rage and Jack's obsessions.

The whole week, I debated. One minute I told myself, *Absolutely not*. While the next, I was thinking, *You probably should*. I was back and forth, back and forth. Until one day, leaving work, I realized that I had assumed the worst of Faye, and why she wanted to see me. What if she wanted to see me to apologize? What if she needed my forgiveness?

I answered my own question by remembering that we all make mistakes, but God forgives us, even if we don't deserve it. He could deny us, but He looks past our transgressions, not only to forgive us, but also so that we may forgive ourselves. I was in the process of forgiving Faye, but more so, I knew that she needed to forgive herself. If she was dying and I denied her that chance, the chance to say sorry, I would be no better than she.

And with that, I decided I would go see Faye and Jack. They might not say sorry, but they might, and I would not stand between them and what God was doing in their lives. People talk about what Jesus would do, and I knew this was it. Though it would be hard, scary, and downright insane in some sense, I would go. For as much as my life experience has taught me, anything worth doing is at some point difficult.

Friday afternoon was the only day I had any downtime. I didn't have any classes, and I tried to schedule it where I didn't have to work at least until seven that evening. I knew that I needed to go and see Faye and get it all over with. I called the hospital where I thought she would be and learned her room number.

As I got into the elevator, I was more nervous than I had ever been. I kept having these moments of panic where I just wanted to stop, run, and never look back. But when I made it to the fifth floor, I knew there was no turning back now. There it was, 508. That was her room number. I walked slowly down the hallway. Cautiously. Not ready for whatever I was about to encounter.

The door was slightly opened. I knocked, but there was no answer. I slowly, hesitantly, pushed open the door, and I was greeted by no one. I turned on the light, and as I looked around the room, I grew… sad.

The bed was empty. There were tubes and various disposable medical supplies on the ground. It was a scene that I recognized. The room looked like a room that had witnessed a code. A room where they were leaving in a hurry, and in more cases than not, they wouldn't be back.

Tears struck my eyes. This foreign emotion that I didn't expect. I was…disappointed that she wasn't there. If she died, she never knew that I forgave her, and she would never know to forgive herself. Again, I was met with that time clock. Much like the clock that I faced when I waited before I talked to my mother. You don't wait for tomorrow; you do whatever needs to be done today, because tomorrow might not show up.

I started to cry. I knew that I had let God down. "God, I'm so sorry. I'm so sorry. You gave me an opportunity, and I didn't take it diligently." My cry was quiet, but it was sincere. I couldn't help but wish that I had done it sooner. Much to my surprise, I was wishing for another opportunity.

Amid my crying, I was startled by the opening of the door.

"Oh, hi, I didn't realize anyone was in here," the nurse said. She was so pretty. She had long dark curly hair and dramatic red lips. Probably in her early thirties. She looked like someone whom I would get along with.

"I'm sorry. I was just here visiting," I said meekly, not really sure of what to say.

"Oh, well, Faye Winters went home this morning," she said.

"She went…home? I thought she was in critical condition?" I offered.

"Yes, ma'am, she is. But she signed a DNR and said that she didn't want to die in the hospital, so she talked to her doctor, and they discharged her. There isn't really anything else left to do, so he let her go home," she said so sweetly, noticing my distress no doubt.

"So she's alive?" I stammered.

"Yes, she is. I'm sure you could call her and see her there." She stroked my back, soothing me.

I was stunned. The Lord, well, I knew better than to put it past Him. And they do say to be careful what you wish for. I smiled meekly while answering her, "Yes, ma'am. I'll do that."

I walked out of the hospital perplexed. I couldn't believe this afternoon. I wasn't excited about going back to the Winters house, but I wasn't going to miss the opportunity. If anything, God was testing me, and I was an A student.

Driving away from the hospital, I was very thankful for my visit there. If anything, it was a little pilot study for me, a preparation for the real thing.

When I pulled up to the old house, my butterflies and anxiety were ever present again. This house was much less safe than the hospital. I was not on neutral territory, and as I got out of my car, I realized that I could be in danger. But I quickly dismissed that. If anything, I didn't think they'd be that stupid.

I reached the door and lightly tapped, knowing full well that they couldn't hear it. *Just a practice round*, I thought. And I knocked louder this time. The door opened, and there stood Jack. Immediately, I felt a wave of apprehension.

"Natalie?" he questioned.

"Hi, Jack. I'm here to see Faye. I hear she is sick," I said simply.

"Oh, okay. Well, she's upstairs in her room resting." He opened the door further to let me in.

"Thanks," I said, and I walked through the door. The smell was all too familiar. The scene was almost identical. I had to force my feet to continue.

I made my way up the stairs, Jack lingering behind me. The door was slightly open, so I gently knocked while pushing it further. Faye was lying there on the bed. She looked…horrible. Her arms were badly bruised from all of the IVs. She was pale but somehow still had a yellowish tint to her skin. Her eyes were sunken in while her mouth was twisted into the frown that was usually there, but this time it had a permanency to it. A sadness. I immediately felt so sorry for her. Even if I didn't like the woman, I remembered the child she once was.

"Faye?" I said quietly before she met my eyes.

Choking, she answered, "Natalie? Is that you?"

"Yes." I knew my appearance had changed very much since the last time she saw me. "You wanted to see me?"

"Hi, Natalie," she said weakly.

"Hello," I responded solemnly. She just stared at me, not giving anything away. I had no idea what she was thinking.

"Your jacket is very nice. Where did you get it?" she asked very unexpectedly.

What? I thought. *What is she doing?* But I answered, "Um, I bought it." Maybe she was trying to lighten the mood.

"Oh, well, it must be nice to have money." Her tone quickly changed into one all too familiar: one of disapproval and hatred. Immediately, I knew this was not going how I thought it might.

"Yes, ma'am," I agreed. But before I knew it, she was ranting and raving.

"You know, you completely destroyed my life. All I did was give you a home when no one in this g-dd—n world wanted you. You know, your dad practically gave you away. I didn't have to pay him that much. I realize now though, I got screwed! You are a f—ing little brat. You always have been."

I stood there silently as she continued. I would not run. I'd let her finish.

"I wish I would have gotten rid of you a long time ago. You are nothing but trash. That's where you came from, that's what you'll always be. You come into this room prancing in your new clothes! I'd bet you're a prostitute or something. That's all you're good for." She was laughing now. "God only knows Jack figured that one out, didn't he?"

The words were like shards of glass ripping and tearing my very being. I swallowed hard, coaching myself to stay put.

"You are just so f—ing stupid. And you think you're going to go to school? What the f— ever. You'll quit. You're not good enough. Never have, never will be." Coughing now, she couldn't keep up with herself. "I don't know what I ever did to you that you think was so bad. Ungrateful! You are just a waste! A waste of life. You know, Charlotte almost aborted you. She should have! I mean, look at you…worthless. A worthless waste." She was hacking now, trying to catch her breath.

My inner patient caregiver took over while I went and handed her a glass of water. "Here. Drink it slowly," I said softly.

"Get out of my room. I never want to see that ugly f—ing face again." She motioned with her arm for me to leave.

I walked toward the door, but I turned before leaving. I listened to her, so now, she was going to listen to me. She wasn't the only one with words.

"Faye, I'm sorry you are so angry. And more so, I'm sorry that you believe that I caused that anger. But I just want you to know that I forgive you. I forgive you for all of the hurt and pain you inflicted on me. I forgive you for the harsh words and severe beatings. I forgive you for starving me. I forgive you for causing me to believe that I wasn't worth living. I forgive you for taking away my childhood. I forgive you for taking away my daddy. I forgive you, and I hope that one day, you'll forgive, too. Yourself and whoever has hurt you so."

There was a look of shock on her face, along with a lack of understanding. I turned quickly, running into Jack but continued down the stairs. I was running down them, as fast as my little legs would allow. I just really needed to get away… from all of this.

"Natalie!" Jack called out. I didn't want to turn. I was almost at the door. I wanted the hell out of that house. Now. But when he called my name again, I heard the emotion. I turned.

"Natalie! I'm sorry. I'm so sorry," he said. I was shocked when I saw that he was crying. His tears were mimicking mine. "I'm so sorry," he said again.

I was at the door now, and I just wanted to run away and never return. But before I did, I turned, my tears flowing steadily as his, and I stated, "Jack, I forgive you, too."

Fast. I was driving fast down the highway. Emotions were surging through me. I was mad, happy, sad, enraged, pleased—all of it. And even though that was probably the worst thing I had ever experienced, I was thankful. I did the right thing.

Faye's heart was hard, but regardless of what she said to me, I knew part of her words were directed at herself. You see, that's what we do when we point out the flaws in others. In most cases, we see the same flaws in ourselves. I knew that Faye, for whatever reason, saw in herself the things she claims she saw in me. She was a broken woman, and that was just something that was out of my hands.

Jack's apology was surprising. But I suppose that's how God works. Nothing is without reason. His apology helped me. It was part of the process that would help me move on.

When I told Jack and Faye that I had forgiven them, I knew that the task wasn't complete. But that's just the thing. In saying those words, I made a promise to them, to myself, that I would continue to forgive them. I couldn't go back on the words I told them. And I wouldn't.

Character is a muscle in a lot of respects. You have to nourish it but challenge it. You have to strengthen it and push the limits. Forgiveness is exercise. It is the run that gives you the strength to merely walk day to day. Character must be conditioned, and forgiveness must be worked at.

A New Generation

*Parents can only give good advice or put them on
the right paths, but the final forming of a person's
character lies in their own hands.*

—Anne Frank

I worked so hard to become a person of character and someone that God would be proud of. In so many ways, I was becoming a new person. But part of me still had trouble moving on. Part of the problem was with my last name. I just hated introducing myself as Natalie Winters. The name *Winters* in my mind just stood for cold people with dysfunctional habits. And in addition, the name was associated with child abuse in the eyes of some of the townspeople. Introductions are forever lasting, and I absolutely hated mine.

So I decided I would change my name. After calling an attorney, I quickly realized after learning the cost involved, that I'd have to be resourceful and do it myself. At first, I thought it best that I take my father's or mother's name, but I decided that neither of them was ever really there for me, and both represented brokenness in my eyes.

I thought and pondered, trying out so many names. Nothing

seemed to fit. Maybe it was strange to want to do this, but I needed it. I began to pray to God. I needed the perfect one. A strong name. I wanted a new generation. One that had values, courage, and strength. One that would start with me. I promised I would break the cycle of drugs and violence, addiction and impulse. I would make a new way, but it would be one He would have to provide.

So after months of researching and prayer, I found the best pick. I studied up on the process to perform a name change in Texas, and it didn't seem too difficult. And, well, it was really my only option. It was going to cost $500, money I didn't have, but I worked to get it. I signed up for every extra shift I could manage and did some extra tutoring. I wanted this more than anything.

My determination paid off. Literally. After months of saving, on April 29, 2010, my court date was set. I was so nervous about the thought of going in front of a judge. But I loved a courtroom. I still had that fond memory of being able to go home with my daddy from that place of justice.

As I arrived, I was dressed in my sharpest clothes: a gray pantsuit and a white shirt. I needed to look professional and dignified. Walking in, a woman asked me what law firm I was from. I couldn't help but smile, comforted by the fact that I must look something close to a lawyer.

I prepared a speech for the judge. In my research, I found that he could deny my motion, and then I'd have to appeal. And, well, there was no way I could afford all of that. This just had to be a one time thing. This was my shot.

I was scheduled for 2:00 p.m. As the lady called me into the courtroom and stated my case number, I was so nervous you would have thought I was on trial. I walked into the room, which smelled of leather and books. The bailiff was at the edge of where the witness usually sits, and a young woman was taking notes. I walked up past the seats where the audience of a trial would sit until I was right in the middle between the prosecution and defense side.

The judge was an older man. His mouth turned into a frown. He looked tired. As he looked up, he was peering over his glasses, evaluating me, no less. For a moment, we just gazed at each other. I, no doubt, was not breathing.

Then I gasped in surprise when he said, "State your name for the record."

"Natalie Elizabeth Winters," I said, my voice shaking.

"Okay, Natalie. Please raise your right hand." He was looking down.

"Yes, sir—I mean, yes, Your Honor." Oh gosh. I forgot to call him *Your Honor*. My nerves were getting the better of me.

"Do you swear to tell the truth, the whole truth, and nothing but the truth, so help you God?"

Yes, help me God, I thought. I was so scared.

"Ms. Winters?" he questioned.

"Oh! Yeah, I mean, yes, sir. I mean, yes, Your Honor. I swear."

He smiled slightly, instantly putting me at ease. He had to know that I was terrified and said, "So tell me why you are doing this. Why do you want a name change?"

Okay, I thought. It was time for the speech. I had it memorized, so I was sure not to mess this up. I had my note card, a trick I learned in my speech class. For a moment, I closed my eyes then took a deep breath.

I began, "Well, Your Honor, throughout my life, I have faced many struggles. Both my mother and father suffered from drug addiction. Needless to say, they couldn't take care of me, so I ended up in Child Protective Services, and a truly long story short, I ended up in the care of Faye and Jack Winters. I stayed there for almost twelve years, and during that time, I endured far too much. It was an unfortunate situation, Your Honor, and I have been on my own since I was seventeen. I am now eighteen, and during the past year, I have earned a high school diploma and an associate degree. I am a tax-paying citizen, and I have worked very hard to obtain what I have. I have never resorted to any promiscuous or reckless behavior, nor any behavior that violates the law of the state. I like to think I have a bright future, Your Honor, and I would like to label it with a name that represents who I am working to become."

"And this name is Krystyne Francis Aleksandr?" he assumed, wearing a smirk.

"Yes, sir—I mean, yes, Your Honor." I was gaining confidence.

"Why did you choose this? The spelling is odd," he stated.

"Well, my first name, Krystyne, means 'follower of Christ,' and that is first and foremost what I will always be: a follower of God. I would like my middle name to be Francis. It comes from the French descent, meaning 'freedom,' and I feel that freedom is the universal principle in which every life has the right to stand upon. And lastly, I choose Aleksandr. The translation of this name is 'warrior or soldier for man' because, Your Honor, that is my ultimate goal in life, to serve, stand up for, and fight for the rights and safety of others. I don't know whether I'll be a lawyer, doctor, speaker, or teacher, but in all my endeavors, I will choose to help other people. This theme is also present in the spelling. It comes from a famous Russian journalist, who goes by the name of Aleksandr Solzhenitsyn. He was a writer during the Russian Gulag. He was one of the only journalists who stood up against Stalin and wrote the truth and told what was really happening to the people. He fought for the rights of the others while risking his own life. At one point, they declared him insane, insisting he was crazy. There have been instances in my life where I feel I have been in the same position. I have grown inspiration from Mr. Solzhenitsyn, so I would like to carry on a portion of that spirit into my new life. This may seem odd, Your Honor, but I feel this is necessary for me. I have beaten many odds and overcome many obstacles. And not only for me, but also for my future children. And my children's children. Because ultimately, I believe that's what one should focus on in life. Not on yourself or your decisions, but the people that your decisions will affect. I ask for a name of a new generation—a generation that starts here with me. That will start with this name."

The judge didn't say anything for a moment. He was looking at me as if I had just spoken a foreign language. I begin to fidget, thinking, *Maybe I talked too long. I shouldn't have said so much!* There was such a tension in the courtroom, evoking suspension that almost froze time. I just stood there, finally putting my head down. I felt defeated. I was going to have to appeal.

All of a sudden, he cleared his throat and choked out, "Motion granted."

I quickly looked up in surprise. Studying him, I realized he had become emotional. I couldn't be sure, but I thought there were tears in his eyes. At first I was in shock, but my face slowly altered with excitement. I was now Krystyne Francis Aleksandr! He judged my reaction while smiling at this point, saying, "Are you sure you can handle this? It's going to be a lot of paperwork."

"Yes, sir! I mean, yes, Your Honor! I can handle it, no problem!" I all but shouted.

Grinning, he said, "Of course you can, Ms. Aleksandr. How did you do this without a lawyer? Where did you get the paperwork?"

I froze. I didn't want to tell him that I Googled it, found a real case, used white out on the names, copied it, scanned it back in, and typed over it. I didn't know if what I did was exactly legal…

"Er, I was… resourceful," I said quietly.

He bellowed in laughter. "Yes, I bet you were. Good luck to you, Ms. Aleksandr. I'm sure I'll be hearing about you more in the future."

Returning the smile, I said "Thank you," still not used to the sound of being called "Ms. Aleksandr" yet.

I pranced out of the courtroom. I had a new name. I felt like a new woman. I was the happiest I had ever remembered being. I was Krystyne Francis Aleksandr, and it was such a conquering moment. Yes, I knew that one day I might get married and my name would be changed, but that didn't matter. This was symbolic to my journey. For me this name was like receiving a trophy, a reward for my endurance. I could now introduce myself with confidence and pride. I had a new sense of self-worth, which could never be replaced. My name, Krystyne Francis Aleksandr, meant something to me. And one day, I hoped it would mean something to others.

The Man Whose Name I Never Knew

It was the week before I started the spring session of my junior year of college. In most cases, by the time you become a junior, you have a pretty good idea at what you're good at, what you don't like, and where you should be going. For me, at that point in time, I wasn't certain on any of those matters.

I was good at many things. And if I wasn't good at it, I worked to get better. My saying was always excellence is accepted, but perfection is expected. I applied that philosophy to every point of my life. If I encountered something that was difficult or that I didn't know how to solve, I simply went to the library and checked out the For Dummies book on whatever the matter was. I would research the subject until I felt I could take a test and make an A on it. Being "good" at something was relative. I knew if I wasn't good, I could find a way to get there. There was no "can't," just "not yet learned."

As far as not liking things, well, that too was relative. Most subjects I enjoyed, because so many of them, I felt were related to each other. I will argue all day that mathematics is a government, that economics is seen in biology, English is a physics of the human mind. It was all about presentation.

And where was I going? Well, I had absolutely no clue. There were so many directions. I wanted for a long time to be a physician, and that career wasn't ruled out. However, there were many personal issues that I had to deal with. I shadowed Dr. Brian, and I realized that I had become consumed with the idea of saving children, though I quickly learned that sometimes, there is nothing to do. Those moments took me back to Emily and brought out the anger I had for people who didn't properly care for their kids. I loved medicine, but at that point, I was unsure if I would be a good doctor. For most of my college career, I had been pre-med. But I began taking pre-law and psychology classes. One unexpected turn was my love for psychology. People are crazy, I knew that, but it was interesting to figure out how or why they were that way. But still, I was so unsure of what I should do.

Once I had a professor tell me to "do what makes you happy." Well, to me, that was such an arbitrary point. I grew up a depressed child in a place where smiles were rare, except when I was at school. When you go from day to day, living nothing but sadness, and you escape, everything makes you happy. I could picture myself in many jobs, positions, and professions and know that I would be happy. No one would ever hit me again. No one was ever going to abuse me. No one would tell me that I was worthless. I would never again go hungry. I would never be without a bed. I would never be poor spiritually, mentally, or fiscally. I was already happy and gratuitous to be going to school. Smiling all the time. My life was wonderful.

I was absolutely happy. I knew what the professor meant, but it was hard to grasp.

One Sunday afternoon, I was working a shift at the hotel. It was really quiet that afternoon, and we only had about two guests. I had already finished the work that needed to be done within my first thirty minutes. I still had another seven and a half hours to go, so I decided that I would do a little work. At all times, I had my book bag with me, and for the past few weeks I was literally working on figuring out my life. I had about ten degree plans printed out with complete statistics about them. I had GRE, MCAT, and LSAT prep books and information on about twenty different schools. From a distance, I probably looked like I was trying to invent a new subject. I was frustrated, confused, and not paying a bit of attention to my surroundings., when the chuckle startled me.

I looked up and saw a gentleman. He was an older man. His skin was the color of creamed coffee, and his hair was silver and white. Much like a Denzel Washington type. He was dressed in a navy suit and holding a fedora with a stylish cane. His eyes were a deep brown, but they twinkled somehow behind the lenses of his spectacles. Very distinguished, professor-like. As he looked at me, he had this smirk. It was as if he knew me. And oddly, it was as if I knew him.

"Hello," I said. "How may I help you?"

"Do I look in need of help?" he questioned teasingly.

I smiled wryly. "Well, no, sir. Um, how are you?" I wasn't really sure how to go from there.

"Ha, I'm well, my dear. So tell me, what are you working on?" He looked at my books, then at me.

"Oh, it's just… Well, I couldn't really tell you," I said cautiously. How do you tell someone that you're researching degree plans as a senior? I didn't want the man to think I was crazy. Been there, done that.

"Well, you must know something. You have a library here," he said. "It seems you're researching. What, if I may ask?"

"Well, sir, I'm trying to figure out what I want my profession to be," I stated meekly. He was going to think I was insane.

"Ah, I see. Are you sure you'll find it in one of these texts?"

"Um, well, no," I stuttered, never really looking at it that way. "I suppose I'm just looking for information about certain careers in these books."

"I see. Is this a list of schools?" he asked as he was skimming through the many sets of papers.

"Why, yes, sir. And their rankings."

"I noticed. Harvard, Princeton, Yale. Very good."

"Oh, well, I'm not going to those. I just look at their ratings for, umm, well, to set a scale. I figure if I try to shoot for what Ivy League expects, I'll have a good shot at other schools, too. Kind of silly, I guess, like watching an Olympic runner when you're preparing for a marathon, but I find it helps."

A smile spread on his face. "You're a smart girl."

"Um, well, I guess compared to some," I said.

"No, dear. That was a statement. I wasn't asking you." He chuckled.

"Oh." I laughed nervously. "Thank you."

"So tell me, what is it that you want to do?"

"Well," I started, "I'm pre-med and pre-law. I'm looking into joint programs and trying to figure out the requirements. What schools offer the program and such. But I like psychology and mathematics a lot, too. And—"

Suddenly, I was cut off by his laughter. I was offended. This man was laughing at me. Some nerve.

I suppose he saw the outrage in my expression. He stopped and said, "My dear, that was not the question."

Confused, I asked, "What do you mean? You asked—"

"I asked what it is that you want to do? Not about degree plans and programs. What is your overall goal?"

Oh, I thought, very humbled now. "Well, I want to help people, I suppose. To change things."

"Ah, that is good. There are many ways to do that. Quite a many of them that don't really require a degree."

A philosopher, I thought. *This guy is some kind of philosopher. Weird.* "Yes, that is true," I went on, "but education is important to me. I suppose I want to help people while fulfilling my selfish need of wanting a degree."

Laughing very loudly now, he said, "My dear, helping people is helping people, with or without a degree. Neither one is better than the other." Still holding my top colleges list, he asked, "Which one of these are you going to?"

This time, I was the one laughing. "Well, sir, I don't expect I'll go to any," I said in between my chuckling. "Like I said, they just help me scale."

"But you achieve on the scale that you set from the standards of these schools, yes?"

"Well, yes, most of the time. I try to."

"Then perhaps you are suited for these schools?" He was questioning me now.

"Maybe, but I don't—" I stopped, not knowing how to put it. "I…well…I…" What I wanted to say was that it was a far-fetching dream to go to a school like that. I was far from privileged. I didn't have any money. I was intelligent mostly because I worked hard at it. Harvard was in Boston, and here I was in Amarillo, Texas. And it would take a lot more than a car or plane to connect the two. "I'm not sure I'm well equipped enough for such a thing. It is only a dream, I suppose. One that gives me hope to strive for my best."

"Hmm." He looked as though he was deep in thought. "You know, Americans went to the moon on a dream."

"What?" I was trying to connect the dots in our conversation. I couldn't help myself from wondering if he had Alzheimer's. "Yes, I suppose we did." My tone was full of suspect.

"Do you know how far away the moon appears from the earth, my dear? We used to measure it like you…by dreams. But now, it is calculated and precise, but it didn't get that way until we started reaching for it."

"Well, yes… That is true," I agreed. *Who is this guy?* I thought.

"Tell me, are you scared to reach for dreams? Are you scared to strive?" he prodded me.

"No, I'm not scared. I'm not scared of anything," I stated firmly. Maybe he was a psychologist. This seemed to be going all Gestalt-like. Well, if that was the case, his analysis was way off.

"No fear? I think that you have fear in yourself. I think you fear you."

His words had me heated. Who did this guy think he is?

"No, I don't fear me. I just know that there is a level of reality that one must keep. Logical thinking. You know how many people apply to Harvard, reach for their moon, and they don't ever get there? Suddenly, their moon disappears, and there is nothing but the heaviness of the dark. Sometimes, it's best to keep the moon in the sky." My tone was stark.

He had a smirk on his face. He was looking at me as though he knew everything. As if he knew exactly what I had been thinking. I grew nervous. I realized he was talking subliminally about my greatest dreams and my worst fears to some strange philosopher-psych guy. In either way, I wasn't fooling him. I did have fears, and I just expressed them.

"My dear, this is why we have faith. If you don't achieve, you try again. Faith will light your dark."

I thought for a moment. Humbled, I said, "Maybe so. I just, well, I don't know where my moon is. So I suppose I have fear in shooting for it."

"Yes, but it's interesting." He looked at me with such intensity.

"What is interesting?" I asked questioningly. Maybe he was just crazy.

"You. You know your way around the sky, my dear," he assured.

"What? What do you mean?" my curiosity intensely asked.

"Ah, you pretend you are unaware, like you don't know what you are." He was smiling now in a grandfather-type manner.

"Well, I don't know what you mean. I don't pretend. I am… me," I reasoned. What is this?

"Yes. You are you. You have great talent and skill. Desire and ambition. Your light shines brightly. And you know your way around the sky because you, my dear, you are a star. A beautiful star."

His words struck me into a frozen stance. I knew he probably didn't understand the meaning of what he said, but I did. Tears flooded my eyes. He called me a star, the very thing I promised myself I would be but dared not tell anyone. I never told anyone about those star-filled wishes of mine. I remembered all the times in my life when I wished to be a star, sometimes in the darkest way. I looked down to hide the emotion then turned away toward the back counter. Grabbing a tissue, I was dabbing my eyes. I needed to compose myself.

As I turned slowly, I didn't see him. The man. He was gone. I looked around, calling, "Sir? Sir?" But there was no answer. I looked all around the lobby for him, but I couldn't find him. I ran outside to see if he had stepped out, but the old man was nowhere to be found.

He had a cane, I thought. *How could he move so fast?* I spent the rest of the afternoon looking for him, calling the rooms. I think the guests were a little concerned, but I gave them descriptions. I just had to find him.

But by nightfall, my shift had ended, and I never found him. It wasn't that I wanted to bother him or anything. I just wanted to tell him thank you. He told me something so dear to my heart, and at that time, it was something I needed to hear.

Later on that night, as I lay in bed, I went deep into thought. I realized no matter what career I chose, I would aspire to be someone's light. I would be a beacon. I would be someone who, someday, a person could look up to. I believed that man, whoever he was. He was wise, and he made me feel confident. I wasn't going to become a star. I already was one, and my light was just beginning to shine.

As I look back to that conversation with Mr. Thomas about stars, it intrigues me, its profound relevance in my life. I know that oftentimes my prayer to be a star was much more literal than it was figurative. But I believe that the dream to become a star kept me alive. That's just the thing about keeping one's eyes on the stars—it keeps you looking up.

I looked up and out rather than down and back. I believed that Jesus was the sun. And, well, He is the Son. The Son of God who has led me my whole life, even in times when I didn't know it. The times I was looking around to see if He was there, He was under me, holding me up out of the stormy waters of life. He has started my best days and ended my worst ones. And He has brought me forth, but only to shine as He does.

In all of the things I've learned, one thing I am certain is that life is about perspective. When you're at the base of a mountain and you look up, it's intimidating and discouraging. But if you take the same mountain and look at it in a bird's-eye view, it's nothing but a dot. I think that's the key in life's difficult times, to change perspective when hard times come. Act like that of a palm tree; grow your roots deep into soils of strength, hope, and faith. That way, when the storms come and the ferocious winds blow, you will stand, even if the world around you is lost in its chaos.

For me, I am appreciative of my past and what it has taught me. For I learned lessons that many will never understand. I have lived through more life than most people can handle, and for that I am a strong person. There were times in my life where I believed I had nothing. Now I know that wasn't the case, but I am so thankful for that belief. You see, when you believe you've been there with absolutely nothing, you realize later on that you need nothing. And nothing can break you.

It's so hard to overcome generational curses. Change is not an easy task. But it's not the thing that needs to be changed that's hard; it's the people around you that cause the difficulty. People will tell you that you can't. They will try and limit you because they limit themselves. They bring you down because they themselves believe that they cannot rise.

However, this may be their perspective, but it doesn't have to be yours. Everyone serves a purpose. Everyone has a place in the sky, no matter where you may begin. Others' choices do not have to dictate your life because it is yours. You have the right to do great things. You have the ability to shine. I went through many battles, and I know there are people that go through much worse, but no matter the circumstances, I believe every individual has an equal ability to achieve great things in their own way. Realizing this is the hard part.

And so I say to the people who were ever without a home, to the ones who have fallen in despair, to the souls who believe no one cares, to the persons who know only sorrow, for the hearts who have suffered many a great woe, to the parents who now protect from above, and to you, little child, who hasn't felt love— shine. Because it is simply no secret, that you are a bright shining star.

Endnotes

1) http://babynamesworld.parentsconnect.com/meaning_of_ Allison.html

MAR 2014

CPSIA information can be obtained at www.ICGtesting.com
Printed in the USA
LVOW11s1531110114

369054LV00006B/816/P